LOGAN

The Honorable Life and Scandalous Death of a Western Lawman

Jackie Boor

Brule, Wisconsin

LOGAN
The Honorable Life and Scandalous Death of a Western Lawman

First Edition

Published by:
Cable Publishing
14090 E Keinenen Rd
Brule, WI 54820
www.cablepublishing.com
E-mail: nan@cablepublishing.com

No part of this book may be reproduced or transmitted in any form or by any means, electronic or mechanical, including photocopying, recording, or by any information storage or retrieval system without the written permission of the publisher, except for the inclusion of brief quotations in a review.

© 2014 by Jackie Boor
All rights reserved. Published in 2014

Hardcover: 978-1-934980-35-4
Soft cover: 978-1-934980-36-1

Library of Congress Control Number: 2014930146

 Printed in the United States of America

LOGAN

The Honorable Life and Scandalous Death of a Western Lawman

To Joel Fish ~

Sherry's favorite Lawman —

Jackie Boor
The Sheriff's great granddaughter

THE DA VINCI EYE

FINALIST

The Eric Hoffer Book Award

Sheriff Thomas W. Logan's story is dedicated
to the families and descendants of fallen peace officers.
We become one in our struggle, our healing, and our triumph.

PRAISE FOR LOGAN

"Exceptionally well done, Logan is riveting and hard to put down. Great photos, detailed references, and context for the events leading up to and surrounding the sheriff's death make this truly a Nevada history lover's delight!"
— **Allen Metscher**, President, Central Nevada Historical Society

"Jackie Boor's fascinating story of Tom Logan is a window into part of the mining boom that reshaped Nevada. It also digs into the characters who affected those times, from frontier lawbreakers to a young attorney named Pat McCarran, later one of the most powerful men in the country. Logan reminds us of the dangers of being a lawman in the West, and of life caught in a mining rush. It is also a story of transition from the 19th century to the 20th, from vigilante justice to law and order, and from one Nevada to the other."
— **Michael Green**, Professor of History, College of Southern Nevada

"Nevada's history is filled with great stories that often change as they are told and retold. The story of Tom Logan's life and death is one that has often been repeated, embellished, and distorted. Jackie Boor, Tom Logan's great-granddaughter, has done diligent research and applied a careful, cognizant approach to bring the true story to the page. Family history is especially tricky, because we all bring our own biases to the work, but Logan moves past those biases and offers the reader all the blemishes and good points of a life lived in the rugged, unforgiving desert of Nevada. Law and order, liquor and ladies of the night, and loyalty to family make this book a great read and a fascinating work of Nevada history!"
— **Michael E. Fischer**, Former Director, Nevada Department of Cultural Affairs and Independent Scholar in Nevada History

"This book vividly brings to life the remarkable story of Sheriff Thomas Logan, who once, "without raising his voice, talked Wyatt Earp into giving up his guns." As the current sheriff of Nye County, I was most impressed by how seriously my long-ago predecessor took his responsibility to maintain the peace and protect the public, regardless of the time, location, or politics of the day. Unfortunately, in the end, he paid with his life, as too many dedicated officers tragically do. Author Jackie Boor gives us much more than a graphic history lesson about turn-of-the-century Nevada. She also very skillfully takes us behind the badge and into an extremely demanding time when the West was experiencing enormous growth, and law enforcement had to rapidly evolve in order to respond to all the new challenges."
— **Anthony L. DeMeo**, Sheriff of Nye County, Nevada

"As the story unfolded, I found myself becoming emotionally involved in what is really Old West Shakespeare: cunning, treachery, and murder, with a hint of what just might have been planned vengeance and retaliation. This book has all the makings of a great movie! Sheriff Logan has waited more than 100 years for his story to be told and I believe he helped guide the author as she shined new light on century-old myths and legend."

— **Joni Eastley**, Assistant County Manager, Nye County, Nevada

"Logan is Nevada history at its best and a compelling biography of Nye County Sheriff Thomas W. Logan. However, accomplished free-lance writer and biographer Jackie Boor, Logan's great-granddaughter, has given the reader something more. Her rigorous research and engaging writing underscore her personal odyssey to find the truth for the generations of her family who have been confused and haunted by Logan's controversial and untimely demise in a Manhattan, Nevada, brothel on April 7, 1906. The work's subtitle, The Honorable Life and Scandalous Death of a Western Lawman, captures Boor's efforts to demonstrate that her Nevada-born great-grandfather was a well-respected man and a law officer who died in the line of duty. She is honest and forthright in coming to terms with why Logan, a devoted family man, was at a brothel that fateful day."

— **Guy Rocha**, Acclaimed Nevada Historian and former State Archivist

"My first lingering memory after reading Logan is the harsh life that the Logan family led in traveling around the deserts of Nevada and Arizona to find their destiny. What they took for granted would be considered very difficult survival for people today. The account of the homicide and subsequent trial of Sheriff Logan's killer is accurately portrayed based on discussions with my father and other relatives who lived in Nevada during the time in which the events took place."

— **Peter I. Breen**, Senior District Judge, Nevada

"Whether by journalistic misfire, academic neglect, or unabashed revisionism, much of Nevada's colorful history has often been obscured. This is the case with the remarkable story of lawman Tom Logan. The mystery surrounding his demise has long overshadowed his compelling life story, but thanks to Jackie Boor, the big picture of the tough guy's rugged road has come into focus. Logan: The Honorable Life and Scandalous Death of a Western Lawman at last gives this larger-than-life character his due."

— **John L. Smith**, Las Vegas Review-Journal columnist,
Author of Sharks in the Desert

List of Era Poetry

CONTENTS

"This tale is timeless; how the loss of an officer in the line of duty impacts his family, fellow officers, and his community. As I read, I felt as if I were there as events unfolded, all the while noting how eerily similar one family journey's through grief, over 100 years ago, is to today's law enforcement line-of-duty survivors. So many things have remained the same: the family's struggle to cope, Hannah Logan's tenacious battle to provide for her family, the unanswered questions, and dealing with the criminal justice system. History comes alive with this riveting tale of honor, loss, and family."

— **Madeline Neumann**, President, National President, Concerns of Police Survivors and Line of Duty Widow

"The scent of sagebrush after a spring rain, the sound of wagons rolling down dusty Nevada roads, and the lively music and rough & tumble sounds of a mining camp all entered my mind as I lost myself in Logan. I was drawn into life on the western high desert, the incredible challenges those early settlers faced, and the amazing strength they needed to survive. And in the end, I was given a fresh look at the circumstances surrounding Sheriff's Logan's death at the hands of another. Any way the cards are dealt, Sheriff Logan died a hero performing the duties he was sworn to carry out through his official oath. May he now rest in peace."

— **Doug Gist**, President, Silver State National Peace Officers Museum, Virginia City, Nevada

Nye County
Thos. W. Logan
Sheriff and Assessor
Nye County Nevada

NYE COUNTY, NEVADA

Mar 9, 1906

TONOPAH, NEVADA, ____ 1906

My Dear Daughters,

No doubt you think your Father has forgotten you, but I have not. I have been away far from home for a long time, after jurors and witnesses. This County is getting so lively now that it keeps me going day and night. I received Jesse's letter this a.m. and two or three from Annie after I came home. Do not get disheartened but stay at school all of you. I am trying to shape up for the rest of the family to come down (to Oakland, California) by the middle of next month, although they don't know it, as I expect $500 by the 10th of April and if it comes and will, I will give it to your mother to go and spend, and give her a chance to see something. Do not say anything to her about it because sometimes these things fall through but I don't think that this will.

Annie, it would be hard for you to get anything to do here as there are so many coming in looking for all of these jobs. I want you to stay where you are and go to school. Lot is doing nothing no matter what he writes you or tells you what his chances are and I know what I am talking about. If everything turns out all right, I may come down with the folks to see you. Be good girls and do not worry about me. We will come out all right—before this summer is over your Father has some chances to make money that he never had before. I enclose $50 and will send more before long with all kinds of _love_ to you _all_, I am your affectionate Papa.

THOMAS LOGAN IS SHOT AND KILLED BY WALTER BERIEAU

LOGAN TOOK WYATT EARPS GUN AWAY FROM HIM

AN, APRIL 7.
GAN, SHERIFF OF
Y, DIED HERE AT
K THIS MORNING.
ULT OF FOUR BUL-
S FIRED FROM A
HE HANDS OF WAL-
AU. LATE LAST

BLE OCCURRED IN
HOUSE, A DISREPU-
T SAID TO BE CON-
A WOMAN KNOWN

I CAN BE LEARNED
MAKING TROUBLE
G, AND WAS VERY
. HE HAD BEEN
AVILY ALL DAY
WAS IN THE
HE TIME, WAS
EJECT BERIEAU.
LANG FORWARD
BERIEAU BY THE
HREW HIM INTO

AD THE SHERIFF
HOLD UPON THE
THAN THE LAT-
S GUN, AN AUTO-
R. AND OPENED
OFFICER.

S NO GUN.
ARMED.
BULLETS TOOK
THE CHIN, ONE
ER AND ONE IN
HE LAST

fighter. He was credited with ab
a dozen notches on the butt of
gun. His name was Wyatt Earp,
there was absolutely no doubt th
he was really bad.

"One night Earp became disor
and his wife came into the place
while he was drinking, and tried
get him to go home. The man sh
her get out by way of reply, a
the act roused the ire of a you
miner who was also drinking at t
bar, and who was a little 'canned' h
himself.

"Not understanding the relatio
ship between the couple, he took
cudgels in the woman's defense.

"A fierce altercation followed, a
Earp rushed out of the place and
his own saloon, down the street
little way.

"In a short time he came ba
with two big six shooters swinging
his hands, and breathing blood a
sudden death for the man who ha
defied him. It looked as though
killing would surely take place.

"Tom Logan was told of the ris
and he hastened at once to the scen
Pushing his way to the centre of
the men, he cause

TONOPAH BONANZA

TONOPAH NEVADA, SATURDAY, APRIL 7, 1906

T BROCK
N TONOPAH

opah Mining Com-
s Railroad Will
ded to Bullfrog

POPULAR SHERIFF KILLED!

Thomas Logan is Murdered in Cold Blood by Gambler in Manhattan this Morning

MANHATTAN, April 7, 1906—9 a. m.

To the BONANZA:

Sheriff Thomas Logan was shot at 6 o'clock this morning and passed away a few minutes ago. The shooting was done by Walter C. Barieu, a low Creole gambler.

Barieu and another gambler had been quarreling and creating a disturbance in the Jewell saloon and the bartender called Sheriff Logan, who was passing at the time, to separate the men and prevent trouble. He entered the place and requested the men to go to their respective homes. As he started to leave the place Barieu fired five shots at him point blank, four of ....nk to the floor mortally wounded.

QUESTION MERGER

McNamara mit Prop Compa

The stockholders of the M
mining company met in San F
yesterday to vote on the prop
consolidating that company
Ohio and West End. The co
a bitter one and it was finall
to endorse the proposition, pr
Ohio company accepts 200,0
instead of 250,000, the othe
be given the McNamara etc
making 300,000 in all for the

A wire was ordered sent
town, Ohio, asking the Oh
to accept the proposition,

SIM-SAYLO

ic presi-
ompany,
ad com-
railroad
orations,
y evening
A. Keith,
ral man-
company.
ve had a
the gentle-
ras enthus-
wonderful

much preliminary work was done before
the close of the year, though unforseen
obstacles that could not be overcome at
the time, delayed the commencing of
actual construction work. Everything
has since been arranged, however, and
the road will be sent through with a
rush. John F. Hedden, for many years
superintendent of the Central New
England Railway, has been appointed
general superintendent of this road.
Material has been ordered and is now
on the road to Goldfield and it is safe to
.... will not be many months

EMAINS OF SHERIFF IN STATE
MURDERER IN COUNTY JAI

o'clock this afternoon a
ble, mud-splashed and
rd travel, pulled up in
e court house and three
ed. First, came Deputy
Hickey, and last Deputy
and between them, with his
sed and discolored, was the
t whose name stands the
having taken the life of
omas W. Logan in cold
er Berieau.
ty left Manhattan this
ten o'clock and came the
to this city without

The testimony of the
showed that Bering mixtge
Logan's gun to him, with
latter hand Berieau into h
While Logan was punishi
rmary Scott Hickey cam
scene, and assisted in sep
two combatants.

Story of Piano Pl
Bering's testimony pra
reiterated that of the Bl
He stated that he first f
over the head with Logs
that Logan wrested the
from Bering, and used
the man underneath.
Logan's revolver w
after the melee br A.
taurant keeper, who,
ing the fight, carried i
to his own place,whe
covered it. Drs. Voi
and McIntyre testified
attended Logan un
They stated that dea
the severing of the wi
artery, causing hem
Scott Hickey stat
Logan forcing Berie
and holding both
hands, one of whi
volver. Hickey sai
Berieau was intoxi

Berieau Fal
And while the
from the line of w
the gruesome
hearts of the
Walter Berieau
the shadow
writhed and twis
of penitence
mouth like a wi
ing in frenzy,
with the fright
Berieau with a
fell to the floor
The dignity
dotten, the aw
moment unfrec
utes the room
cries of hor

AST SAD RITES FOR
THE DEAD SHERIFF

arrangements for the
mas Logan have been
services will be held
house at three o'clock
noon. The eulogy
by C. H. McIntosh,
s will be under the
Odd Fellows. The
rve the last sad rites

narch for the funeral
the direction of
grand marshal.
of Odd Fellows,
Daughters of Re-
Eagles, the Miners
ard of honor com-
emen. Then will
borne on the hook-
and attended by
re department, and
hree chosen from

Berieau Is Calm
Walter A. Berieau, the man accused of murdering Sheriff Thomas W.
Logan, is most cool and unconcerned
as he sits in his cell in the county
jail.
Only once since he was brought in
from Manhattan; since his collapse
in the court room at his preliminary
hearing, has he shown any sign of
emotion, say the men who guard
him.
That single exception to his calm
assurance, was when his sorrowing
wife flung herself against the bars
and wept bitterly yesterday evening.
Then, and then only, did this man of
iron give way to his feelings, and
the tears sprang to his

from a depth of 1,000 feet. As soon as it is in operation the working force is to be increased and the greater portion of mining energy to be devoted to driving the shaft well down into the sulphide zone which was tapped in the old shaft at a depth of 85 feet.

A. J. Woodward, W. P. McCarthy, J. H. Pierson, George Hilgalogh and Louis Koberg have located 11 claims in the Toyabe range about 16 miles west of Manhattan. On one of their prospects the ledge is showing from 75 to 100 feet wide and 15 assays taken from across it returned gold values ranging from $6 to $18 the ton. About one mile from this group they have located a number of other claims and on one of them the ledge is 50 feet wide. For the first 10 feet of this width gold values average $9 per ton. Their acreage includes two springs, one of which has a flow of 10,000 gallons per day.

STRUCK A GOOD ORE SHOOT

It seems some few days ago that considerable dissatisfaction was felt among leaders at Phillipsburg and for a while things at the camp seemed blue. Harry Stimler, of the Stimler Leasing Company, who has been superintending the work in person, was one of the dissatisfied parties. The Stimler ...

LOGAN'S SLAYER IS FOUND "NOT GUILTY"

The Jury so Declares After Deliberating from 12:25 Friday Until 9 A. M. Today.

The jury in the case of the people of the State of Nevada vs. Walter Barieau, charged with the murder of Sheriff Thomas W. Logan in Manhattan on the morning of April 7th, brought in a verdict of not guilty this morning at 9 o'clock a. m.

Barieau who followed gambling for a living, shot and killed Sheriff Logan in the Jewell saloon in Manhattan, a place kept by one May Biggs, on the morning of April 7, about 6 o'clock. The facts of the killing briefly outlined are as follows: Logan was in bed in the house when Barieau and others entered the saloon. After having drinks Barieau and the Biggs woman got into a difficulty and the woman ordered him to leave the premises. He went ...

sheriff into the house, the case for the prosecution was closed.

Attorney Pitt___ who opened the case for the defense, outlined the course they proposed to pursue, which was substantially to the point that the defendant Barieau had reason to believe his life in imminent danger and that his action was justifiable from the standpoint of self defense.

The defendant, Walter Barieau, was called to the stand to testify in his own defense. He stated in effect that on the fatal morning he, in company with others, went to the Jewell saloon where he took one drink of wine, which made him sick and he went ...

THE TONOPAH DAILY SUN, TONOPAH, NEVADA, SATURDA

WEEK'S GOLFIEL MINING REI

Good Progress Being Made Rich Mines of Our Nei boring Camp.

The prosecution of work in the at Goldfield is continuing leaved the following notes from the Nev

The great Mohawk mine st___ tinues to pour out its golden wi over-increasing quantities. One ___ two others are producing a ___ amount, and still others are expe daily to break into the ore. The ___ A Mexcette still continues to be prowder of all. It is this leaser is producing 140 tons daily, which considerable increase over any prev time. The grade is about the ___ of past weeks. The hoist has been able to take care of all the ore the broken down and 10 men __ from so ...

Two Mile Fissure Lode at Go

(Continued From Page 1.)

to fifteen feet wide and is true and strong. There is something so decisive about it as to cause the non-miner to take notice and remark. At the sixty-foot level a twenty-foot stope accounts for the pile of sacked ore at the top. Drifts north and south reveal the same true form of the fissure and add to its strength. On the 105 level the ledge matter is more solid. It is less broken and augurs well for what may be its situation at the four or five hundred. Every miner in camp is elated over

ford fourteen That ground i James H. L. Patrick did outlook strike it w tivity.

A portion is on the ledge, and that is th the Cliffo ind the pany are

JURY FINDS BARIEAU NOT GUILTY OF MURDER

Logan's Slayer Given Freedom After Seventeen Hours' Deliberation-- Affecting Scene in Court

Walter A. Barieau was declared not guilty of the murder of Sheriff Thomas W. Logan by the jury in the district court this morning.

The verdict was reached only after seventeen hours of deliberation. The case was given into the hands of the jurors just before 12:30 o'clock yesterday afternoon and it was 5:30 this morning when the twelve men, worn out with an all night struggle to come to an agreement, finally decided that the evidence introduced by the prosecution was not sufficient for the conviction of the accused.

Immediately after the retirement of the jury a ballot was taken and ___ six for con-

the shadow of the gallows with the reading of the verdict, who unflinchingly looked District Attorney Pittman in the eye during the terrible arraignment yesterday, now gave way and bending over with his head in his hands, Walter A. Barieau wept and his lips moved in audible thanksgiving to his lawyers who rushed over to congratulate him.

By order of the court the jury was polled and as each name was called an answer of "not guilty" was given. The jury was thanked by the court and discharged and Barieau walked for the court room a free man.

Seldom if ever in the history of Nye county has there been such an interest displayed over the verdict as that displayed in the ___ of a jury as that displayed the sole

RESERVE SHAFT AT GOLDEN A TAIN

It has shipped three tons that $80 to the ton, but that would ___ $80 to the ton, but that it is not

INTRODUCTION

MY GRANDMOTHER, HAZEL Margaret Logan Barton, rarely mentioned her father other than to say he had been a sheriff in Nevada and was shot to death in 1906. The fourth of Sheriff Thomas Logan's eight children, she was 14 at the time. When Hazel married a miner from Maine in 1914, they boarded a train for Oregon that very day. She never returned to Nevada except to attend her mother's funeral in 1942. My grandmother died in 1974. We'll never know how much she knew about her father's death, his killer, or the controversial murder trial that set him free.

One of Hazel's daughters, Bethany, was my mother and the seventh of eleven siblings who grew to adulthood conveying a variety of scenarios under which they thought their grandfather had been killed: He was ambushed escorting a prisoner to jail; he was struck by an errant bullet when a gunfight broke out between warring miners; he was shot in the back by a highwayman who had wrestled away his gun; or he had been summoned to the aid of a woman fending off a disorderly gambler with a short fuse and a fully-loaded pistol.

Raised in northern California, I was unfamiliar with any of these narratives until 1985 when, at the age of 34, I attended my first Logan Family reunion in Central Nevada. What I knew then about our history wouldn't fill the back of a postcard, and I was anxious to learn more. About 30 aunts, uncles, and cousins, many of whom were meeting for the first time, set up camp within the gritty folds of the high desert ghost town of Belmont, about 50 miles northeast of Tonopah, the Nye County seat. Some were in motorhomes, others in travel trailers, and a few, like me, my mother, and two-year-old son, roughed it in tents. An uncle constructed a makeshift outhouse and gravity shower. The weather was scorching hot but breezy, meals were potluck classics, the music country, the yarns enthralling, and the favorite watering hole, Dirty Dick's Saloon, stayed open late. Also invited to the reunion was the nephew of my great-grandfather's killer, who added his version of what happened that blood-soaked morning at the Jewel—making it impossible for me to know what to believe.

One afternoon, I wandered a short distance from camp into the undulating expanse of parched and twisted sagebrush. A furnace-born wind rushed up from the valley, sweeping away the sounds and trappings of modern days, coaxing into view hazy images of long ago—when the same moaning gusts and incessant whipping currents tormented those seeking fortune from the land or, even more promising, from another man's pocket.

What secrets had time packed into the dusty crevices of the past about Sheriff Thomas Walter Logan—husband, father, cowboy, rancher, businessman, and public servant? Was my great-grandfather to blame for his demise, or was there something more sinister lurking in the shadows? If so, should I search for answers or leave this recalcitrant mystery undisturbed? Even his long-suffering wife Hannah had made known to inquisitive family members that it was best to "let the dead stay dead."

But what about *his* voice?

What might Tom Logan have to say about his final hours? What would he want his family to know? What unfinished business might he have left behind? As his beating heart slowly surrendered to eternal silence and his fondest hopes and dreams drained away with his blood, the excruciating pain he suffered was likely due as much to burning regret as it was to the bullet holes in his flesh.

Should I retreat or move closer?

To be sure, in that summer of 1985 at the Logan family reunion, there floated in that warm, beseeching wind an undeniable, distant whisper nudging me to "keep looking." Beyond mortal curiosity, I was driven by an indescribable longing to know more about my roots and the context of the lives that contributed to my being. Never did I imagine all I would find and the profound impact of those discoveries on me, other Logan descendants, and Nevada history.

Clan Logan is represented by the heraldic crest
of "a passion nail piercing a human heart"
with the motto HOC MAJORUM VIRTUS,
Latin for "this is valour of my ancestors"
and the slogan *Druim-nan-deur*,
Scottish Gaelic for "the ridge of tears."

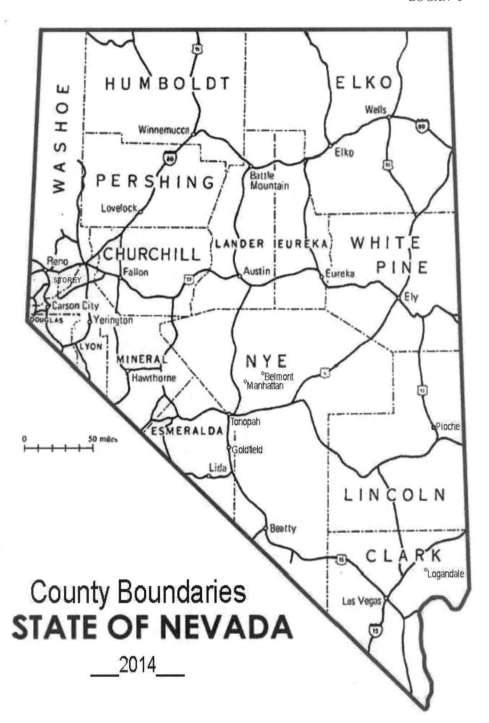

County Boundaries
STATE OF NEVADA
__2014__

The Old Covered Wagon

Beside an old junk pile so sad and forlorn
Stands an old covered wagon, all rusted and worn.
It's in an out-of-way place, this vacant old lot,
Where stands this old wagon, forgot, yes, forgot.
Its tongue is all splintered, its lead-rod is broke,
The double-trees rattle and the old neck-yoke
Has fallen to pieces—just the irons are there.
Whenever I see it, I just stop and stare.

The wheels seem to be leaning as if unable to stand;
The reach is held together with one rusted band.
Its body is sagging, all splintered and marred,
The box shows hard fighting, with bullets it's scarred.
And I look back to the days long, long ago
When this old covered wagon with the top white as snow
'Way out o'er the prairie, like great ship of state,
This wagon was coming with great load of freight.

The oxen that drawed it panted 'neath the load,
While they patiently toiled on the long winding road.
And the dust of the prairies hung like a cloud
While the shout of the drivers sounded so loud,
And all of the passengers would walk up the grade—
At noon-day they rested 'neath the great wagon shade.
But those days are gone like the old pioneer
And oh, what changes have come year by year.

Along the old trail where there wasn't a shack
We now see cities and a railroad track.
And autos a-speeding and airships so high,
Like swift birds of passage they mottle the sky,
But like you, old wagon, sturdy and strong
We give our years of service, then pass along
At last, for our portion is but one little lot—
Like you in the junk pile, forgot, yes, forgot.

—James W. Whilt, Mountain Memories, 1925

1

A NEVADA SON: 1861-1898

"The sidewalks are crowded with rough-bearded men, gathered from all quarters of the continent. These men are the pioneers of civilization, the advance guard of the army of occupation in all new lands. Enterprising to a degree, brave, patriotic, self-reliant, and honest in their way, they prepare the ground where others till and mow and reap the harvest. Rest is something they utterly abhor, and the man who will remain quietly in one place for a year is to them an object of supreme contempt...."

New York Tribune, "Our Hidden Wealth: The White Pine Silver Mines"
New York, New York, August 10, 1869

THE SPRING OF 1861 will always loom large in the annals of North American history. Newly elected President Abraham Lincoln had been in office less than two months when a conflict between Union and Confederate forces at Fort Sumter, South Carolina, launched a divided nation into four agonizing years of civil war. That same spring, far removed from the blood-soaked battlegrounds, beneath the eastern slope of the majestic Sierra-Nevada, an adventurous young couple welcomed the first of their seven children on May 29. Robert Howard Logan and Mary Elizabeth Perkins had married in Sacramento, California, on July 4, 1860, before moving to Franktown, a small Nevada Territory* community located about 25 miles south of present-day Reno. Not quite age 17, Mary was 12 years younger than Robert.

Thomas Walter Logan was born into a family well-fortified by pioneer gumption and ingenuity along with, attributable to his father, a restless nature, a penchant for fair play, and a haunting weakness for cigars and liquor. Like his siblings to come, Tom would grow to treasure his devoted, long-suffering mother and respectfully tolerate the headstrong father forever in pursuit of status and prosperity. In time,

Tom would come to exemplify his mother's kind heart and soft-spoken ways as well as his father's entrepreneurial pluck and civic sensibilities. From his parents he learned when to offer a hand, when to take a stand, and most importantly, when to fight back. Like so many others of his era, Tom's life story epitomizes the best and worst human traits prevalent during Nevada's tumultuous boomtown years—when the lure of precious metals begot schemes and dreams, and the loosely drawn line between success and failure shifted with random disregard.[1]

---

* The Territory of Nevada became the 36th state on October 31, 1864.

Mary Perkins Logan with infant Thomas Walter Logan, 1861
(Logan Family Collection)

Tom's father was born in Genesee County, New York, on April 29, 1833. As a young man, he briefly worked as a blacksmith in Northfield, Michigan, before joining the westward movement to California. Like tens of thousands of others, he sought the bountiful fortunes thought to be lying in wait, only to discover such opportunities were few and far between. At the time of his marriage to Mary in 1860, he was working as a bartender.[2]

Mary's journey westward began at the age of 12 in 1856. Her father, Robert Perkins, and his wife of 16 years, Susannah Donaldson Perkins, gathered up their four children and joined a wagon train out of Des Moines, Iowa, bound for Sacramento. The arduous trip via the Beale Trail running through the future states of New Mexico and Arizona into southern California would take more than two years. Tragically, along the way, Mary's youngest sister accidentally shot herself in the abdomen while looking for a needle in a sewing box to mend her torn dress. Delilah lived only two hours before her grief-stricken family laid her to rest in an isolated grave along their path. Death, in one form or another, was no stranger to the pioneers.

While roving bands of Native Americans posed an ever-present threat, hunger was frequently of even greater concern. Many times in later years, Mary recounted to her own children how their wagon train had run short of supplies and all would have surely perished if a Zuni village had not housed and fed them through a winter layover. During that stay, Mary tucked away a piece of cornbread, which the Logan family preserved for more than 25 years as a cherished, albeit rock-hard, relic of a trying time forever blushed with gratitude.[3]

Mary's father was a hot-tempered, fifth-generation Virginian with piercing blue eyes and dark red hair. Her mother was one of fifteen children born to an Ohio household supported by a cobbler father who was also a part-time Methodist preacher. Susannah was a sturdy, God-fearing woman whose grandfather served in the Continental Army and was among those who crossed the icy Delaware River at Valley Forge with General George Washington during the American Revolutionary War.[4]

The Perkins family eventually settled south of Sacramento, California, where they took up farming. When Robert Logan asked Mary Perkins to be his wife, her father raged against his 15-year-old daughter marrying a man 12 years her senior and with unproven prospects. The day Robert arrived at the Perkins farm the summer of 1860 in a shiny buggy and wearing his best suit, Mary's father warned he would disown her if she left with him. The moment Mary settled into the seat next to Robert, her father kept his promise and turned his back on her forever. Only her mother attended the marriage ceremony performed by Rev. Shuck on July 4, 1860, in Sacramento.[5]

Robert Howard Logan with sisters, Detroit, Michigan, c. 1867
(Logan Family Collection)

About ten years later, when Robert and Mary Logan's three oldest children were youngsters, she took them back to California to meet her parents, hoping to mend fences. When she knocked on the front door, her mother answered, gave her daughter a brief, cold stare, and abruptly closed the door between them. Mary promptly returned to Nevada and never went back.[6] Susannah's decision to reject her daughter may very well have been survival-based given her husband's unyielding nature; any perceived act of defiance might result in her also being discarded. The pervasive subservience of women and the overwhelming demands on men to provide for their families could harden the most tolerant soul. From a letter written by one Tom Logan's cousins in 1935 to his sister, Clara:

Poor Grandma had a hard time. Grandpa was not good to her.* [Once] he took all his cattle up to Truckee for the summer.. and lo and behold, he was up there and had a woman living with him. Poor Grandma got word of it so she went up there and stationed herself in the house. He told people Grandma was not his wife and took everything out of the house but the cook stove. Grandma kept it so hot they could not move it and she asked for a settlement. He was to give her half of all he had and he was pretty well fixed. He got her to sign some papers that caused her to lose all and he even put her in jail. Well, some men who had never seen her before went [sic] her bond and she did not have to stay in jail.[7]

NOT LONG AFTER Tom's first birthday, his mother gave birth to a brother, Jay Calvin Logan, on August 8, 1862. Now living near Carson City, his father had become a man on the rise. He had taken up ranching, was invested in a mining corporation, and had been elected county tax collector. As Tom would experience more than three decades later when he too held public office, Robert Logan soon found himself the target of critics. After being indicted by the Grand Jury for failure to properly process a $25 license fee, he wasted no time fighting to clear his name and, after several months of legal maneuvers, prevailed in the Appellate Court.[9] In so doing, he demonstrated what he would instill in his children—a sense of obligation to never hesitate to right a wrong and, in so doing, be willing to go the distance.[10]

Among one of Robert's most forward-thinking ventures was creating a partnership the summer of 1863 to purchase a square-mile section on the eastern shore of what was then known as Lake Bigler. Located in the Carson Range above Carson Valley and named for California Governor John Bigler (1853–58), the vast, sparkling emerald body of water would later be renamed Lake Tahoe. From Edward B. Scott's *Saga of Lake Tahoe*:

By the summer of 1864, Logan's large two-story hostelry had opened its doors and was doing a brisk business. Logan House stood on a bluff above the lakeshore, one and one-half miles south of Glenbrook House, and its outlook was so promising that Wellington Stewart left Genoa to enter into the suggested partnership. The owner-proprietors rates of $15 a week were $6 less than the stylish way station at the head of Glenbrook meadow, and they catered primarily to the wagoner and foot traveler…offering "fine meals, fishing and sailing skiffs…."[11]

---

* Susannah would eventually reach a breaking point with her husband's cavorting and filed for divorce the spring of 1882 in Sacramento, CA. She lived out her days toiling against the elements with meager means until her death in 1906. Robert Perkins, also with little to show for his lifelong ventures, died five years earlier in Los Angeles at the age of 83.[8]

That same summer, Robert and Mary's second son, Jay Calvin, died just short of his second birthday on August 1, 1864.[12] Adding to the surge of misfortune and perhaps a direct result of its remote location, Logan House, the first hotel on Lake Tahoe, failed to prosper and was soon cited for delinquent taxes. The property was eventually purchased in 1870 for its timber by Henry Marvin Yerington of the Glenbrook lumbering combine. By the turn of the century, Logan House had vanished into the earth and today, the shoreline below the bluff where it once stood is known as Logan Shoals, the last public memento to Robert Logan and his unsuccessful attempt to enter the hotel business. The Lake Tahoe region would eventually develop into the world-class resort it is today – an ever-luminous reminder to modern-day Logan descendants of what might have been.

Unsuccessful in the lodging and mining businesses, Robert Logan looked eastward, attracted by the enthralling tales of the pulsating new boomtown of Austin, Nevada, 175 miles away. According to western historian, Oscar Lewis, Austin "shot up fast and had only a few years of prodigious growth" following the chance discovery in 1863 of some promising quartz samples by a Pony Express rider looking for stray horses.[13] Soon, Robert, Mary, and four-year-old Tom had joined the swelling population of Austin. Robert elected to invest in one of the more proven moneymakers in any mining camp—a saloon. Bob Logan's Saloon, located on the northeast corner of Main and Virginia Streets, was in full swing by the fall of 1865. In addition to advertising the best wines, liquors, and cigars to always be on hand, he guaranteed "barkeeps with high foreheads, smiling countenance and winning ways."[14]

Austin furnished Tom with many of his earliest memories and was the perfect environment in which to observe both the benefits and hazards of boomtown life. A visiting correspondent for the *New York Tribune* during this time reported:

At night the brilliantly lighted gambling saloons, with open fronts, are filled with a motley crew. Women conduct the games at several monte tables, shuffling the cards and handling the piles of silver coins with the unruffled serenity of professional gamblers; while men of all classes fight the tiger [house odds] with the usual earnestness of that fascinating pursuit.[15]

On October 10, 1865, Tom's only sister, Clara Marcella, was born, weighing in at a healthy 11½ pounds."[16] As the mining claims around Austin played out and the heavily dependent saloon trade subsequently declined, Robert next set his sights on a new strike 100 miles to the south. Located in the Toquima Mountains at an elevation of about 8,000 feet, the budding camp of Belmont would be the birthplace for Tom's brother, Charles Hugh Logan, on March 31, 1867.

Predictably, tents or canvas cabins had first been erected in Belmont, followed by wooden and brick structures as soon as the mines began to deliver in irrefutable volume. By September 1868, as the demand for a courthouse and other official county facilities increased, the local *Reporter* newspaper observed that the Nye County seat was "without a single public edifice: no place for officers and no place of safety for valuable archive records which we owe to posterity." It was recommended that taxpayers no longer accept this shortcoming and build a new structure to house municipal services.[17] As community leaders wrangled with issues related to modernizing their community, seven-year-old Tom went about his boyhood business wholly unaware that, three decades later, he would be elected Nye County's sheriff and would be the last lawman to occupy the stately two-story courthouse now under construction.

It is not known what enterprise busied Tom's father in Belmont or how long the family lived in the area before relocating to Hamilton, where son George Melvin Logan was born on March 30, 1869. A bustling town of about 4,000 people, Hamilton was about 230 winding miles northeast of Belmont, and nearing the peak of its boom. A *New York Tribune* writer reported:

Hamilton looks, when viewed from the surrounding hills, like the winter encampment of an army, which may be torn down and removed or burned at an hour's notice…. All day long it is thronged. Great covered wagons, hitched two or three together, one behind the other and drawn by 12 to 35 large mules, laden with freight of every kind from Elko, pass along, the rows of bells suspended from an arch above the shoulders of each mule, jingling musically as the train moves on with military precision. O' the cursing![18]

His restlessness unabated and the ever-tantalizing lure of good fortune to be had if a man just kept at it long enough, Tom's father yet again relocated his family. This time, they headed south 100 miles to Pioche. Now with four children between the ages of one and nine in tow, Robert worked as a laborer in the mines.[19] Nothing was certain. Daily life was a relentless, hand-to-mouth struggle to provide food, shelter and clothing.

One of the most pulsating silver-mining towns in Nevada at the time, Pioche sprung into being after Paiute Indians showed William Hamblin, a Latter Day Saint's missionary scouting for new settlement sites, several silver deposits in the area in 1863. (Hamblin's niece, Hannah, would later marry Tom Logan.) San Francisco banker Francois Pioche purchased Hamblin's claims in 1869 and developed the town, which quickly became known as the most lawless camp in the state, rivaling even the legendary Wild West gyrations of Tombstone. Numerous historical accounts note how some 75 men were killed and buried before anyone who had died of natural causes was ever added to the Boot Hill population. Hired gunmen were reported to be arriving at the rate of nearly two dozen a day to "intervene" as needed in mining claim disputes, and the sheriff's office was alleged to have collected some $40,000 a year in bribes to guarantee "certain" outcomes.[20]

On September 15, 1871, Pioche suffered the effects of a horrific fire. Having started at the rear of a restaurant on upper Main Street during a celebration of Mexico's independence from Spain, the blaze soon spread to a mercantile store where 300 kegs of blasting powder were stored in its cellar. The resulting explosion "shook the mountains to their center" and showered the town with flaming debris that burned buildings to the ground, killing thirteen, wounding 47, and leaving more than 1,500 homeless.[21]

Pioche rebuilt within six months, but the Logan family, believed to have lived there at the time of the fire, chose to leave behind the literally explosive bedlam of that untamed city. It was in the harsh environment of the Muddy River Valley, 150 miles to the south, where they finally put down roots – but not without paying a soul-searing price.

At the age of ten, Tom had now lived in at least five Nevada mining camps and gained position as the ever-reliant older brother to three siblings: Chisse (Clara), Charley, and George. Besides also functioning as "the man of house" when his father was away, Tom had surely been exposed to numerous frontier calamities and hardships. Life was a grueling, often bloody struggle for saint and sinner alike. Fatal diseases, murders, suicides, and mining and range accidents were commonplace. Local headlines were packed with sensational offenses courtesy of those who cheated, robbed, maimed, and killed at will.

Although a guaranteed fascination to any growing boy, the evils of drinking, gambling, and consorting with women of easy virtue were constantly warned against by Mary—an iron-willed perspective held by most mothers of the day. Her fundamental religious convictions coupled with her husband's proclivity for civic engagement greatly influenced their children. All would grow into hard-working, big-hearted, enterprising adults, which, in Tom's case, worked mostly to his advantage until the morning of April 7, 1906.

ROUGHLY 60 MILES northeast of what is now Las Vegas, the Muddy River or Moapa Valley region was initially colonized in 1865 by Mormons looking for land to grow cotton and other pioneer staples. Under the direction of their leader, Brigham Young, the settlements of St. Thomas and St. Joseph were established in what he considered part of the state of Deseret and within the Territory of Utah. Drawn to what some characterized as an oasis setting at the confluence of the Muddy and Virgin Rivers, Mormon settlers streamed into what would become southeastern Nevada.

St. Thomas had a post office within two years and, by 1867, the regional population had reached 500. However, it soon became obvious that the seemingly idyllic environment fell far short of their expectations. Despite treaty agreements, adversarial encounters continued with area Native Americans. The salty Muddy River, fed by a mineral hot spring, proved to be a poor source of irrigation for crops. Include drought, fires, floods, and maladies like dysentery and malaria, and many settlers either perished or retreated to more hospitable establishments in Utah.

In 1870, a state boundary survey determined the town sites of St. Thomas and St. Joseph to be in the new state of Nevada and not in either Utah or Arizona Territories.* Unwilling to pay back property taxes that had erroneously gone to Utah and by direct order of Brigham Young, some 600 Muddy Valley colonists packed up wagons and returned to Utah. They left behind dozens of homes and hundreds of acres of orchards and crops consisting of sugar cane, wheat, cotton, corn, vegetables, and grapes.[22]

Tom's father acquired one of the abandoned Mormon ranches in exchange for a wagon and a team of horses near St. Joseph in 1871.[23] Author Arabell Lee Hafner wrote about the Logan family's arrival in the valley in her book, *100 Years on the Muddy*:

The mother was ill and the father quit working in the mine he was employed at to care for his wife and family. The Logan family came and settled in an adobe house…There was one room 18 by 20 feet built by the Mormons for protection from the Indians. A brick could be taken out [of portals] at intervals to shoot through. The walls were two feet thick and underneath was a storage place for food. Out in another adobe house was a canvas bellows for a blacksmith shop. The homes were all connected, had dirt floors and tule, with dirt roofs and logs and packed dirt ceilings.

After a while, Mrs. Logan began feeling better as the climate was good for her and she used to ride horses a great deal. One day she rode through the valley and the horse didn't go fast enough for her, so she stopped for a branch off a tree. When she arrived home, she stuck the stick into the ground, and it grew into a beautiful tree that stood until 1954, giving shade to many people.[24]

During the 1872 election, Tom's father served as the Lincoln County (later Clark County) Registry Agent for the St. Thomas precinct. Remembered by neighbors and descendants to have not been "very serious and kind of a character," Robert also served as a census marshal, one of the Inspectors of the Election for the St. Thomas Precinct, and was elected Justice of the Peace, an office he held for many years.[25]

The Logan family farm produced alfalfa, grain, sorghum, and practically

---

* Utah became a state on January 4, 1896; Arizona did the same on February 14, 1912.

all the grapes grown in southern Nevada and Utah. Robert's vineyard was on a hillside above the swampier lowlands, and he soon became known for his wine-making skills. In addition to a large wine cellar well-shaded by cottonwood trees, Tom's father also operated a still in a thicket of bushes where the stealthy Logan boys snitched their first taste of alcohol.[26]

Mary Logan, the only woman in St. Joseph (now known as Logandale) at the time and its first postmaster, gave birth to Frank Logan on February 17, 1874. The population of this remote enclave would reach 34 by 1880.[27] Few inhabitants had money in their pockets. Most bartered for services and merchandise. Clothing was either handmade or traded for with wheat or barley. Frank would later tell his own children that he wore moccasins until he was 17, only then getting his first pair of cowboy boots.[28] In hard times, when Robert was away and Mary was alone with her brood of children, area Native Americans would bring them corn and other provisions to get by.

Tom's younger brothers (left to right) Charles, Frank, and George Logan, c. 1881 (Logan Family Collection)

Before a school house was built, lessons were taught in a grove of cottonwoods with a blackboard nailed to a tree trunk. Children of varying ages sat on crudely fashioned wooden benches during class time. However, should a flock of ducks swoop by, a boy or two would grab a shotgun and, despite the teacher's objections, momentarily abandoned their studies to chase after the unsuspecting fowl or any other potential meal that ventured close.[29]

Community dances and basket socials afforded women the opportunity to showcase cooking skills and vie for the attention of a potential suitor. Ladies wore calico dresses and the men, often dressed in their finest overalls, bid on baskets with undisclosed contents, hoping at the end of the evening they would be dining on fried chicken and pie and not some dried-up cheese sandwich. Proceeds were often split between the cook, the church, and the musicians typically outfitted with either a fiddle, banjo or juice harp. A barrel of beer, 72 quarts worth, cost between $6 and $12, and whiskey went for about $1 for a quart.[30]

On July 27, 1881, ten years after coming to Muddy Valley, the last of the Logan children, Robert, Jr., was born. However, when Mary failed to fully recover, Tom's father placed him in charge of the farm and family, and bundled his stricken

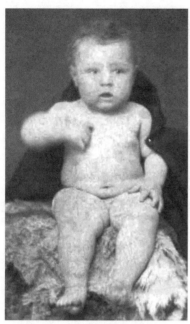

Tom's youngest brother, Robert
Logan, Jr., 1882
(Logan Family Collection)

wife and new baby into a springboard wagon bound for medical services in San Bernardino, California, some 300 hundred grueling miles away. After a week had passed, one or the other of the older Logan children rode a horse up to a rise in the road every day, expecting to see their parents returning and anxious to hear their beloved mother was on the mend. Nearly a month later the wagon driven by their crestfallen father finally arrived home with Mary in an even more fragile state.[31] From the *Pioche Weekly Record*:

It is my very painful duty to announce through your columns, the death of Mrs. Mary E. Logan of this place, which sad event took place on the 5th instant [March 5, 1882]. Mrs. L. and her husband had but just returned from a visit to Pioche. On the Monday preceding her death, upon her arrival home, she complained of fatigue and weakness. During the remainder of the week her symptoms created no alarm until Saturday night. On Sunday, at half-past 1 o'clock, she sank quietly to her eternal rest, surrounded by her family and many friends...her funeral to-day was very largely attended and her loss will be deeply deplored by all who knew her. The grief-stricken family have [sic] the profound sympathy of the whole community.[32]

Tom's mother was the first valley dweller buried in St. Joseph. Her heartbroken husband arranged a ring of large white rocks around the grave and planted a circle of cottonwood saplings. Now needing assistance to care for his younger children, Robert brought in 23-year-old Hannah Mariah Hamblin, a self-professed Mormon defector, who had been working as a servant for a household a few miles to the south in St. Thomas. She was the third of ten children born to Edwin and Hannah Ann (Cook) Hamblin, on December 12, 1859, in Santa Clara, Utah Territory. Her mother hailed from Gloucestershire, England, and her father from Bainbridge, Ohio. Edwin's older brother was Jacob Hamblin, a prominent associate of Brigham Young and responsible for introducing the Mormon faith to his parents and siblings. As a respected Native American diplomat, Jacob gained renown as the "Buckskin Apostle."[33]

Hannah's grandfather, Isaiah Hamblin, fought in the war of 1812 under General Henry Dearborn, but her most famous ancestor was a fourth great-grandmother, Hannah Emerson Dustin. Born in 1657 in colonial Massachusetts,

Hannah Dustin was the first woman in North America to have a monument erected in her honor in 1874. Still standing in Boscawen, Massachusetts, the statue memorializes an incident that occurred during the French and Indian War in 1697 when Abenaki Indians from Quebec raided a colonial settlement, killing 27 and kidnapping 13 — three of whom were Hannah Dustin, her newborn daughter, and nursemaid. After two weeks in captivity, during which her wailing baby was bashed to death against an apple tree, Hannah Dustin conspired with four other hostages to successfully kill and scalp their captors before returning to their distraught families.[34]

In no uncertain terms, Dustin's namesake, Hannah Hamblim, would also endure mishap and misfortune with comparable courage and resilience as the wife of Tom Logan. From the *Pioche Daily Record*:

Quite a fashionable wedding took place in Pioche last Sunday morning [May 27, 1883]. Justice Young, in the most approved style, tied the knot that bound Thomas Logan of St. Joseph, and Miss Hannah Hamblin of Clover Valley, as husband and wife. Three sisters and three brothers of the bride stood up. The number of crusty old bachelors hanging out in Pioche would do well to follow young Logan's example, thus securing the services of a competent female to do their summer washing.[35]

Hannah was a consummate homemaker. Trained since early childhood in the proficiencies required of the woman of the house, her duties included cooking, baking, quilting, sewing, growing and preserving food; making butter, cheese, soap, candles, clothing, and rag rugs; and tending to any number of children

Thomas Walter Logan, age 22, 1883
(Logan Family Collection, James
Hildreth Traveling Photographers,
Mineral Park, Mojave County, AZ)

Hannah Hamblin Logan, c. 1895
(Logan Family Collection)

engaged in chores, lessons, and antics. Such skillful hands, in motion upon rising and until the last light of night was extinguished, set a standard for generations to come. Few personal traits exemplify the legacy of Tom and Hannah Logan in their descendants as does a willingness to work hard, partake in honest enterprise, and sustain self-sufficiency—frequently, to the point of pure obstinacy.

For a brief time, the new Mr. and Mrs. Thomas Logan continued living and working on his father's ranch, where Tom also temporarily assumed his mother's duties at the St. Joseph post office. Their first child, Anna Elizabeth Logan, was born some 170 miles to the north in Clover Valley on April 4, 1884, presumably at Hannah's parent's home.

About this same time, Tom decided to strike out independent of his father by hitching a ride out of Muddy Valley on a load of provisions headed to Mohave County, nearly 200 miles to the southeast in the Arizona Territory. That decision was probably forged during a trip Tom and his father had recently taken to that area, likely peddling meat, wine, and produce from their farm. At one point, when they stopped for Tom to grease an axle, he discovered a bottle of concealed whiskey. Exasperated by Robert's increased drinking since Mary's death, Tom smashed it over the wheel. This ignited a heated argument that may have been heightened by Robert's tendency to disappear for weeks, leaving the family to fend for themselves. Had it not been for the local Native American women taking food to the Logan children during their father's prolonged absences, they would have starved. Now married and a parent himself, Tom's priorities and loyalties had shifted considerably.[36]

For the better part of the next decade, Tom and Hannah moved about Mohave County as opportunities ebbed and flowed. Tom first hired on as a ranch hand for Sam Crozier, a prominent cattleman who ran a butcher shop in Kingman,

Anna Logan, c. 1892
(Logan Family Collection)

Mohave County, c. 1885

which supplied both the ever-transient mining enterprises as well as the Atlantic & Pacific Railroad under construction between 1880 and 1883. Chasing wages like so many others during this time, Tom was gone much more than he was home, forcing him to leave Hannah alone with baby Anna. Their first house, believed to have been located near Peach Springs, was a crudely converted milk house without windows. The nearest woman was 60 miles away. Hannah hung blankets over cracks in the walls to prevent lantern light from shining through and unintentionally inviting a passing vagabond or hostile-type to stop.

One morning, with Anna in her arms, she opened the front door to discover a man with an ax about to chop his way in to look for food. Hannah frightened him almost as much as he did her, but was soon relieved when he began gently speaking to her startled baby. It became Hannah's belief that if a stranger spoke first to Anna, she need not be afraid. However, if he ignored the baby, her guard went up because that meant "he was crazy."[37]

Tom soon relocated his family to Mineral Park, then the Mohave County Seat, and formed a brief partnership with James Smith to open a grocery market. Shortly, Tom became full owner and, apparently back on civil terms with his father, he stocked many staples from the Logan ranch 130 miles to the north, including the choicest of bacon with a "reputation for rapid sale."[38] From "Local Brevities" in the December 14, 1884, *Mojave County Miner*:

Thomas Logan's four-horse team came late to town on Thursday loaded with live turkeys, sausage, fresh pork, lard, raisins and various other luxuries, the product of the St. Joseph farm where he formerly resided. These luxuries and many others are on sale at his market on Main Street.[39]

A favorite family memory from this period involved one of Tom's horses. Bred and raised in St. Joseph, the horse was sold to a new owner in Mohave County but soon broke free, swam across the Colorado River, and returned to the Logan ranch. After waiting a period of time for the owner to claim the fugitive animal,

Tom resold the horse, which promptly repeated the same feat. Tom's brother, Frank, estimated that single horse was sold at least five times.[40]

By January 1, 1885, Tom had enough capital to purchase the Willows and Fairview ranches in Mohave County for use as a stock range. He moved his family from Mineral Park to Quail Springs where they lived for about three years.[41] That same year, at the age of 19, Tom's only sister, Clara, married Phillip (Klingen) Smith in Pioche. Besides working as mail rider and day laborer, Smith would be elected sheriff of Lincoln County in 1907.[42]

With the impending dawn of the 20th century, rampant lawlessness perpetrated by those who ignored principles of human decency—let alone the emerging laws of the land—began, however excruciatingly slow, to recede. A major component of the evolving law enforcement system was the justice court.

Tom's only sister, Clara Logan Smith, c. 1881 (Logan Family Collection)

Whether elected or appointed, a justice of the peace was not required to have any legal training to hold the office and had jurisdiction over, for instance, debt disputes, vagrancy, assault and battery, and other petty crimes. They could also perform marriages. To best function in a non-trial setting, a justice needed to be a good listener, a keen student of human behavior, and fair-minded.

As a J.P. and now age 52, Tom's father had earned the respect of the Muddy Valley community in which he had lived for more than a decade. However, that reputation did not prevent him from being swept into a bizarre legal fray with the U.S. Government. The situation began simply enough when a former employee of the Moapa Indian Reservation brought suit in justice court for the purpose of foregoing red tape in order to collect a salary still due him. Agents from the reservation were uncooperative, so Robert Logan placed a levy on some of their cattle, which the constable sold to satisfy the debt. This action was reported to the authorities in the nation's capital and U.S. Marshals were dispatched to round up Robert, the constable, and any accomplices for transport to Carson City, 600 miles away, to be "tried, condemned, and hung by the U.S. Circuit Court for meddling with Uncle Sam's horned stock."[43]

Once before the tribunal, it was ascertained that Tom's father had acted within his jurisdictional duties, and all were released but given not one dime for the long trek home. "The most of these prisoners were compelled to walk from Carson to their homes on the Muddy," reported *The Pioche Weekly*

Record, May 1, 1886, "which was superior exercise for the development of the muscles of the legs, but hard on patience and shoe-leather."

A principled man with a potent sense of how he chose to dispense justice in his court, Robert found not a sliver of humor in the heavy-handed usurping of his authority by the U.S. Government. To make known his outrage, he traveled to the nation's capital, hell-bent on prosecuting the U.S. government for $50,000 in damages. As word spread of his monumental undertaking, *The Albuquerque Journal* speculated on April 28, 1886, that, "Mr. Logan will return home sometime in the twentieth century with the statement that the committee had reported favorably on his claim."[44] Robert was back in Nevada by August 1886, the outcome of his mission heretofore unknown.

Tom Logan, (far left) Cash Grocery Store, unknown location, c. 1890
(Logan Family Collection)

Meanwhile, Tom Logan was making plans to open a much-needed butcher shop in Mineral Park and take in his two youngest brothers for the coming school year. Frank and Robert, ages 12 and 5, were among the Roll of Honor students recognized in the local newspaper the spring of 1887.[45] Only months earlier, on January 4, Hannah gave birth to a second daughter, Jessie, in Kingman. A rapidly expanding town, due in large part to its proximity to the Atlantic & Pacific Railroad, Kingman was now the Mojave County Seat. That same winter, the first rail shipment of cattle left Kingman, bound for Los Angeles, projecting certain success as a vital southwestern commercial hub.[46]

With each business prospect, Tom thoughtfully weighed his chances. Growing up amidst droves of voracious miners, speculators, and gamblers betting on being one step ahead of the competition, he had gained appreciation for the more reliable vocation of catering to basic and predictable needs such as food and transportation. Adapting to fluctuating local economics, social trends, and transient populations, he distinguished himself in the cattle trade. In addition to his butcher shop, he also operated the Mineral Park and Kingman Express Line, which hauled passengers and freight along the heavily traveled 20-mile road between the two towns.[47] As his business prospects and partnerships expanded, so did Tom and Hannah's family. Daughter number three, Josephine (Joie) was born in Peach Springs on April 22, 1889, just before the Logans moved into Kingman.

Descendants speculate that Tom left Arizona and returned to Nevada when his father's health began to deteriorate. Daughter number four, Hazel, was born in Overton, just a few miles south of the Logan's Muddy Valley ranch on September 29, 1891. Hazel once confided in one of her daughters that with her birth, Tom gave up hope of ever having a son. Aware that her birth had been a disappointment to her father, Hazel endeavored to impress him by excelling as a horsewoman, which often garnered special praise from Tom.[48]

In early 1892, Tom's father transferred ownership of a substantial portion of his land to daughter-in-law Hannah as a gesture of appreciation for her efforts in caring for his children following Mary's death.[49] During his final years, Robert maintained his duties as justice of the peace and didn't hesitate to speak his mind if provoked. In June, 1893, he appeared before county commissioners to dispute the public's access to a "private" road on his property.[50] A year before his death, battling cancer, and described by the *Pioche Weekly Record* to be "rusticating," he filed a suit in district court contesting certain land rights in Muddy Valley. Even though the case was dismissed and, looking back on other causes he undertook, it appears as if winning wasn't nearly as important as making a statement about some perceived inequity.[51] Robert Logan believed in having his voice heard.

Just two months before his death on July 18, 1896, Robert sold his prized 600-acre ranch to, "an Eastern gentleman who intends to settle a colony in this fertile valley."[52] He was buried in Panaca, Nevada. A dual marble headstone with a connecting arch marks his grave. On the left column is inscribed: *"Amiable and beloved father, farewell! Not on this perishing stone but in the Book of Life and in the hearts of thy afflicted friends is thy worth recorded."* To the right, in anticipation of his wife, Mary, someday being moved from her resting place in Logandale to his side, the column reads: *"God's unseen angel O'er our pathway crossed – looked on us all and loving her the most straightway received her to the heavenly fold."**

---

* To date, Mary remains buried in Logandale.

Tom Logan, c. 1890 (Logan Family Collection)

The new patriarch of the Logan family was now Tom Logan. A native Nevadan, he was accustomed to a climate that could stop a man and horse in their tracks as easily with a brilliant sunset or a razor-edged blizzard. He knew well the splendor and perils of a terrain abounding with untold riches and heartache. As to the excitable, often reckless culture fixed on testing the limits of social norms and disobedience, Tom would rely on the formative influences of his parents and the grueling lessons so typically associated with boomtowns and the open range.

One particular point of guidance imparted by his father was based in a story about a lawbreaker who took a point-blank shot at an unarmed sheriff standing across the street. Speaking in a low voice, the officer calmly walked toward the shooter and soon had him under arrest. "If you go after a bad man," Robert Logan cautioned, "you're better off without a gun, because you can generally talk to them and work things out without anyone getting killed." [53]

The Ranchman's Song

Afar from the tumult and turmoil of fashion,
Away, far away, from the throng that intrudes;
I am free from all envy and malice and passion
For my spirit expands in the wild solitudes.

I love the broad prairie, the nother's sad sighting,
The whispering stars, the owl's lone hoo,
The mocking-bird's song when the twilight is dying,
The cayote's weird call as it echoes "ki-oo."

Wild nature to me is a thing that I cherish;
I hate the dull discords that cities have shown;
For there out of tune my free spirits all perish;
Let me dwell near to nature with my ideals alone.

Better live rich at heart on a crust in a garret,
Than languish in mansions impoverished with strife;
There is joy in a dugout, if fancy but share it
With hope and fond memory to brighten thy life.

There's a zest amidst hardship which some natures treasure
A charm on the prairies that care cannot cloy;
So, avaunt! ye dull follies of fashionable pleasure,
Give me the wild pleasures that ranchmen enjoy.

—William Lawrence "Larry" Chittenden (1862-1934)

2

CALL OF DUTY: 1899-1900

"Sheriffs and their deputies shall keep and preserve the peace in their respective counties, and quiet and suppress all affrays, riots and insurrections, for which purpose, and for the service of process in civil or criminal cases, and in apprehending or securing any person for felony, or breach of the peace."

An excerpt from *The General Statutes of the State of Nevada*, sec. 5, 1861

SETTLERS JOURNEYED WESTWARD in the mid-1800s to build lives on their own terms, and conventional thinking presumed a stranger to be trustworthy until proven otherwise. A fellow traveler was welcome to stop in for water, food, or lodging. Locks symbolized an impeachment of mutual honesty and integrity. A man's word was his bond, and treating others as one would like to be treated was the default law of the land.

The discovery of gold generated the bulk of lawlessness that made the West wild and the Colt six-shooter often more powerful than any law book stored on a shelf. Between 1850 and 1890, approximately 20,000 men were killed in gunfights, an all-too-frequent method for settling disputes. Sheriffs could at-will declare a renegade desperado as "bearing the wolf's head," thereby granting permission to kill on sight as they would a wild animal. Translation: Wanted Dead or Alive, legal rights optional.[1]

Sheriffs were usually elected to office, although occasionally appointed. Previous law enforcement experience was not required, but both job and life depended heavily on being a quick study. Entrusted to tackle vice and all manifestations of disorder, the frontier sheriff relied on personal prowess, gut instinct, steady nerves, and recurrent strokes of ingenuity. He also had to be amply skilled with a sidearm, proficient with horses, and able to round up a posse in swift fashion. Some were certainly more capable than others, and more than a few succumbed to bribery and other corrupt enticements. Still, history attests the majority stood firm and stalwart in their oaths to protect and serve. In the latter half of the nineteenth century, these often forgotten lawmen served at the forefront of converting unruly encampments into civilized municipalities. With constantly evolving duties, they fought and cajoled, jailed and punished, sacrificed and bled for the common good.

And some, like Sheriff Tom Logan, died in the line of duty.

Just before the turn of the century in 1899, Tom Logan became fully engaged in the Nye County's rapid transition from the creak and rattle of the horse-and-buggy days to the hissing clank and grind of the Industrial Age. Having settled in the area some four years earlier, he and Hannah welcomed Amy, daughter number five, on July 3, 1894. Between 1895 and 1898, they ran a ranch near Duckwater with about 75 head of cattle. During this period, at long last, their first son, Jay Edwin (Ted), was born January 3, 1897. A sixth daughter, Thelma Kate arrived less than two years later on November 11, 1898. That same month, Tom, now 37 and father of seven, was elected sheriff.

Hazel, Joie, and Amy behind Ted and Kate Logan, c. 1900, Belmont, NV
(Logan Family Collection)

The eleventh Nye County sheriff and assessor since the first was appointed in 1864, Tom narrowly defeated fellow Silver Party member and four-term incumbent Charles McGregor by a vote of 120 to 113. He was sworn into office on January 3, 1899, at the first county commissioners' meeting of the new year.[2]

The county's population was barely more than one thousand and, dwindling, in a region that was "almost as free of crime as it was taxes."[3 & 4] More and more, it was getting harder to cobble together reasons to stay in a place teetering on the verge of being reclaimed by earthly elements. Once thriving mines had long ago played out, and formerly verdant rangelands had been depleted by over-grazing.[5] Other than the ever-rosy visions of diehard prospectors obsessed with striking it big, there was not the slightest hint of the world-class mining camp about to burst into being from what was then termed the "unexplored desert."

More than 18,000 square miles in size, Nye County is named after James Warren Nye, a one-time district attorney and judge from Madison County, New York, whom President Abraham Lincoln appointed the first governor of the

Nevada Territory in 1861.[6] The county is hammer-shaped and about the size of New Hampshire and New Jersey combined. From *The History of Nevada, Vol. II*, 1912:

The topography of [Nye County] differs little from that of the major portion of Nevada, consisting of valleys running north and south and of mountain spurs and ranges. In its earlier years, Nye was considered fine grazing country and thousands of cattle grazed annually upon the bunch grass and white sage which grew profusely over the large portions of the county, the white sage in particular constituting a very valuable winter food. For many years, however, the greater portion had been looked upon as desert, inhabited by the lizard and horned toad, while the slinking coyote is monarch of all he surveys.[7]

The Nye County seat in 1899 was Belmont, a name derived from "beaumont," a French word meaning "beautiful mountain." Roughly to the west was Smoky Valley, to the east Monitor Valley, and in between, stretching about 70 miles south to southwest, the saw-toothed Toquima Mountain Range, with the highest summit being nearly 12,000 feet. In the higher elevations, trout populate the snow-fed streams and small lakes. On the valley floors, the scalding run-off of hot springs etch networks of steaming ditches tinged with green and rust-colored algae. Native people composed mostly of the Western Shoshone, along with explorers like John C. Fremont in 1845, and eventually ranchers and miners, were adept at routing boiling spring waters into tepid pools ideal for year-round human indulgence.

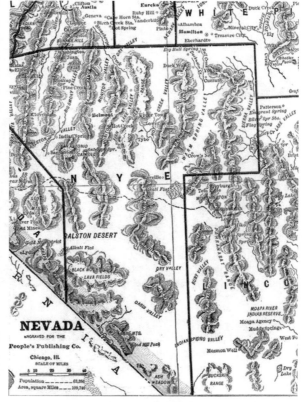

Nothing so enlivens the incessantly drab landscape as does a wash of crimson Indian paintbrush in the spring and the brilliant yellow bloom of brittlebush in the fall. Howling coyotes slink through the nights stalking antelope, rabbits, and sage grouse. And overhead, the Nevada sky, from a stunning, amber-colored sundown to the fitful wrath of a midnight thunderstorm, rarely disappoints. Yet within the seductive splendor of the high desert resides a ubiquitous caveat. This magnificent environment can become so brutal that, upon stealing a fallen man's last breath in the blistering heat of summer, it will commence reducing flesh and bone to dust before the next day's sun peeks above the horizon. And in winter time, frantic icy winds can so thrash an unprotected man that, upon collapse, the last sensation he feels is likely nothing but his pitiful soul taking flight.

People like the Logans, who chose to live in and around remote Belmont long after the silver boom of the 1870s, were an especially hardy breed. In truth, when Tom took office on January 1, 1899, his biggest daily challenge was most likely the weather with which he had to contend while traveling about his far-reaching jurisdiction. The business of running the county had so slowed that whole sessions of the district court sometimes passed without a single case to adjudicate.[8]

Cosmopolitan Saloon & Hotel, Belmont, NV, c. 1895
(Central Nevada Historical Society, Tonopah, NV)

Still, as the loosely hinged service center for mining camps and ranches, Belmont hosted a reliable cluster of shops and saloons, a newspaper, bank, livery stable, telegraph office, and church. On the outskirts of town were tall abandoned brick smokestacks and stone-built shells of the stamp mills where small mountains of ore had once been noisily broken apart to extract precious minerals. The preferred social hub was the Cosmopolitan, a hotel and dancehall. Upon hearing piano music and bursts of laughter from within its walls, many a curious child was drawn into the evening shadows along Main Street, hoping to spy through an undraped window ebullient couples dancing or, better yet, witness some forbidden spectacle.

At one time or another, most of Tom and Hannah's children attended the Belmont School. To encourage regular participation, each student's attendance record was published in the local newspaper. In the winter of 1899, the oldest Logan daughter, Annie, age 15, scored 97 percent. Her younger sisters, Jessie and Josephine, ages 12 and 10, had 94 percent, and Hazel, age 8, 90 percent.[9]

Belmont School, (Back row, l to r) Lottie Hughes, Katy Hughes, Jessie Logan behind Viola Brotherton, Della Gilbert, Kate Logan, Annie Bradley (teacher), Francis Brotherton, Roslie Hunt, Nevada Bell Butler behind May Hunt, (Front row, l to r) Brotherton boy, Freddie Hughes, Hazel Logan (author's grandmother), Ruth Hunt, Amy Logan, (Behind front step row, l to r) Francis Gilbert, Ted Logan, Essie Brotherton, Robert Hughes, Joie Logan, Belmont School House, Belmont, NV, c. 1902 (Logan Family Collection)

Just up the hill from the school, northwest of town, was the courthouse. Completed in 1876, the majestic two-story brick and granite building housed the county's administrative offices, including that of the treasurer, recorder, district attorney, and sheriff. A two-cell jail with flat-iron strap doors was attached to the rear of the building. Upstairs was a spacious courtroom with an adjacent judge's chambers, all generously lighted by rows of high, arched windows. Atop the peaked roof, a glassed-in cupola, accessible by a steep, plank stairway, offered a bird's-eye view of the town's patchwork of earth-toned rooftops and, to the southwest, the vast and barren expanse of the treeless desert. The more daring Logan children took any chance they could to sneak into the tiny tower, more times than not at the cost of a stern scolding from their mother.

Nye County Courthouse, (sheriff's office occupied the lower right corner) c. 1889, Belmont, NV (Nevada Historical Society, Reno, NV)

Visitors entering the courthouse would find the sheriff's office to their immediate right. Earning a meager $55 a month in scrip,* Tom continued to generate alternate sources of income. In April 1899, he partnered with George H. Sharp to purchase a 150-acre ranch, roughly 20 miles northeast of Belmont in Monitor Valley, for $1,450. Frequently away on business, Tom hired a foreman to help run the ranch in his absence.[10] During both growing season and harvest time, the Logan family stayed in the valley to work the crops, but when the weather turned cold from October to April, they moved up to Belmont, where they lived in a small brick house near the courthouse.

Life for the Logan household, as with most Nye County families at the turn of the century, was a relentless exercise in adaptation, self-sufficiency, and conservation. Clothing was passed down from sibling to sibling. Fabric scraps, as small as a square inch, were pieced into crazy quilts. Outfits for clothespin dolls with button hats were crudely stitched together with leftover strands of thread rarely longer than six inches. Soap was made from wood ashes and fat, and perhaps hair shampoo made, as Hannah had learned as a child, from powdered yucca root mixed with water.

The laundry was soaked in a large kettle on a wood-burning stove, scrubbed clean against a corrugated rub board, rinsed, and hung outside to dry on lines or inside on hooks and racks by the stove. Flour sacks were fashioned into curtains, mattresses stuffed with down feathers, and tin cans cut and pounded flat to patch roof leaks. Root cellars were stocked with homegrown produce and

---

* Scrip functions as an alternative to cash or other forms of legal tender, and guarantees the payee credit for certain services per an agreement between the issuer and merchant.

pantry shelves with jarred preserves. Nothing was wasted, and everyone had chores from churning butter to hauling water, hoeing weeds to milking cows, stacking wood to slaughtering livestock, and picking crops to pitching hay. The work was never done, but time was still made for brief excursions and social events, usually associated with a holiday.

The *Belmont Courier* regularly documented Logan family activities and Tom's travels from one end of the county to the other gathering jurors, delivering subpoenas, assessing property, collecting license fees and taxes, chasing down an occasional lawbreaker, and performing any other duty deemed in the community interest. The following samples from the *Belmont Courier* reflect various facets of Tom's first year as sheriff:

May, 13, 1899: *Sheriff and Assessor TW Logan informs us that nearly the entire fruit crop from Eastern Nye was destroyed by frost last month.*

June, 3, 1899: *Mrs. Rose Bradley and Misses Ida Brougher and Nellie Goldbach were visiting TW Logan and family in Monitor Valley this week.*

June 10, 1899: *Mrs. Thomas Logan was quite ill this week at her home in Monitor Valley.*

June 17, 1899: *Sheriff and Assessor TW Logan returned from Western Nye on the 12 (instant); brought a large specimen to Belmont from the new mine south of San Antonio. The quartz is rich in gold and silver and there is no doubt that Messers Bell and Court have discovered a Bonanza.*

July 15, 1899: *The first new hay which has arrived in Belmont this year was brought to town on Tuesday by Sheriff and Assessor TW Logan from his ranch in Monitor Valley. (The crop was light this year.)*

August 5, 1899: *Sheriff and Assessor TW Logan and Postmaster FR Brotherton visited the southern Klondike last week and report the mines being worked there to be most valuable properties.*

March 24, 1900: *The Masque Ball: The large and motley throng of masqueraders that crowded the Cosmopolitan Hall on the night of the 16th created great sport for the many spectators present. There were no elegant, and very few costumes on the floor, but the ridiculous suits and funny faces made an amusing spectacle and every one of the characters were well sustained...[including] T. L. Oddie (Fool), John Nay (School Girl), Lottie Stimler (Topsy) George Hughes and John Clifford (Twin babies), Jessie Logan (Sister of Charity), Annie Logan (an Old Woman), P. J. Bradley and F. G. Humphrey (Irish Dudes)....*

At the end of summer 1899, Tom received the heartrending news that his brother Charley, the only one of the five Logan brothers still in Arizona, was dead. For the last three years he had struggled with a "disorder of the stomach" thought to be cancer and had traveled as far away as Los Angeles and San Francisco for treatment. A miner-turned-rancher and active in his community, Charley's failing health was the motivation behind his decision to pursue a less demanding vocation two years earlier when he, his wife Lizzie and young daughter moved from Kingman to Hackberry to build and operate a hotel.[11] Charles Hugh Logan died on September 12, 1899:

Charles Logan, a young man about thirty-two years of age, and well and favorably known in Northwestern Arizona, died at Hackberry Tuesday of stomach trouble from which he had suffered for years. In his untimely departure from this life Mojave County loses an honest, upright citizen, and one whose impulses were always good. Born and raised in the west, he grew up, married and had his home among our people and was always considered a worthy man....[12]

Charles "Charley" Logan, c. 1895
(Logan Family Collection)

Back in Nye County, with winter fast approaching, Tom moved his family from their Monitor Valley ranch up to Belmont in October, where the children would attend school for several months. The threat of illness was ever-present and even Tom, as the following entries from the *Belmont Courier* reveal, occasionally succumbed to the harsh elements:

October 7, 1899: *Sheriff Logan and Treasurer Warburton were confined to their rooms this week with sickness.*

October 21, 1899: *Sheriff Logan was taken down by a severe bilious attack the fore part of the week, but is much better now.**

November 4, 1899: *Sheriff and Assessor TW Logan visited Smoky Valley this week.*

November 18, 1899: *Sheriff and Assessor TW Logan was in Western Nye this week.*

November 25, 1899: *Sheriff and Assessor TW Logan returned from Eastern Nye on Sunday last.*

---

* A "bilious attack" was a catch-all term during this time for an upset digestive system usually caused by eating something "disagreeable." Symptoms include severe headache, vomiting, diarrhea, constipation, fatigue, and a sour disposition.

DURING THE SECOND week of January 1900, Tom and Hannah had just returned to Belmont after a visit to the Barley Creek Ranch (on the other side of Monitor Valley) when young Jim Clifford* rode into town with breathless news for the sheriff. Richard Breen, the old Irishman who owned the cattle ranch south of the Clifford spread in the Kawich, was dead. Jim claimed that he and his older brother Ed Jr., both in their mid-20s, had stopped by the man's ranch and became alarmed when Breen was nowhere to be found. After searching for hours well into dark, they discovered his badly injured body in a meadow not far from the stone and sod-roofed house, where he lived alone.

In her book, *Jack Longstreet: the Last of the Desert Frontiersmen*, renowned Nevada historian Sally Zanjani meticulously described the ensuing tangle of events associated with Breen's suspicious death. To summarize, upon learning that Richard Breen had been found dead, Tom promptly loaded an empty coffin into his wagon and asked County Public Administrator Charles Anderson and Joseph McCann, a young miner, to accompany him and Jim Clifford back to the Breen ranch, some 85 miles southeast of Belmont. Breen's new neighbor, the inscrutable Andrew Jackson "Jack" Longstreet, in his 66th year and remarkably spry, had also been summoned. He and Ed Jr. stood watch over the old man's body while waiting for Sheriff Logan.

Jack Longstreet, c. 1905 (Central Nevada Historical Society, Tonopah, NV)

A tall, whiskered, and leathery southern-born man who kept to himself unless incited to do otherwise, Longstreet was handy with a gun and had a knack for skirting the law. During a failed attempt to steal horses in his youth, he had had one ear cut off in lieu of a hanging. Consequently, he wore his graying blond hair long to cover the disfigurement. Purported to have been a Pony Express rider, one of Mosby's

---

* The powerful Clifford family was among Nye's most prominent pioneers. With a houseful of children, they had ranched in the area nearly 20 years and were widely respected by the community. According to historian Sally Zanjani, "scarcely an issue of the *Belmont Courier* went to press without relating their sociable comings and goings."

Raiders in the Civil War, and a veteran of the Indian Wars, Longstreet sported five notches on his pistol.

Whether his reputation was earned, fabricated, or a combination thereof, Longstreet was an imposing, grizzled force to be reckoned with. In 1882, he and his Native American wife had homesteaded 120 acres in Moapa Valley and opened a combination saloon and drug store in St. Thomas. There he also raced horses and, apparently without noteworthy incident, first crossed paths with the Logan family. His later advocacy for Native American rights became legendary.

Longstreet's Red Rock Ranch, in the otherwise unpopulated Kawich region of Nye County, was just six miles north of Breen's property and about 20 miles south of Clifford's. Breen's body, besides being badly bruised, was in such a battered state that Tom could not be certain if he was looking at the victim of a tragic accident or a murder. His elbow was lacerated, skin was worn off one toe down to the bone, and his neck was broken. Footprints indicated Breen had been walking around with only one boot on. Nearby, grazing peacefully, were several horses and a mule with a rope dangling from its neck. Tom concluded the old rancher had been drug behind a horse or the mule. Anderson and Longstreet concurred.

Longstreet confided in Tom that Breen had told him the Cliffords had been pressuring him to sell them his ranch and he had refused. Later, during probate proceedings, Breen's will revealed that he had left all his stock and the ranch to Ed Clifford, Jr. Although suspicious, there was no proof one way or the other that the document was forged. Still, there was enough mystery and doubt that the coroner recommended an investigation.

In April 1900, the Grand Jury found that Breen was "of unsound mind, and came to his death through wandering around, and from exposure." It would take more than two years for the court to deem the will genuine. Neither outcome quieted rumors that the Cliffords had maliciously orchestrated the acquisition of Breen's ranch. Sheriff Logan and Charles Anderson remained convinced that foul play had transpired, but it was Longstreet who eventually acted upon that festering sentiment.

During the winter of 1902, Longstreet encountered Ed Jr. in Tasker Oddie's new office in Tonopah. Scathing words were exchanged and, when the old gunslinger drew his pistol, a scuffle ensued. Oddie, the recently elected Nye County district attorney, wrote of the clash in a letter to his mother on February 24, 1902:

A shooting scrape occurred here today, and the consequence is that I will have to go to Belmont tomorrow to prosecute the man who did the shooting.

It is disagreeable business as I know both men. They are ranchers. [Fred] Siebert and I were standing close by, as it happened in our office. Nobody was hurt, as Siebert grabbed [Longstreet's] arm and turned it down, so the bullet passed through the wall into my front office, and did not hit anyone. [Longstreet] tried to fire a second shot, but I got my finger under the trigger of the gun and it did not go off. It skinned my finger though, but did no damage....

Longstreet was arrested but posted the $2,000 bond and was back at his ranch in short order, still breathing fire.* However, on March 11, 1902, Ed Jr., Jim Clifford, and their brother-in-law, Joe Nay, "happened upon" Longstreet and his friend Jim Smith in the still-frozen hill country below his secluded ranch. Bullets flew, as did subsequent accusations as to who fired first. Nay, for whom Longstreet held no contempt, was seriously wounded in the leg. Once again Longstreet landed in "Logan's Bastille." Bond was set at $3,000, which he posted with ease.

Indicted for assault with intent to kill, Longstreet lamented the likelihood that jurors would show favoritism toward the influential Clifford family. Consequently, he hired three attorneys: W.N. Granger, George Bartlett and, most notably, Key Pittman, a future U.S. Senator newly arrived from the Alaska Yukon. At age 29, Pittman was eager to build a legal career. Such ambition frequently translates into being willing to take on any client—even one with the scurrilous propensities of Jack Longstreet.

Jury selection commenced in Belmont on June 19, 1902. To the dismay of the prosecution team, they encountered a stubborn procession of prospective jurors who freely divulged they believed Longstreet was innocent. This unforeseen development was the first signal the case against the bull-headed recluse, considered evil by some and merely eccentric by others, was not as one-sided as first thought.

Once the trial was underway, Longstreet spewed every contemptible thought he had for the Clifford family. Convinced Ed Jr. and Jim had killed Richard Breen and counterfeited his will, Longstreet claimed they had even threatened to kill him unless he stopped broadcasting his accusations about their underhanded ways. Without wavering, Longstreet maintained that the Cliffords had been the aggressors and shot first, thereby forcing him to return fire in self-defense.

Acutely aware of the commanding prestige enjoyed by the Clifford family and equally familiar with the easily riled one-eared rogue, Sheriff Logan— who took no advantage testifying one way or the other—corroborated Longstreet's testimony. He also had unrelieved doubts about Breen's death and the far-too-convenient content of a will bequeathing his coveted ranch to Ed Jr. The jury's verdict was "not guilty."[13]

Somewhere between the legend and the reality of Longstreet's checkered life there pulsed a rare combination of fearless gall and moral gumption. Perhaps those core characteristics, however frequently summoned to push the boundaries of law and order with his personal brand of justice, are what gained the respect of Tom Logan and his brothers. They also shared a heightened appreciation for

---

* To date, any subsequent court action has not been located.

fast horses. Frank Logan, in exchange for a gallon of wine, would jockey for Longstreet in horse races.

During a Labor Day celebration in Tonopah in the early 1900s, Frank had come down from Belmont to enjoy the festivities and was quickly approached by Longstreet to replace the rider on a horse he had entered in a race. Frank declined, claiming he had put on too much weight and didn't know the horse. Longstreet wouldn't listen and informed the other rider that Frank was taking his place. Considering who was giving orders, no objection was raised from either man, and Frank promptly took the horse down to the starting line. A "tin-horn gambler" approached him and asked if he was going to ride the Longstreet horse. Frank replied, "I'm going to try to."

The shifty-eyed man then offered Frank $800 if he would pull his horse short and lose the race. "You're riding the fastest horse and my boys have money on the brown mare." Without hesitation, Frank told him, "If I am riding the fastest horse then I am going to win this race."

Frank crossed the finish line in first place and soon encountered a "pretty sore bunch" of losers. Apparently, they had earlier succeeded in bribing the other rider but Frank or, more accurately, Longstreet himself, had thwarted the diabolical ploy.[14]

The inhabitants of Nye County were accustomed to gambling on horses and cards, but they also bet on the weather, on the contents of a bucket of ore, and often on another man's word. Risk was everywhere, while reward, a constant seductress, danced just out of reach. Clever schemes, both small and large, were hatched with one eye on a prize and the other on whoever might unhinge even the most iron-clad plan. That person could have just as easily been Jack Longstreet as it was Sheriff Tom Logan. And likewise, if one's guard was down, either man, however seasoned and alert, could be done in by the unexpected. That day came for Longstreet the summer of 1926, when he shot himself in the shoulder while cleaning a gun.*

For Tom Logan, nothing would be more unexpected than a riled gambler pulling a revolver from beneath his coat the morning of April 7, 1906.

---

* While Longstreet survived the initial gunshot, this time the Grim Reaper held the stronger hand, and one of the most incorrigible frontiersmen of all time would die from a festered wound and resulting stroke on July 26, 1928.

The "Cross-L" brand was originated by Tom Logan and later conveyed to
George H. Sharp (Jeanne Sharp Howerton)

To the Unknown Heroes of the Pick and Pan

Work that's done, and the prize that's won—
These be cheerful tales—
There's a minor note that grips the throat;
What of the man who fails?

Pledge a health to the hard earned wealth,
Hail to the men who win—
And to those who wait at the golden gate
For the ship that never comes in.

That unsung horde whose ranks are broad,
Knights of the pick and pan;
They toil and sow, and the next who go
Harvest what they began.

The sort that stays for the endless days
In the Never Never Land;
The golden dream is a vanishing gleam
Like the phantom like in the sand—

Till the grind is past, and they set at last
Out on the last long trail,
Where the sun has set and beyond it yet—
Here's to the men who fail!

—Ruth Comfort Mitchell, c. 1900

3

QUEEN OF THE SILVER CAMPS: 1900

"Mining is fascinating work when one is working for himself with good prospects ahead, as he is always expecting to strike it rich. It is somewhat of a gamble though, but it is a clean business, as when a man makes money at it, he is benefiting the community and himself and hurting nobody. It is not like so many others lines of business where one will succeed at the expense of someone else...."

Tasker Oddie, January 2, 1900

"I HAVE BEEN enjoying myself a good part of this week," wrote 27-year-old Tasker Oddie on April 9, 1900. "I went down Monitor Valley, Wednesday, with Sheriff Tom Logan, and returned Saturday evening."[1]

A tall, gentle-mannered man with an astute intellect, Oddie was a new arrival in Belmont and arguably the most educated man in Nye County at the time. He had earned a law degree in New York yet, instead of pursuing that profession chose to take his chances in the mine fields of Central Nevada. After quickly securing a lease to operate a small-scale mining enterprise, he soon embarked on what would be a lifetime of public service.[2] As Nye's deputy recorder and superintendent of schools, Oddie also filled in as the assistant district attorney.

Based on reports from the D.A.'s office to the State Attorney General from 1897 to 1900, the Nye County prosecution schedule

Tasker Oddie, 1901
(Nevada Historical Society, Reno, NV)

demanded little of the local judicial system. To follow is a four-year summary of the county's underwhelming crime statistics:

Offense	Convicted	Dismissed	Pending
1897			
Murder			1
Assault with a deadly weapon	1		
Assault to do bodily harm	2		
Assault and battery		1	
Misdemeanor	1		
Grand larceny			
1898			
Murder		1	
Housebreaking		1	
Assault to do bodily harm		1	
Robbery		1	
Grand larceny			1
Changing marks and brands			1
1899*			
Grand larceny, ignored by Grand Jury		1	
Assault, escaped jail		1	
Assault with a deadly weapon, ignored by Grand Jury		1	
Assault, defendant escaped jail			1
1900*			
Obtaining money under false pretenses, fine $1, or imprisonment in county jail until fine is paid.	1		

In a letter to his mother on February 20, 1900, Oddie grumbled about the slack and antiquated practices of the local purveyors of justice, detailing the outrageous, if not comedic, behavior of Judge Harry Stimler, Sr.:

The trial was very amusing as old 'Stim' the judge, knows absolutely nothing, has a wooden leg, is always drunk, or nearly so, and has a gait like an umbrella rolling downhill. He knows nothing about keeping order in the court, but he did refuse to allow the contesting parties to get a bottle of whiskey while in court...Old 'Stim' is the man taken home on a two-wheeled truck. He gets too drunk to walk with his own leg. I believe the wooden one will work all right, whether he is drunk or sober. He plays the fiddle for dances.[3]

---

*Activity logged during Sheriff Logan's first term.

Oddie's opinion of the local sheriff was much more positive. An enduring and loyal friendship with Tom Logan began to take form the spring of 1900 when they paired up for a trip to gather jurors from outlying areas of the county. Along the way, the sheriff acquainted him with various landmarks and many of the robust souls who called the region home. Oddie wrote of this outing:

We went to Mosquito Creek Ranch, where the McCann's live, the first night, about twenty miles from Belmont. The second and third nights we spent at Potts' ranch, about twenty miles further from Belmont. The roads are excellent in Monitor Valley, so we are not long on the road. Logan's team is a fine one and averages eight miles an hour on such roads. He can easily drive them sixty miles a day. Logan was out after grand jurors, so I went with him, as I felt the need of a change and wanted to see Monitor Valley. I enjoyed the trip very much.

I saw the "Devil's Punch Bowl," which is about five miles from Potts' ranch. It is a wonderful curiosity, and would be of world-wide fame if it was near civilization or railroads. It is an unassuming hill or mound….When you get to the top you suddenly find yourself on the rim of an immense well about eighty feet in diameter. The walls are perpendicular, and about thirty feet down from the rim is the water, which is at the boiling temperature…. If a snake is thrown in, it stiffens right out and is cooked in a short time….We had quite an uncomfortable snow and wind storm on the way home, but as it was in our backs we did not mind it.

Tom Logan is a very pleasant man, and has been a cowboy and rancher all his life. He has been in Arizona a good deal, riding after cattle. He has to travel a great deal on his trips through this county. The wagon road from the northern end to the southern end is about 360 miles in length, and the road from the eastern end to the western end is about 250 miles long. It takes eight days to go from Belmont to the southern end of the county, as there are so few places where a man can stop, and it is such hard traveling on the team….

There will be a great excitement in town tomorrow, as the judge, and twenty-four jurymen, and several lawyers will be in town. It means a great deal to Belmont to have such a crowd here. Court meets on Wednesday. It will only last a few days this time, as there is very little business to be done. Every room in town is engaged ahead, so families double up considerably in order to rent their rooms….[4]

Later that year, Oddie joined the Logan family and some 90 others at the Rogers' Smoky Valley ranch to celebrate Independence Day. People came from as far away as 50 miles—including Belmont belles Annie, Jessie, and Josephine Logan—bedding down in haystacks and bedrolls under the stars.[5 & 6]

Also by this time, Tom's brother, Frank, age 26, was married with two children and farming and raising stock in eastern Nye County near Duckwater. He would soon take ownership of the Silver Bend livery stable in Belmont. Residing in the same area was brother George, 31, single, and working as a stock rider.[7]

Silver Bend Livery Stable once owned by Frank Logan, Belmont, NV
(Central Nevada Historical Society, Tonopah, NV)

The youngest of Tom's brothers, Bob, barely 19, had decided to try his hand working Nevada's Klondyke mines with other buckaroos.[8] Among his ventures was going in one-third on a mining claim with two future historical icons—a former Nye County sheriff, Wilson Brougher, then the county auditor and recorder who would become a state senator, and Tasker Oddie, a future governor of Nevada and U.S. senator. They, like most of their compatriots, were prime examples of the versatility required to cobble together a living in that day and age. From the *Belmont Courier*, October 21, 1899:

Recorder Brougher and (Bob) Logan started for the Southern Klondike on Thursday taking two wagons loaded with lumber and provisions. They will work on their claims this winter and have gone prepared to live comfortably. Their friends hope that their slumbers will not be disturbed by visions of the horrors that haunted many an oldtimer drinking beer brewed in the old brewery, the walls of which are to be used in building lumber houses in the Klondike [Klondyke] Camp.

Bob Logan's partnership with Brougher and Oddie was short-lived and, as providence would determine, he would not be among the fortunate ranks to cash in on the colossal stroke of luck that awaited his associates. Like so many others, he would move from one venture to another and generally experience more toil than profit; the fruits of their labor instead made golden by their affable temperaments and fair-minded ways. Well-respected by most esteemed personalities throughout the region, Bob and his Logan brothers were held in high regard by even some of the less law-abiding citizens such as one Black Jack Kelly.

Robert "Bob" Logan, Jr. (seated) with two unidentified fellow buckaroos, c. 1900, Nye County, NV (Central Nevada Historical Society, Tonopah, NV)

Black Jack was a local, chronic horse thief who broke jail in Belmont and "hit out over the hills" on foot toward Smoky Valley where he planned to steal a horse from the Darrough Ranch, alter the brand, and high-tail his way toward Arizona Territory for a quick sale. A sheriff's posse caught him before he got far. Curious as to why Kelly had struck out for Smoky Valley rather than "procure" a more convenient horse from Frank Logan's livery stable, Frank personally asked him, "Did you lose your nerve?" Kelly simply replied, "I wouldn't steal a horse from you."[9]

AMONG TOM LOGAN'S closet allies was District Attorney Jim Butler, an agreeable, rotund man with a walrus moustache, known to friends as "Lazy Jim." The nickname came about because he much preferred sitting with cohorts and swapping stories to any type of physical labor. Born on February 2, 1855, in El Dorado County, California, he had moved with his father and two brothers to Nevada when he was thirteen. His mother, as did many wives averse to accompanying their wanderlust husbands to parts unknown, remained behind and eventually secured a divorce.[10]

During the fall of 1888 and while living in Tybo, Nevada, Butler drew the ire of Maurice Donahue when he intervened in a domestic dispute between him and his wife, Belle. Claiming Donahue had abused her and their children, Belle filed for divorce and began keeping company with Butler. That relationship allegedly caused Donahue to seethe with jealousy. Accounts vary as to who fired the first shot when the two men met on Main Street, but after the grappling and gunplay, Butler's cheek had been grazed by a bullet and Donahue was dead from gunshots to his abdomen and head. Butler would receive a judgment of

James Butler, c. 1902
(Central Nevada Historical Society,
Tonopah, NV)

justifiable homicide, marry the widow six months later, become a step-father to her three children, and move to a small ranch in Monitor Valley.[11]

Jim Butler was elected Nye County district attorney in the fall of 1896. Absent a law degree and likely to acknowledge he was ill-suited for the office, he was often otherwise occupied at his ranch or off prospecting. He had nearly completed his second two-year term when he made the strike "felt 'round the world." In early 1900, sometime between haying season and prosecuting a man for stealing a bottle of whiskey, "the placer tailings stirred in Jim's blood." With packed burros in tow, he headed off to the Southern Klondyke to try his luck in that new camp. An essay by an unknown author written in the early 1920s captures the charmed happenstance of Tonopah's beginning:

It was a long trip and Jim took it easy over the Manhattan Mountains to Rye Patch, where there was a little desert spring known to the Indians as Tonopah. Jim camped there for the night and the next morning discovered his burros were gone. He started out to search of them. A brisk breeze with an ounce of sand to each cubic foot was blowing. The burros had found shelter behind a ledge where Jim found them. Appreciating their wisdom, he sat down to wait out the wind, and as he sat, chipped idly at the rock. The specimens looked promising so he dropped them in his pocket. This was on May 19th, 1900….[12]

On the way back to Monitor Valley, Butler picked up more samples, but it wasn't until several weeks later that he approached Oddie in Belmont. Even though Oddie once described Butler as "an ignoramus" in regard to his legal proficiencies, the two men had cultivated a solid personal relationship outside the courtroom and would soon both be catapulted into incomprehensible wealth and notoriety. "Here's some likely looking rock, Tasker," said the future Father of Tonopah. "I'm broke, but if you get it assayed, I'll give you half interest."

Oddie took the offer, but didn't have even a dollar to pay for the assay. However, he did have a friend in Austin who was a part-time assayer. Oddie sent the samples by stage to Walter Gayhart with a note promising half of his interest to test the ore. When Gayhart processed returns yielding $75 to $575 per ton he was left gasping for air and immediately sent word to Oddie, who dispatched an Indian runner to the Butler Ranch.

Busy bringing in hay, Butler had to delay a return to his discovery site. In the meantime, word leaked about the assay figures. Prospectors from Klondyke hastened to the area, hoping to make a similar find, but "Lazy Jim" had not bothered to erect a monument or follow any routine location protocol. Had he done so, his exclusive rights would have expired and someone else could have easily and legitimately relocated the claim, relegating Butler to his ranch where he rarely had one penny to rub against another.

Original locators, (left to right) Tasker Oddie, Capt. Jenkins,
Belle and Jim Butler, 1900
(Central Nevada Historical Society, Tonopah, NV)

On August 25, he and Belle outfitted a buckboard and hit the trail. They located the "Desert Queen" claim for themselves and "The Burro" for Oddie. In pursuit of another fugitive burro, Belle located the "Mizpah," which proved to be the richest in their group of eight initial claims. Two months later, after raising $25, Butler, Oddie, and Wilson Brougher (brought in because he had a hauling wagon and team) were on site working claims that would birth Tonopah.*

---

* For a brief period of time, Tonopah was known as Butler. The actual town site of Tonopah, situated between Mt. Brougher to the west and Mt. Oddie to the east, was first surveyed in early 1901 by Walter Gayhart, who outlined about 20 blocks of small lots. To the southwest is Mt. Butler.

The first sack of ore was loaded into a wagon and hauled some 100 miles north to the nearest railroad service. An $800 return from the smelter assured their fortunes and made it possible to hire labor.[13]

The same week that Jim and Belle Butler were staking claims, Tom and Hannah Logan hosted a community gathering at their Monitor Valley ranch. As reported by the *Courier*, September 1, 1900, "A large party of young people from Belmont attended and report having a most delightful time. A midnight delicious supper was served and it was daylight before dancing ceased." Shortly thereafter, Tom announced his candidacy for a second term.[14] His opponent was Belmont native James Power, one of his deputies and, according to the *Courier*, "a young man of exemplary habits." The following commentary appeared regarding Sheriff Logan:

Mr. Logan is the present incumbent of the office. He has been a most accommodating and hard-working officer and has spared no pains to his duty. He is a staunch Silver Party man and a supporter of all principles advocated by the friends of the Republic. He is strongly opposed to imperialism…. If elected, he will continue to discharge his duties of his office to the satisfaction of the public.[15]

Oddie ran unopposed for district attorney and wrote his mother on November 10, 1900, "Tom Logan is probably re-elected sheriff in the county. I am much pleased, as he is quite a friend of mine."[16] Tom won by a vote of 124 to 94.[17] These balloting results would be the last in Nye County history to number in the low hundreds. By the next election in two years, votes cast would exceed 1,000.

Even though winter was fast approaching, more and more aspiring prospectors drifted into Tonopah. With an elevation of slightly more than 6,000 feet, temperatures would soon plummet and cast a virtually inescapable icy chill over the camp. Tents sprang up, and makeshift shelters were assembled out of a menagerie of barrels, oil cans, tarps, and packing crates. Amazingly, in those first few months, Butler granted more than 100 oral leases without the slightest scratch of a pen. Oddie was in charge of management and meticulously logged pertinent details and figures in a memorandum ledger. Hundreds of thousands of sacks of ore were shipped, checked, and paid for by Oddie from the smelter returns, and in the final settlement there was not one dollar in dispute.[18]

As for how Tom Logan fit into Butler's enterprise, no records were found documenting any formal interest in these early claims, but that is not to say he was not involved. Handshake agreements were commonplace and, with about 20 years of freight-hauling experience, Tom made quick use of his wagons and teams. The *Courier* reported on December 15, 1900, "Sheriff TW Logan started for Eureka on Tuesday last with a load of ore from the Tonopah District. This is the second load of ore shipped from Tonopah."

The Brougher Brother's Mizpah Grill and Saloon, Tonopah, NV, 1901;
the tallest man standing on the porch roof, seventh from the right, is
Tom Logan's brother, Robert, Jr.
(Central Nevada Historical Society, Tonopah, NV)

In the near future, Tom would invest in more than 20 Nye County mining locations. However, in the first few months of his second term as sheriff, while those around him were focused on the ground, he was perhaps watching the horizon. Opportunists of both the law-abiding and conniving sort were about to stream forth in droves, pressing him into service far beyond his present scope of duties. Nevada-born and forged, he had learned how to take matters in stride and trust instincts born of trial and error. As with any impending desert storm, seasoned travelers prepared long before the first gust of wind tugged at their hat, but even Tom Logan could not have predicted the all-consuming turbulence about to materialize.

As 1900 came to a close, Tom went about his routine business, often arriving home in the dead cold of night, a shadowy figure wrapped in buffalo hide, his boots softly scuffing over the wood floor, only to be gone again in a day or two. From the *Courier*:

November 24, 1900: *Frank Wilson was unhitching a team at Rye Patch in Ralston Valley when the animals became frightened and ran away with the neck yoke. Joe Scuffy who started in pursuit found a horse uninjured at Logan's ranch where they had been caught by TW Logan.*

December 22, 1900: *Misses Annie and Jessie Logan, Kate Hughes, Rosalie Hunt, and Lottie Stimler (and others) attended the dance in Smoky Valley.*

December 29, 1900: *The people of Belmont celebrated Christmas in a quiet way. The dance held Christmas Eve was well attended and on Christmas Day many fowls were eaten at the Christmas board. The day was pleasant and the children played with their toys out of doors; Sheriff TW Logan left for Austin on Thursday last with a load of concentraits and hides. He will bring back provisions.*

January 12, 1901: *Sheriff Logan and George Sharp were the first persons in Belmont to take a sleigh ride this winter.*

Such was the proverbial calm before the storm.

FOR AS LONG as each would live, Tom and Hannah's children never forgot the unnerving intensity of their parents' quarrels about the saloon business. For Hannah, raised to abhor the poisonous dalliances of those who indulged in sinful behaviors, her aversion to the evils of smoking, drinking, and gambling was unwavering. When Tom decided to sell his interest in their Monitor Valley ranch* during the winter of 1901 and invest in one of Tonopah's first saloons, Hannah was certain that by catering to the gluttonous underbelly of society, her husband was doing the devil's work and asking for trouble.

However, where Hannah saw debauchery, Tom saw a mining camp vibrating with economic opportunity. Running a saloon made good business sense, and, as the father of seven children and soon to be eight, he was keen on generating another source of income. Whether depending on the ever-changing weather to produce a bountiful crop of hay or the fickle promise of a mining investment to yield generous returns, odds had to be weighed and chances taken. Tom weathered the point and persevered, which left Hannah to pray that none of her predictions would ever come true.

As a place of sanctuary and camaraderie, saloons were always among the first commercial enterprises to appear in a new camp. One could be erected in a matter of hours. Any ambitous fellow could throw up a tent, situate a pine plank across two barrels, and pry open a crate of whiskey ready for service. If labeled spirits were scarce, a privately brewed concoction in unmarked bottles would suffice, guaranteed to inebriate though surely with less relish. Predictably a rambunctious environment, saloons also helped keep the peace by occupying

---

* The sale included the rights to Tom Logan's "Cross-L" brand, which is still owned by Sharp family descendants.[19]

clientele during their idle hours when, if left to personal inclination, were more likely to court mischief.

Although the line between recreation and vice was a perpetual and confounding blur, Tonopah's early "drinking houses" functioned as the favored headquarters for routine socializing and deal-making. Amid the muffled flutter of playing cards, the plink of coins on a table top, the gurgling pour of liquor, and the pungent, enveloping haze of cigar smoke, the house endeavored to maintain order by posting preferred rules. These guidelines minimally included: no credit, no fisticuffs, no cheaters, and no brandished firearms, plus all spit must be confined to a cuspidor. Since an officer of the law was not always nearby, this rudimentary system of self-governance relied on the occasional mustering of collective muscle and brawn to toss a rabble-rouser out of the premises. Any hard feelings were usually defused by a good night's sleep and a slack memory.

Saloons operated on the basis of demand, regardless of the hour, as confirmed by the *Courier* on March 2, 1901: "W. J. Rice and Ramsey opened a saloon there Saturday noon and it had not closed for a moment when Messers McCann, Rice and Logan left there Monday...without doubt Tonopah will be a permanent camp."

Composed of mostly local inhabitants and tradesmen, many of whom had pre-existing relationships, Tonopah's initial harmony was about to radically change. Fast-talking financiers, ruthless gamblers, and women of the more adventurous persuasion with powdered bosoms and perfumed hair would join the incoming flood of prospectors and laborers. Infused with this movement would also be shopkeepers, cooks, blacksmiths, carpenters, bankers, teachers, paperhangers, and laundrymen along with a doctor, undertaker, and a preacher or two. Tents soon transformed into fixed structures, trails became streets, and the law of the land shifted from a hastily dashed notice tacked on a saloon wall into the hands of the local sheriff's office.

At the intersection of Main Street and Brougher Avenue, on the southeast corner, Tom Logan acquired lot numbers 11, 12, and 13 of Block E from Jim Butler for his saloon site. Partnering with Edward Emmett Saylor, a 42-year-old railroad man newly arrived from Pennsylvania known as a "jolly good fellow with a roaming disposition," they either purchased lumber—a scarce commodity at the time—or used deconstructed building materials Tom had hauled down from Belmont to erect the single-story "Logan-Saylor Sample Room."[20]

Next door, south of Tom's saloon, a bath and steam house with a barber would soon open. The standard price for a shower, given the scarcity of water, was fifty cents. Grubby patrons stood on a wooden grate that rocked back and forth like the treadle of a sewing machine. This action pumped about five gallons of water from the sump barrel beneath to the perforated kerosene can above. The same water would be used over and over for about a week. Only when the perforations began to plug up did the barber change the water.[21]

Early Tonopah, 1901 (Central Nevada Historical Society, Tonopah, NV)

The first boarding house in Tonopah was operated by a daughter and son of Nye County's colorful Judge Stimler, Lottie and Harry, Jr. She credited the "dreary monotony of life in Belmont" and Jim Butler's promised financial assistance as motive enough to relocate to Tonopah the winter of 1901. On opening night, instead of the dozen men for which they had prepared, 30 crowded into the 14x15 feet tent to feast on beans, sauerkraut, steak, and biscuits.

Days later, a ferocious blizzard immobilized the isolated population of about 80 residents for two weeks. With passages blocked, water wagons from Rye Patch or freight haulers from Sodaville—the closest rail point about 90 miles to the northeast—could not reach Tonopah. Snow was melted for drinking water and food rationed. Staples like flour, bacon, and ham vanished and were replaced by canned sardines, corned beef, dried peaches, and rice until also depleted. Men would rotate positions standing close to one of the few stoves. Precious lumber earmarked for construction was used to heat and cook. Soon, Tonopah experienced its first crime wave: wood theft. Frost collected inside tents while fierce gusts of wind clawed from every direction. Necks that once craned, searching for shipments of whiskey and building materials, now stretched above the frozen landscape hoping to spot incoming food and firewood.

When the sky finally cleared, the snow thawed so quickly that in Lottie's boarding house, "the water was ankle deep all over the floor and she had to wade through clay mud to serve up the dinner." Even then, teams with provisions were slow in coming and the pressures so overwhelming that one day Lottie lost heart, ran into the cellar, threw herself upon a sack of potatoes, and

The Butler Saloon (far left) shared the southeast corner of Main and Brougher with the Logan-Saylor Sample Room, 1902. (James W. Travers, *Tonopah, Past, Present, Future: History of the World's Greatest Mining Camp*)

wept uncontrollably. "I became so discouraged," she remembered. "I would have quit the business, but we could get no one to take it off our hands…and the men were all dependent on me for a place to eat."[22]

Gradually, women of varying prestige made their way into the promising camp. At the bottom of that hierarchy were the prostitutes and dance-hall girls. Above them were the "poor but decent" wives or widows with little education or social refinement.[23] Between those less fortunate and the more sophisticated high society ladies was Hannah Logan.

Savvy in her own right and equipped with unfathomable internal fortitude and physical stamina, Hannah rarely had the opportunity to participate in social affairs frequented by the female elite, such as founding a library or organizing a community beautification project. Laden with responsibilities that could drive a lesser spirit insane or worse, she was among the many who relinquished girlhood beauty and short-lived dreams to tend a family. These frontier matriarchs with calloused hands and wayward hair answered their own call to duty with courage and humility. In their weathered faces can be found the tell-tale lines of drudgery frequently interwoven with twinkling traces of pride, for they know—if no one else does—the enormity of their unsung sacrifice and contributions.

Nevada's New Camps

Then have ye seen the mining camp
They're building over yon,
'Twas suddenly created there
Between the night and dawn.
They built it by the glinting light
Of gold beside the street.
And they built it on the desert
Where the desolations meet.

And mountain rocks and lesser rocks
Berib the rugged scene,
And some are hard and golden rich
And some are hard and lean.
There's not enough of water there
To bicker down a rill,
But stronger drink, of vicious red
Flows even up the hill.

And have ye seen the fling of chance
The men that luck will choose—
The tyros here who win the gold,
The pundits there to lose?
And have ye see the ancient shame
Of women lost to hope
That may not even walk to hell,
But weakly toward it grope?

And have ye heard the lusty shout
Of rudely snatched success
That drowns the quiet moaning of
The hearts that know distress?
And don't ye hear that laughter's god
Is loud and full of cheer
To hold the world's attention lest
It sadden at a tear.

Yet when you see that mining camp,
(You cannot miss the trail;
It's blazed with empty bottles and
With signs of fierce travail.)
Regard the homes, the garden spots—
That on the desert probe
Where men of strength with woman's aid
Subdue the wilderness.

—Phillip Verrill Mighels,
Tonopah Daily Sun, March 26, 1905, (condensed from original)

4

KEEPING ORDER: 1901-1902

"A fearless press is always an instrument for good in any community…. Fond hopes go out that Tonopah, the queen city of the new Nevada, may astonish the world and riches pour into the lap of every one of her citizens, and upon the city the prosperity which nature generously gives and which men, parties or policies cannot keep back."

Tonopah Bonanza, February 8, 1902

UPON ENTERING HIS second term as Nye County sheriff and assessor in January 1901, Tom Logan's responsibilities seemed to compound with each new surge of humanity that spilled into his district. Besides expanding law enforcement demands, his work as tax collector was also increasing. In that capacity, he was summoned to participate in the first annual meeting of Nevada county assessors hosted by Governor Reinhold Sadler in Carson City in early April. A legislative enactment approved the previous month had mandated an Assessors' Board be formed to develop a more uniform valuation of property throughout Nevada.[1]

Agenda items for the fourteen assessors in attendance included, for instance, fixing a standard rate per head on beef cattle, stock horses, and mutton sheep throughout the state. Members also took on the contentious task of railroad assessments. Their rather robust discussion concentrated on determining whether to tax profits earned by a railroad company, a property's full market value, or establish a fee per mile of rail track. As to how to classify railroads, they considered doing so on the basis of gauge, location, and usage. A variety of scenarios and calculations were considered. Based on the meeting transcript, Tom did far more listening than speaking in this new 20th century setting until the last day, when he contributed his personal brand of cowboy reasoning in the following exchange:

The Governor: *The law provides for all assessments to be the full cash value of the property.*

The Controller: *The law is on the statute books, but has never been enforced. The cash value of the road can be arrived at by considering the value of its stocks and bonds, which are about one hundred and twenty odd millions, and its net income, which is about seven and a half millions now per annun. It is for you to decide on this matter by investigating these figures. You have raised cattle from $25 to $32.50 a head, and the question of deciding whether the railroad or the cattle is nearest the true cash value within the meaning of the statute. This is the true way of getting at a somewhat complicated question,* *and the percentage of the raise cuts a comparatively little figure. The main question is: How near are you to the true cash value after the raise?*

Mr. Logan of Nye: *It looks to me as if the road had been assessed about one-fifth of its cash value, as it had been mortgaged for $100,000, and it must be worth that much. If we are working on the 6 per cent plan, it would amount to about $33,000, instead we have assessed it at $20,000. I have no desire to work any hardship on the Railroad Company, only to do what is fair and just. The railroad had been paying about 10 per cent of the actual value of the road, while the cattlemen have been paying about 75 per cent.*[2]

Sheriff Tom Logan with deputies, Nye County, NV, c. 1902
(Logan Family Collection)

Not surprisingly, railroad assessment fees became a routine topic of debate. Viewpoints were generally divided between the interests of the more developed communities in northern Nevada and the more remote southern regions, like Nye County. Lawsuits were filed by Central Pacific Railroad and the Virginia & Truckee Railroad contending, among other issues, that they were being over-taxed and it was the function of individual assessors, as defined by state statute, "to fix values on classes of property, but not to make values on the property...."[3]

About two months after the Board of Assessors' meeting in Carson City, Tonopah's first newspaper, the *Tonopah Bonanza*, published its inaugural edition. Considering the number of saloon advertisements alone in the newspaper, establishments like The Tonopah Club, The Mizpah, The Silver Star, The Chloride, and The Logan-Saylor Sample Room were apparently doing brisk business.[4] Because Tom traveled so frequently about Nye County, often bringing along one or two of his older daughters, he served as a valuable field correspondent for the newspaper, commenting at one point that "reporting is a harder job than assessing."[5] Given Tonopah's growth rate, that opinion was about to change.

The camp's first annual Fourth of July celebration was declared "a howling success" by the *Bonanza*, and apparently transpired without incident. "Sheriff Logan arrived on scene," the newspaper reported, "just in time to take part in the Fourth. He supposed his services would be needed but was agreeably disappointed."[6] This, of course, would not be the norm for long, as even trash and garbage patrol were added to his list of responsibilities:

Sheriff Logan has posted notices throughout the town notifying people that they must keep their premises clean. The sheriff means what he says and anyone found maintaining a nuisance will be arrested.[7]

In August 1901, shortly after the completion of a "fine, strong" city jail in Tonopah, Tom appointed nine more deputy sheriffs: B.C. McCann, Dr. Al Hudgens, Wm. Rice, P.J. O'Brien, Cal Brougher, W.J. Sinclair, H. Ramsey, Tom Kendall, and W.W. Booth. He named James Power, his one-time opponent for the office of sheriff, as Tonopah's night watchman.[8] A freshly painted sign tacked above the entrance to the new jail read "Pioneer," as an assigned new identity for evil-doers that, upon release, "would do well to hike themselves to more enticing climes."[9]

Interspersed with fever-pitched mining news, the latest developments along Main Street, and the comings and goings of locals and visitors alike, the *Bonanza* did not shy away from unrestrained editorial commentary reflective of the time, such as:

The Tonopah Bonanza *advocates the proposition that the school trustees of that new camp employ none but old maids to teach in the schools at that place for the reason that the chance of their getting married will be slim...that's right old gals, send in your applications. The older, the wiser you are.*[10]

Newspaper headlines also revealed how the disheartened and despondent were choosing to deal with failure. For example, "A Man Sits on 25 Pounds of Giant Powder and Applies Match."[11] While some saw fit to kill themselves, others decided to take out their frustration on someone else. But unlike the bullet-ridden boom of Pioche 30 years earlier, Tonopah was earning a more appealing reputation. With nine deputies in town, the *Bonanza* observed on September 28, 1901: "New mining camps always attract a considerable quantity of the lawless element, but the number of peace officers in Tonopah indicates a greater quantity than the usual proportion of that class...they keep things straight, all right."

In addition to now having its own newspaper, another symbolic indicator of the camp's assured permanency was the arrival of a large safe for Tonopah's first bank.[12] This overdue necessity heightened security for the vast amounts of cash and other valuables passing from hand to hand. Few men had the personal resources to undertake a business venture on their own and relied on loans from the bank or an associate. Partnerships of all caliber and intent flourished.

For more than 20 years, since first striking out on his own in northern Arizona, Tom Logan had engaged in several successful joint ventures. In 1901, he was not only aligned with Saylor in the saloon business, but he also partnered with Robert (Bob) Gilbert, co-proprietor of Belmont's Cosmopolitan, to build a butcher shop in Tonopah.[13] While most property transactions were eventually filed with the county recorder, many went no further than a gentleman's handshake and a swig of whiskey. Perhaps as poetic testimony to the magnitude and frequency of business transactions being conducted, by the end of summer, there was not a sack of flour to be found in town. However, "wet merchants" continued to receive regular shipments of whiskey and beer, and ice was hauled in from Belmont, which kept the saloons operating around the clock.[14]

During the last quarter of 1901, Tom was responsible for collecting business license fees and managing the completion and operation of Tonopah's new jail. At the County Commissioners September meeting, he was also a strong advocate for road repairs. With public needs exceeding the county's available financial resources, the matter, like many others, was "laid over" to the next meeting.[15]

In the meantime, complaints poured in regarding businesses being inundated with "small checks of no value." The *Bonanza* did their part in trying to deter the practice by reporting on October 5, 1901, "The bogus men are at work in Tonopah and when found out they will be made a horrible example. They will be given the frying pan brand, a gift they will always remember."[16]

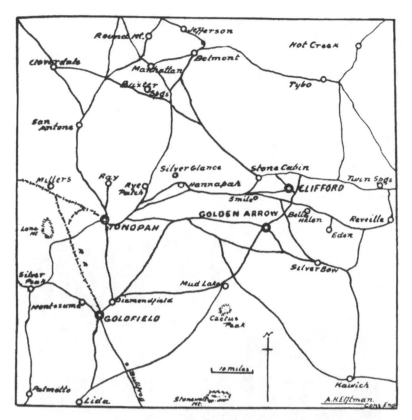

Nye County mining camps, c. 1906

Before the end of 1901, Tonopah's population reached 1,300, and total assessed property values increased by roughly 10 percent, from $373,340 in 1900 to $419,412.[17] The *Bonanza*, ever-watchful of county coffers, happily reported just before Christmas that, "It will not be long before the county will be paying all bills against it in 'long green.' The bullion tax of 1902 will wipe out all indebtedness."[18]

Tonopah had also recorded a multitude of firsts in 1901: a baby's birth, a wedding, a masquerade ball, and a death. The camp's first funeral had been for John Weeks, a 45-year-old miner from California, who died from an apparent heart attack while chopping wood on May 9, 1901.[19] With no undertaker in town, a carpenter from Belmont hastily constructed a pine coffin, and Lottie Stimler organized a small choir that included Tasker Oddie and all of the women she could round up. A buggy was commandeered for the grieving widow and teenage son. A buckboard functioned as the hearse. Several members of fraternal organizations marched in columns behind the water wagon carrying women and children. The somber, improvised procession followed Main Street northward down the hill and curved around a gentle bend toward the west before stopping at a desolate plot of land on the edge of town. Here was laid to rest the first of many occupants, including in but a few short years the body of a soft-spoken sheriff who, on this day, was likely among those expressing condolences to the sorrowful family.[20]

Soon Tonopah would have a school, a library, and a hospital. A fire bell was on order and, along with electricity and telephones, the railroad was coming. With routine frequency, San Francisco investors cycled in and out of Tonopah. There were now eighteen licensed gambling games "running full blast" and at least six more expected before year's end. With ten saloons and four planned, the *Bonanza* quipped, "This would be a warm place for Carrie Nation and her little Tomahawk."[21]

Interior of unknown saloon, Tonopah, NV, c. 1902
(Central Nevada Historical Society, Tonopah, NV)

Competition among the various drinking and gaming establishments was intense. Before the end of the year, Logan and Saylor had renovated their saloon and hosted a grand opening on New Year's Eve. "This is a handsome resort," reported the *Bonanza* on January 4, 1902. "The bar is of antique oak, the glass a quarter-inch thick. The proprietors are both popular and meeting with success." Subsequent advertisements read: "The CHOICEST Liquid Refreshments and the Finest Brands of Cigars. Comfortable Club Room, Courteous Treatment, A Gentle Tiger* in the Club Room. Be Convinced by a Visit."[22]

---

* The term, "gentle tiger," was a customary way of promising generous odds at the gaming tables.

A good portion of the hopeful miners, businessmen, and gamblers coming into Tonopah were from the Alaskan goldfields. Within that population was Wyatt Earp and common-law wife Josephine, more commonly known as Josie or "Sadie." Born in Iowa in 1848 and one of six brothers, he attained legendary status after surviving a 30-second gunfight at the O.K. Corral in Tombstone, Arizona, on October 26, 1881. Killed that day were three apparent "outlaw cowboys" by the gun-toting quartet of Earp, brothers Morgan and Virgil, and friend John "Doc" Holliday. Although debate continues as to who fired the first shot, from that moment on, Earp's reputation took on a life of its own. According to biographer, Casey Tefertiller:

The real Wyatt led a life that was authentically Western. He was a gambler and a saloonkeeper, and enjoyed the charms of several women, even leaving his common-law wife to take up with a dancer. Most of all, he was as tough as men came when toughness earned respect. He was loved and hated, a man who drew allegiances and made devoted enemies. Wyatt Earp was a natural leader with a coterie of followers and friends who always believed he did right….

He was not a mankiller who delighted in death, and he was never a gunfighter, at least in the sense that later movie generations would understand the word. He fought only two standup gunfights, one with a pistol and the other with a shotgun. There were no fast draws, no fancy shooting. Wyatt Earp faced a challenge and responded.[23]

Before coming to Tonopah the end of January 1902, Wyatt and Josie had joined the gold rush to Alaska late in 1897. There he also managed saloons and ran gambling concessions before partnering with Charlie Hoxie to operate The Northern saloon in Nome. Rarely out of the headlines along the West Coast, Earp prospered and could not resist trying his luck in Tonopah. "He has a big wagon," reported the *Bonanza* on February 1, 1902, "loaded down with soft hardware and, as soon as he and his partner Mr. Martin secure a location, they will be home to all. They are good citizens and we welcome them to Tonopah."

Earp's new saloon, also called The Northern, opened on February 8

Wyatt Earp, San Diego, CA, c. 1887 (Nevada Historical Society, Reno, NV)

and was located on the north end of Tonopah, just two doors below the Miners' Exchange Hall. During his brief stay in Central Nevada, besides prospecting, he also served as a U.S. deputy marshal under Marshal J. F. Emmitt, mostly serving summonses on federal court cases. He was also hired by mining engineer John Hays to lead a private police force to run off claim jumpers.[24]

Author and early Tonopah resident, Marjorie Moore Brown, once asked Tasker Oddie to tell her his best claim-jumping story. As it turned out, Sheriff Logan may very well have been responsible for Oddie's decision to employ Earp's "security services." From *Lady in Boomtown*, as told by Oddie:

I can tell you the one that meant the most to me. Some ruffians moved in from Salt Lake and tried to jump the Mizpah, the original claim. Ralph Wardle and I went up the hill to put them off and found three men down the fifteen-foot shaft. Wardle and I climbed down the ladder, and before we knew it, we were in a hand-to-hand scrap, three of them against two of us. People down in town got wind of trouble on the hill, so the sheriff* rounded up some men to go up there with him. He poked his head over the edge of the shaft, looking to me like the Angel Gabriel, and yelled, "Hey! You fellas got no business on this property. Quit fightin' and get outta that hole!"

One of them let go of me long enough to yell back, "You can't stop us, Sheriff. You gotta have a warrant to stop us, and you can't get it. The court house is seventy miles away in Belmont." The sheriff yelled back, "You come outta there and we'll talk about it." By this time half the town was up on the hill. We all scrambled up the ladder.

Then the sheriff said, "Now I'll show you coots whether I can do something about this or not. All you fellas who are in favor of the Tonopah Mining Company's claim [come] over here." About fifty men came over and stood by me.

"Now all you rattlers who think these men are not thieves join up with them over there. Now, Oddie, I'll arrest anyone that comes over there. You go hire a man to ride to Belmont and get out a warrant for malicious mischief, and we'll file that suit. And while you're at it, Oddie, hire enough men to keep these coyotes outta that hole. I'll stay here until you get back."[25]

All culminated peacefully and in Oddie's favor, and he wasted no time finding the right man to guard his claims. For six days, Oddie paid $20 a day to Earp and the nearly two dozen men he had enlisted. "That was an expensive bit of litigation," Oddie told Brown, "but I never spent money more effectively."

Josie Earp described a similar incident involving Oddie in her autobiography, *I Married Wyatt Earp*. Two claim jumpers had kicked down some of Oddie's location stakes. Short on options, Oddie had hopped into the shallow hole and defied them to move him just as Earp and Al Martin happened upon the scene in a spring wagon. One of jumpers accused him of being a "butinsky" and asked, "Who the hell do you think you are?"

---

* Although not specifically named, Tom Logan was the sheriff in 1902.

Wyatt Earp's Northern Saloon in Tonopah, Jim Butler (center) and presumed to be Wyatt Earp to his right. c. 1902 (Nevada Historical Society, Reno, NV)

"I'm Wyatt Earp," he answered. Trading on his reputation and pointing toward the wagon where Al had taken aim with a double-barrel shotgun, Wyatt said, "I'd size up the odds if I were you fellows before you head into a lot of trouble you may not be able to handle."

The offenders immediately surrendered, but Earp did not allow them to leave until they had re-positioned the claim stakes. Josie observed that Earp believed once a man had an upper hand it was prudent to, "rub their noses into it. That way they don't forget." Earp had rescued one of Nevada's future governor's without even reaching for the pistol under his jacket. However, it was not as if he had a choice. That day, Wyatt Earp was unarmed.[26]

While it is impossible to know how often Earp and Sheriff Logan's paths may have crossed, the two must have taken time to size up the other. Each was a lawman of notable stature and influence, and both had brothers in the same line of work. However, they differed in one striking regard: Earp, now 54, had a reputed dozen notches on his gun (allegedly acquired during acts of self-defense), and Tom was never known to have shot anybody. The following encounter between the two appeared in the *Tonopah Daily Sun*:

One night Earp became drunk and his wife came into the place in which he was drinking, and tried to get him to go home. The man slapped her face by way of reply, and the act roused the ire of a young miner, who was also drinking at the bar, and was a little "ginned up" himself.

Not understanding the relationship between the couple, he took up cudgels in the woman's defense. A fierce altercation followed, and Earp rushed out of the place to his own saloon down the street a little way. In a short time he came back with two big six shooters swinging in his hands, and breathing blood and sudden death for the man who had defied him. It looked as though a killing would surely take place.

Tom Logan was told of the row, and he hastened at once to the scene. Pushing his way to the center of the mass, he caught Earp by the arm and without raising his voice, talked him into giving up his guns. And I can tell you that it was not only on that occasion that Tom acted as peace-maker. It was a common occurrence. The man did not know what fear was, and he always tried to stop trouble by peaceful means, although there was no better hand with a gun in this country than he."[27]

Whether convincing Wyatt Earp to relinquish his guns or advocating for equitable livestock assessment fees, Tom apparently preferred a diplomatic approach. Halfway through his second term as sheriff, he attended the board of assessors' second meeting in Carson City on January 13, 1902. The state controller reported, "the assessment roll for 1901 was, in round numbers, $28,000,000 as against $24,000,000 for 1900… Nevada was going uphill instead of down." Ever considerate of the state's southern farmers and ranchers, Tom expounded how the stock cattle in Western Nevada, being closer to shipping points, were worth more than those from Esmeralda, White Pine, Lincoln, and Nye counties, and proposed a reduced valuation from $17 to $15 per head. The motion carried.

As had occurred the year before, spirited discourse erupted when attentions turned to railroad valuations. Regarding the Board's mission to establish standardized figures throughout the state rather than defer to the discretion of individual assessors, Tom offered this cautionary observation: "I think the majority of assessors are jumping at conclusions in placing the valuation on this [rail]road… We wish to do what is just to the railroad and what is just for the people…." A Central Pacific Railroad representative responded: "Last year our road was placed at $20,000 per mile….We did not consider that fair, and we did not consider it an equalized assessment according to the law."

Following more discussion, William Kinney from Ormsby County made a motion to set the amount at $16,000 per mile. Washoe County assessor George Holcomb moved to change the amount to $15,000. Reflecting the frequent divisiveness between Northern and Southern Nevada, assessors from Churchill, Elko, Eureka, Humboldt, Lander, and White Pine Counties supported the amendment. Acutely aware of the rapidly escalating demand for public services in Nye County and neighboring municipalities, Tom joined Douglas, Esmeralda,

Lincoln, Lyon, Ormsby, and Storey Counties in holding firm to the $16,000 amount. After a third day of deliberations and the threat of a lawsuit from Central Pacific if either "inflated" figure were adopted, the fourteen board members could not break the seven-to-seven impasse and adjourned. For yet another year, county assessors would proceed at their own discretion.[28]

DURING THE WINTER of 1901-02, Tonopah was struck by a horrific plague. The mysterious malady, many attributed to days of incessant massive dust storms, came on suddenly and took but a few tortuous days to run its course. Victims, most of whom were miners, first experienced a crippling pain as their liver became so enlarged it virtually pushed the heart and lungs out of place, strangling patients to death within less than 48 hours. Bodies would quickly swell to an enormous size, turn black and spotted, and have to be buried at once. After about a month had passed, a massive snow storm blanketed the land, at which time the vicious outbreak ceased almost as quickly as it had begun.[29]

The State Board of Health reported 17 deaths from pneumonia between December 31, 1901 and January 13, 1902.[30] Jim Butler and the county commissioners donated more than a $1,000 to the Miner's Union to help bury those who were not members and without means.[31] Like the town itself, the population at the Tonopah cemetery was also growing. A six-year-old child who succumbed to complications related to measles so moved Mrs. D.A. McDonald that she composed a heart-tugging poem for the *Bonanza*, which read in part: *"Put away the marbles, the top and ball. No little voice for them now will call. No little footsteps will run to greet Daddy's return far down the street...."*[32]

Ironically, the first person to die of "unnatural" causes was shot to death by a French gambler just before dawn. Samuel Findley, a barkeeper from California, had entered into an altercation with William Lavelle, reported the *Bonanza* beneath the headline, "Samuel Findley Fails in His Endeavor to Kill Wm Lavelle and in Return is Shot Through the Head:"

The man shot had played a $20 "spiel" against the faro bank of Lavelle and was given cash for it. Lavelle upon discovering the counterfeit said nothing, and when Findley came in this morning asked him about it. As near as can be ascertained the dead man had his right hand upon his gun in his overcoat pocket, and without any provocation raised the pistol and coat together, intending to shoot through the garment at Lavelle, whereupon Lavelle grabbed his arm and a scuffle ensued. In the meantime, Lavelle to save his own life, drew a 41 Colt revolver from his pocket and fired a bullet into the brain of Findley.[33]

A coroner's jury ascertained Lavelle acted in self-defense and was justified in protecting his own life.[34]

With some 5,000 people expected to descend on Tonopah by summer's end, previously infrequent incidents of assault and theft were becoming more commonplace.[35] On any given day, Sheriff Logan might be at the courthouse in Belmont—a seven-hour trip from Tonopah—testifying in a criminal case, making reports to the county commissioners, or appointing yet another deputy sheriff to help keep pace with public demand.

"The deputy sheriff of this camp," wrote the *Bonanza* on January 18, 1902, "should be compelled to make people keep their premises clean. It is a shame and an outrage that an officer will allow filth to accumulate as it does in Tonopah."

Assessing property, collecting license fees, serving warrants and subpoenas, tracking the wanted, and supervising deputies scattered throughout his vast and ever-changing jurisdiction—not to mention tending to his own business affairs—all meant Tom was missing more than ever Sunday suppers with his family.

Nye County District Attorney's Report to the State Attorney General, 1901*

Offense	Number of Cases	Convicted	Acquitted or Dismissed
1901			
Grand larceny	3	2	1
Petit larceny	2	1	2
Assault with intent to kill	2	1	
Jail breaking	1	1	
Threats against life	2	1	1
Threats against life and property	1		1
Drawing a deadly weapon	2	1	1
Disturbing the peace	2	3	
Disturbing the peace and resisting an officer	1	1	
Attempt to commit arson	1		1
Selling whiskey to Indians	1		1
Forgery	2		2
Assault	2	2	
TOTAL	22		

* Logged while Tom Logan was sheriff.

Early days in Tonopah, from a period postcard (Logan Family Collection)

In less than two years, the D.A.'s caseload had grown from one to 22.* Besides rounding up lawbreakers and monitoring the accumulation of garbage and rubbish, Sheriff Logan, for obvious reasons, was next ordered by the commission to prevent the "storage of explosives within the city limits and to prosecute all who did not comply."[36]

By early June 1902, Tonopah citizens recognized the need to share the mounting burden carried by county officials, and convened a citizen's committee to explore additional methods for restraining the "vicious element" becoming more numerous by the day. On June 14, 1902, the *Bonanza* issued the following admonition:

That a certain class of people who live below the "dead-line" in every town of any importance are tolerated, is a matter beyond discussion. But it is not altogether the evils spread abroad by women of the demi-mode, but the male associates (the he prostitutes) who live upon the earnings of these scarlet women, and like human vampires that they are, suck the life of their victims, that are a public menace…. An opium joint was raided last Tuesday and four hop fiends pulled and fined. This damnable blot upon our modern civilization will, if left unmolested, like the devil-fish fasten it tentacles upon every home in the country, and not only will this evil be stamped out, but the non-producing, uneasy virtue class of male habitués of the red light district will be given short shrift by our officers and court: "A word to the wise is sufficient."

At the next county commissioners meeting in July, Tom Harney was appointed Tonopah's first constable and charged with spearheading nuisance abatement. During this same session, Sheriff Logan was ordered to get five voting booths for the upcoming election in the fall.[37] Such "other duties as assigned" surely competed with the more urgent pressures to protect life and property. The old-world landscape upon which he had taken the oath of office just two years earlier had changed with breathtaking velocity. How well Tom responded to increasing violence, bloodshed, and vagrancy along with keeping the town clean and orderly would determine whether or not he would be elected for a third term. A sampling of his activity for August 1902 included:

***Tonopah Bonanza*, August 2, 1902**: *John Lowe, better known as "Dutch Chris," asked Chas. McLeod to share or live in the cabin belonging to him. On Thursday eve Chris accused McLeod of having robbed him of $25.75. This McLeod indignantly denied and*

---

*By 1905, that figure would skyrocket from 22 to nearly 1,000 cases on file with the Nye County district attorney.

a savage fight ensued, in which Chris wielded a sharp short-handled axe, inflicting a severe cut across the head and face of McLeod, besides dealing out a general beating.

Sheriff Logan promptly took the axe wielder into custody and a hearing was had almost immediately before Justice Peters. The blood-stained axe was produced in court, and upon search, the officers found the money in Chris' cabin exactly where he had placed it himself. Including this incident, there were three fights that evening within fifteen minutes. The others were street scraps in which fists flew with more or less damaging effect. The participants were run in and one of them upon a plea of guilty was allowed to contribute a fine of $5 and costs.

Daily Nevada State Journal, August 12, 1902: *Sheriff Getchell of Nevada County, California, arrived from Tonopah Sunday night with Bick Ballestero, of Nevada City, who is wanted for rape. It is the theory of the officers that Ballestero and one Schenk planned to send young girls from Nevada City and Grass Valley to Tonopah houses of ill-fame. Both of the suspects have been arrested on the rape charge. The case of Ballestero is an interesting one. He was arrested a couple of weeks ago by Sheriff Logan... on a telegraph warrant from Sheriff Getchell.*

Reno Evening Gazette, August 13, 1902: *A special to the* Evening Bee *from Tonopah, Nevada, says last night at 10:30 o'clock Wells, Fargo & Company's mail safe was robbed by a lone highwayman one quarter of a mile from town. Dan Robbins was the driver and there were no passengers on board. The robber had stretched a rope across the road and also covered the driver with a shotgun. He broke open the treasure box with a sledge hammer, but it is not known how much he got. Sheriff Logan and Constable Sullivan tracked the highwayman into town and they regard his capture as certain.*

Entering the fourth quarter of 1902, the *Bonanza* reported Sheriff Logan's books had been reviewed and "there are 133 business licenses sold and collected quarterly, in sums ranging from $7.50 to $100 each. That source of revenue aggregates about $1,200 per month on the average, or $40 per day."[38] The last week of August, Tom was reported to have left Tonopah for Belmont "where he will enrich the treasury of Nye County in the sum of $7,000. Of this, something over $5,000 was derived from the bullion tax, or rather the tax on proceeds of mines."[39]

While all funds collected by Tom were eventually turned over to the county treasurer, there was no protocol for how to hold those resources before that transfer occurred. Common practice was for the sheriff to lock money in a convenient safe, deposit into his personal bank account, or store elsewhere. Often, it was the far-off jingle of coins nestled in his saddlebags that first signaled the Logan children that their father was approaching, at which time they dashed off to greet him.

As sheriff and assessor, Tom earned $66.67 per month, a substandard sum that did not go unnoticed by the *Bonanza*. "Officials of Nye County," it had reported the previous year, "are the poorest paid public servants in the U.S. The next legislature will be asked to give these officials enough to sustain life on. The district attorney of the county is paid $50 in scrip and waits seven years for his pay."[40] With expanding revenue streams, salaries would modestly increase in the coming years as well as finance much-needed additional personnel.

Logan-Saylor Sample Room, First Railroad Days, Tonopah, NV, 1902 (Central Nevada Historical Society, Tonopah, NV)

In its transition from an improvised camp to an established town where roaming chickens laid eggs with flecks of gold and silver in the shells, Tonopah launched a campaign to "buy local" as opposed to mail order. Logan and Saylor had installed gasoline arch lamps in their saloon, touted to be the very best in town. Assistant District Attorney Charles Richards was leading an effort to establish an ice plant and open a brewery. Tom Kendall was building an addition to the Tonopah Club, and the much-anticipated Palace Hotel just south of Tom's saloon would open before the end of the year. A county hospital was under construction, and the Tonopah Water and Improvement Company was about to start digging wells and laying pipe. Plans were forming to erect an electric power company and expand telephone service. The town's first electric call-bell system was installed in Tom's saloon, but perhaps nothing was more indicative of his faith in the future than the three sapling shade trees he planted on Main Street in soil where trees had never grown.[41]

The Town of Nogood

My friend, have you heard of the town of Nogood
On the banks of the river Slow,
Where blooms the Waitawhile flower fair,
Where the Sometimeorother scents the air
And the soft Goeasys grow?

It lies in the valley of Whatstheuse,
In the province of Leterslide.
That tired feeling is native there;
It's the home of the reckless Idontcare,
Where the Giveitups abide.

It stands at the bottom of Lazy hill
And is easy to reach, I declare.
You've only to fold up your hands and glide
Down the slope of Weakville's toboggan slide
To be landed quickly there.

The town is as old as the human race,
And it grows with the flight of years.
It is wrapped in the fog of idlers' dreams.
Its streets are paved with discarded schemes
And sprinkled with useless tears.

The Collegebred fool and the Richman's heir
Are plentiful there, no doubt.
The rest of its crowd are a motley crew
With every class except one in view—
The Foolkiller is barred out.

The town of Nogood is all hedged about
By the mountains of Despair,
No sentinel stands on its gloomy walls,
No trumpet to battle and triumph calls
For cowards alone are there.

My friend, from the deadalive town of Nogood
If you would keep far away.
Just follow your duty through good and ill!
Take this for your motto, "I can, I will,"
And live up to each day.

—W. E. Penns, *The Coconino Sun*, Flagstaff, AZ, November 19, 1898

5

ANOTHER SHERIFF: 1903

"Nevada bad men must give up their shooting irons, for this state is no longer in the list of those forming the wild and wooly west. The last legislature passed a law against carrying concealed weapons and it is now in effect. Violators punished with a fine of $20-500 and imprisonment in the county jail 30-60 days."

Tonopah Bonanza, May 9, 1903

NEVADA SILVER PARTY Chairman, W.J. Westerfield, called to order their 1902 convention in Reno with the pound of a silver gavel on a card table draped with the Stars and Stripes. Despite rumblings that the once-vibrant political party was in decline, he ardently assured they were still strong, still had the welfare of the citizens of the state at heart, and *still* "stood for SILVER, first, last, and all the time!" Westerfield's speech received enthusiastic applause from the audience, which included 11 Nye County delegates—one of whom was Tom Logan.[1]

The next week, on September 6, 1902, the *Bonanza* confirmed Tom's decision to seek a third term as sheriff, writing:

Elsewhere appears the announcement of Thos. W. Logan, submitting his name to the Silver Party convention as a candidate for re-election to the office of sheriff and assessor. Mr. Logan needs no introduction to the people of Nye, he being one of the best officers the county ever had.

Tom's challengers were former opponent, James Power on the Democratic ticket, and Republican-Labor candidate James Cushing.[2] Heavily supported by the "working men" of Tonopah, Cushing was known for his unyielding loyalty to the principles of unionism.[3] Far different than the last election, this race for top lawman would be determined by those who had lived in Nye County less than two years. Issues of the day had drastically changed since 1900, and any candidate who evoked pre-Tonopah norms was in jeopardy of losing to one considered to be a more contemporary operator. As an incumbent, coupled with the *Bonanza* declaring support for Cushing and the Republican ticket, Tom Logan's re-election was a long shot:

The Labor Party with the hearty endorsement and cooperation of all regular Republicans has in the field a candidate for sheriff and assessor a man whose executive ability cannot be questioned. Combined with innate honesty of purpose is the moral and physical courage essential to the performance of such duties. James G. Cushing is a sturdy native of Wisconsin and 28 years of age, the past 12 of which he has found employment in the mines of the west, as a competent, intelligent worker, and staunch union man. His popularity is evinced by earnest effort to secure his election by those who know him best.[4]

The *Tonopah Miner* did not share the same viewpoint and was chastised by the *Bonanza* for indulging "in a lot of prevarications" related to Cushing's actual qualifications.[5] Amid what had to have been stout political posturing on all sides, Tom was defeated by just six votes. Cushing supporters were ecstatic and reasoned the new sheriff had been "elected squarely and won't be bounced out of office." The *Bonanza* proclaimed, "Hurray! Jas. G. Cushing is the next Sheriff of Nye County. Three cheers and a big tiger!"[6]

Tom was encouraged to contest the results but concluded there were no grounds upon which to do so.[7] Consequently, he accepted the outcome and finished his second term by successfully completing his assessor duties, which included valuating real and personal property in Nye County.[8] He also welcomed the arrival of his eighth and last child, Roy Walter Logan, born on November 18, 1902, in Belmont. Soon-to-be former Sheriff Logan next set about the business of life as a private citizen—at least, for the time being.

Main Street, Tonopah, c. 1903
(Central Nevada Historical Society, Tonopah, NV)

District Attorney Tasker Oddie was elected to the state senate. His replacement was Nevada native, 26-year-old Charles L. Richards, a graduate with a law degree from California's Stanford University. A Democrat, he had come to Tonopah in 1901 to begin what would become a lengthy legal and political career with terms in the state assembly and the U.S. House of Representatives from 1923 to 1925.[9]

Although the 1903-04 slate of fresh-faced candidates had snatched the reins of local government from the old guard, they were soon hampered by inexperience. The fiercely active and increasingly unruly populace, that had more than quadrupled in the last two years, was about to test the sheriff's office as never before. Still, the *Bonanza* advanced the most optimistic of hopes as Cushing assumed command in January 1903:

Belmont, the old seat of the county, new in life, industry and population, gets considerable of a change in the court house personnel, as a result of the biennial election. Sheriff and assessor Thos. W. Logan, a justly popular officer, gives way to Jas. G. Cushing, who will be found equal to the official demands.[10]

The 1902 election stirred up an unprecedented flurry of concerns and expectations related to Tonopah's future. A self-appointed voice of reason and conscience for the region, the *Bonanza* spared little ink calling attention to community issues, such as the need to expand the fire department, improve the jail, and organize a more responsive local governing body. However, the newspaper's strident support for local unions and caustic condemnation of Chinese workers only intensified the simmering racial tensions about to reach a full boil:

BE IT KNOWN TO ALL PERSONS: That the Miners' and Labor of Tonopah, Nevada, view with alarm the inroads that the Chinese labor is making on our fair city, by securing the work that should be done by the willing hands of our own people, especially in laundries, restaurants, hotels and as household help….[and] do hereby appeal and request all union men and women and the public generally in and around our fair city of Tonopah who are in sympathy with organized labor, to cease their patronage of Chinese restaurants, laundrys [sic], and all places where Chinese is [sic] employed, thus giving our own race a chance to live.[11]

The *Bonanza* further advocated that Tonopah businesses post notices in their windows stating they did not employ Asians. In early February 1903, the *Bonanza* reported a restaurant, "formerly owned by Chinese," had been forced out of business by local labor organizations and purchased by Mr. Wentworth. "In time," wrote the *Bonanza*, "John Chinaman in Tonopah will be a thing of the past."[12]

Racial strife was but one of the adverse byproducts of the unstoppable surge of inhabitants that would boldly test both Sheriff Cushing and District Attorney Richards. Not only was crime increasing, but the culprits were becoming more brazen, and Tonopah's reputation as one of the most peaceable boomtowns in history began to erode. Even the saloon next to Tom's, and named for Jim Butler himself, was not immune:

At 12:30, when the house was comparatively quiet, two masked men entered the back door leading in from the avenue, with two pistols in hand, the first robber ordered all then present, to the number of eight, to throw up their hands; to put them on the bar, as though they were all taking a drink, and for them to remain in that position and no one would be hurt. He was very deliberate and methodical, by his coolness proving himself to be an old hand at business....

Finding [the safe locked] he proceeded to the cash register, rang up the "no sale" button and appropriated all the gold and silver, amounting to $85 which he dumped into a barley sack. He then started for the roulette wheel when he noted a fine diamond ring worn my A. R. Graham, remarked that it "looked good" to him and took it off his finger. He then placed the stacks of silver in the bag, which amounted to $400.[13]

When the bartender tried to make a run for the back door, one of the robbers shot him in the neck before making a clean getaway. The *Bonanza* assured citizens that law enforcement had "good clues and expect to capture and put a strong case against the perpetrators of this daring villainy. All pimps, rounders, and check guerillas will be compelled to leave the town at once."[14]

The Butler saloon hold-up was but one of several motivating factors for a group of local citizens to form their own protection agency and publicize their resolve to assist Sheriff Cushing in "driving out the undesirable class who are becoming quite numerous in Tonopah."[15]

In turn, Cushing pressed commisioners to fund an addition to the Tonopah jail and was promptly informed "there was not enough money in the treasury to build anything."[16] The *Bonanza* was quick to back the new sheriff's request, writing: "The town jail of Tonopah is in a very dilapidated condition. The floor of the building is covered with water, owing to the leaky conditions of the roof and the seeping accommodations are anything but inviting. This abode of refuge should be at once repaired."[17]

With ninety percent of Nye County business now being conducted in Tonopah, momentum was building to relocate the county seat from Belmont, where there were, at best, 150 residents.[18] By the end of March 1903, the honeymoon was over for Sheriff Cushing. Hard-pressed by routine duties, he was now charged with enforcing a new state regulation mandating what could be considered "the impossible" and close all dance halls in Tonopah.[19] In two short years, a one-time staple of entertainment in any flourishing mining camp had been downgraded to that of a public nuisance by more urbane and staid mentalities.

Additionally, like his predecessor, Cushing was barraged with directives to strong-arm compliance relative to local health and sanitation laws. Underscoring the hazards of overflowing trash as a breeding ground for pestilence, local leaders urged Cushing to take immediate action against offenders or they would form a committee of citizens to "see that something is done."[20] The next week, the *Bonanza* intensified the community's appeal by writing: "...a little judicious hustling on the part of authorities will expedite matters and will be a performance of duty which the people have a right to expect."[21] One month later, the *Bonanza* lost patience:

The public streets are still in a littered and filthy condition, and there seems to be no effort on the part of authorities to have them cleaned. Where is our district attorney? Not long ago, when the town consisted of mainly shacks and tents, before broad sidewalks, balconies and plate glass fronts came into vogue, Main St. was cleaned regularly. Now that businessmen have gotten rich nothing of the kind is done. What's the matter, anyhow?[22]

In short order, whether intentional or due to a lack of capacity, or a combination of both, Cushing was about to slip from the pedestal so hastily erected by his supporters at election time.

SINCE BEING RELIEVED of his official duties, Tom remained active in the community and shifted his attention to a variety of business and family matters. Still living in Belmont, the Logans began 1903 busily preparing for oldest daughter Annie's marriage to Thomas H. Warburton, Jr., the fast-talking, blue-eyed son of former Nye County Treasurer Thomas Warburton.[23] Despite Tom's firmly held misgivings regarding his future son-in-law's work ethics and prospects as a provider, his opinion did little to change the course of events. The wedding, held at the Belmont courthouse, was a lavish affair complete with a red carpet. As suspected, during the next year, young Warburton failed to impress. Subsequently, Tom convinced Annie to join her sisters Joie and Jessie at a business college in Oakland, California, where they could learn respectable skills to support themselves if need be.[24]

In the coming months, Tom partnered with several friends and associates to invest in a number of quartz mines in the Pactoles District and sold a couple of vacant lots he owned on South Street in Tonopah. He and Saylor remodeled the façade of their saloon and constructed Tonopah's first bowling alley next door, as featured in the *Bonanza* on April 4, 1903: "The arrangements and outfit are of the latest kind, while the game of tenpins is gaining renewed popularity everywhere."

Among additional business transactions for Tom in early 1903 was a quitclaim deed granted to R.C. Taylor for a right-of-way across agricultural land in the Rye Patch area along a road linking Tonopah and Belmont. The purpose of this agreement was to accommodate the construction of a desperately needed water pipeline. A few months later, Tom sold his entire interest in 160 Rye Patch acres — previously acquired as state contract land — to the Tonopah Water Company. Their plan to start drilling mid-year could not come fast enough for the thirsty masses in and around Tonopah.[25]

Other significant developments included construction of an opera house and the town's first automobile stage-line, which promised to transport up to 16 passengers 60 miles in six hours. District Attorney Richards selected a site to build a new jail in Tonopah and put merchants on notice to keep sidewalks clear under penalty of arrest and prosecution. Shortly, the *Bonanza* happily reported Main Street was "undergoing a raking and sweeping and cleaning as it has not had in months." However, their satisfaction did not apply to the back streets in town, which they described as being "in a filthy condition and our D.A. who is paid a comfortable salary sitith down and sayeth nothing. Is it because he hasn't the ability to prosecute?"[26]

As "finger pointing" escalated, even relationships among law enforcement officials began to unravel. From a *Bonanza* article titled, "Nightwatchman Booth Arrested on Flimsy Pretext:"

The culmination of a long series of official outrages was reached last night when Night-watchman M. P. Booth was arrested by Constable Scott Hickey and Deputy Sheriff Barr Francis on the trivial pretext of carrying a concealed weapon and thrust into the calaboose....

Booth has been the nightwatchman in Tonopah for about ten months and his zeal and watchfulness have attracted the attention of a big majority of property owners on Main Street and caused them to stop pay of the constables which the latter have been drawing, but not earning, and transfer the same to Booth. This aroused the anger of the officers and is the animus of the charge against him.

The county and precinct police have been running things with a high hand in Tonopah the past few months, winking at open violations of the law, and making demands on citizens that savor strongly of extortion.... It is a shame and disgrace to a civilized community the way things have been carried on here lately. This town started right and its good citizens propose that it shall continue on those lines.[27]

Disharmony between a sheriff and district attorney was far from uncommon; Logan and Oddie appeared to have been an exception. Generally, discord stems from law enforcement's disappointment in prosecutors they believe fail to adequately hold offenders accountable. On the other hand, prosecutors often find fault with officers who mishandle suspects and evidence, thereby weakening their ability to try a case. For Sheriff Cushing and District Attorney Richards, the integrity of their relationship came under strong scrutiny following the Walter Dunn killing the summer of 1903 and raised serious doubts as to the effectiveness of the local justice system.

The saga began when more than 6,000 people crowded into Tonopah to celebrate Independence Day. Spectators vying for vantage points packed the streets and lined rooftops to watch two days of festivities. Following a drilling contest on the afternoon of July 4, 23-year-old Walter Dunn, an employee of the

Tonopah Mining Company and prone to youthful tomfoolery, directed an off-color comment at Frank Smith. A blacksmith working at the North Star Mine and nearly twice Dunn's age, Smith took offense to the insult and lashed back with his own "vile epithet." Dunn reportedly threw the first punch, and the ensuing grapple was quickly broken up by bystanders. Still hankering for a piece of Dunn, Smith grabbed a drill and started after him again just as officers arrived and escorted the irate man away.

"The Winning Team in the Fourth of July Drilling Contest" at the intersection of Main and Brougher Streets, Logan-Saylor Sample Room in the background (right), July 4, 1903 (Central Nevada Historical Society, Tonopah, NV)

After Smith promised to remain peaceable, he was released but later spotted passing The Butler Saloon with a large pocket knife. Again, he found himself in the custody of local lawmen, again promised to lay off, and was again released, plus allowed to keep his knife. The next evening, Smith found Dunn outside the Tonopah Club and took a swing. Dunn fought back and as the two men exchanged blows, onlookers were unaware that Smith's uppercuts had the advantage of a knife-in-hand. Dunn was stabbed six times, and a deputy hastening to break up the fight sustained a superficial wound.

Walter Dunn died the next morning, and Sheriff Cushing whisked Smith off to the Belmont to put distance between his prisoner and a lynch mob.[28] A coroner's jury found Frank Smith "had willfully, feloniously and with malice of fore-thought murdered Walter Dunn." Under pressure by Richards to bring Smith back to Tonopah for the preliminary hearing, Cushing refused, indicating he was acting under the advice of "those other than the District Attorney" and if served an order, he would ignore it.[29] More than a few voiced concern about what appeared to be preferential treatment by the sheriff's office both before and after the killing.

Fourth of July Parade, July 4, 1903
(Central Nevada Historical Society, Tonopah, NV)

The first week of August, in what popular opinion characterized as a "woeful miscarriage of justice," Justice Henry Hancock presided over the hearing and reduced Smith's charge to manslaughter. "The whole thing savors of jobbery," the *Bonanza* reported. "It is the general impression that the whole transaction was fixed before the case came up."[30]

Smith was scheduled for trial in December.

Cushing's brand of law and order was again called into question after another murder the third week of September. Although not yet a matter of public discourse, many were privately beginning to regret their choice for sheriff, opening the door ever so slightly for Tom to consider running in the next election. Even the unapologetic anti-Chinese *Bonanza* exhibited a change of heart with this headline: "Gang of Thugs Attack Chinese Quarter: Kill One, Murderously Assault Others and Attempt to Drive Them out of Town:"

Nothing has ever transpired in Tonopah that created as much excitement among the populace as did the announcement early Wednesday morning that a mob of men the night previous had invaded Chinatown, which occupies the west corner of the city, and commanded the [Chinese residents] at the point of guns to leave town instantly and never return. All kinds of rumors were afloat—that the men, after ordering the Chinamen to go, had accompanied them to the outskirts of town, had robbed and maltreated them…."[31]

The greatest damage was inflicted by a small group of about ten men who invaded, ransacked, and looted nearly every Chinese household in Tonopah. Under the leadership of Labor Union No. 224 President and local laundry owner, E.M. "Al" Arandall, the marauders kicked, cuffed, and pistol-whipped many of the inhabitants while demanding they leave town or they would be hanged. The most brutalized victim was a wash-house operator, 66-year-old Chong Bing Long, who was beaten and marched into the desert. Left alone, he staggered for hours in the darkness before he collapsed and died three miles west of town.[32]

News of the riot spread to several neighboring states. Jim Butler telegraphed from San Francisco: "If what I read be true regarding the abuse of Chinese, it is an outrage to the people of Tonopah. If the people do not fight this case I hope they may never prosper. I will give $500 to any fund for prosecution of the mob, and an additional $500 in case of conviction."[33]

Public viewpoints regarding the culpability of the perpetrators were severely divided. Union leaders denied involvement, and horrified citizens denounced the event as a crime against humanity. In an abrupt turnabout from his one-time exuberant support of Cushing, *Bonanza* editor, William W. Booth, penned the following condemnation of the man who had dethroned Tom Logan:

MUST COMPLY WITH THE LAW: Ever since early summer the sheriff's office in Nye county has been conducted in such manner that it has invited and received deserved criticism from the people of Tonopah, and the gentleman occupying that office has displayed such utter disregard for the statues of the state and has allowed his prejudices such latitude that the purposes of the law—the enforcement of which he swore to respect when elected—are liable to be defeated in one or more criminal cases now pending before the courts.

In July last, when the deplorable murder of Walter Dunn occurred, the sheriff, in direct opposition to the advice of the district attorney and in direct violation of the statue, had the murderer committed on a warrant issuing from the magistrate at the county seat, ignoring and refusing to serve the one that was issued from the magistrate's office in Tonopah, where the crime was committed. Then, with flaunting effrontery, he declared that he would be guided by the advice of his attorney who had been retained by the murderer as one of his counsel. But as these facts are pretty well known in Tonopah, and as the Supreme Court will soon pass on them, it may be out of place to expatiate on them now.

His latest exhibition of incompetence and stubbornness—to call it by no more severe name—has been the cause of more censure, however, than any previous action and has paved the way to well merited condemnation. In searching for evidence that would incriminate any person with participation in the murder of the poor old defenseless Chinaman, who was so brutally beaten last week, he has signally failed; in apprehending persons for whose arrest warrants had been placed in his hands, he has proven himself unsuccessful; when suggestions were made to him, he has refused to take cognizance of them; when advice was deemed necessary, instead of going to the district attorney, to whom he should pay heed in all criminal matters, he listens to the words of other advisers; and last, but not least, he dismisses from his staff deputies and calls for the star of the one officer who has been the most efficient and most zealous in his efforts to run to cover the perpetrators of the most heinous crime that has ever been committed in Tonopah.

For these and other reasons which can be addressed if occasion demands it, the sheriff has proven his utter unworthiness to hold the responsible position which he occupies, and the time has come when he must perform his duties, fairly and conscientiously, and in compliance with the instructions of the law, or he must be forced to resign. His methods have provoked his bondsmen to the extent that one of them, James L. Butler, withdrew his bond last month; and it is more likely that at the next meeting of the board of county commissioners two more will be asked to be released. It is more in sorrow than in anger that we feel constrained to give publicity to these facts concerning Sheriff Cushing, but as his actions tend to reflect discredit on the county and odium on the people, it is time to call a halt, and sentiment must give way to the demands of right and justice.[34]

Two weeks later, in a follow-up column, Booth elaborated on how he had approached Sheriff Cushing several times and "expostulated with him for the course he was pursuing." Believing he had a public duty to expose derelict behavior by an elected official, Booth was blunt in his summation:

As for Mr. Cushing, we can only express our regret that we ever advocated his election, for had he not proven total incapacity for holding the position of sheriff previous to the attack of the Bonanza, *he has certainly demonstrated it since that time, notably in his failure to materially assist the district attorney in his prosecution of the Chinese cases."*[35]

Following Butler's decision to withdraw as one of Cushing's bondsmen in the wake of the foregoing developments, the imperiled sheriff regrouped and in early October, 1903, furnished a new bond with, among others, Tonopah Club owner, Tom Kendall, and county treasurer, Robert Gilbert, as sureties.[36]

At the mob-killing trial in Belmont in early December, District Attorney Richards and Key Pittman appeared on behalf of the state. California attorney Samuel Vermilyea, one of the lawyers retained by Frank Smith in the upcoming Walter Dunn murder trial, represented several of the accused. After more than 40 witnesses testified during a two-week period, the jury deliberated for less than two hours before handing down a full acquittal in the beating death of a Chong Bing Long.[37] The *Gazette* was quick to unleash their condemnation of Nye County justice:

The evidence against them was complete. Before any jury of intelligent and unbiased men anywhere in the country a conviction would have been a certainty, if not for murder in the first degree at least for murder in the second degree. There was no excuse for it other than ignorant stupidity and brutality....[38]

On December 14, 1903, knife-wielding Frank Smith was also acquitted on the basis of a plea of self-defense. His attorneys secured their client's freedom with the assistance of two suspiciously convenient witnesses who swore they had seen Dunn strike the first blow on the day of the fatal stabbing. Additionally, Sheriff Cushing and Deputy Barr Francis bore witness as to Dunn's quarrelsome nature, thereby imputing him blameworthy in his own death. "Owing to all circumstances attendant upon the case," wrote the *Bonanza*, "the acquittal of Smith was entirely unexpected."[39]

As Sheriff Cushing's first year in office continued to fuel controversy and disapproval, Tom Logan was undoubtedly watching from the sidelines, but not averse to being of assistance if needed:

Word was received from Belmont Thursday night [October 8, 1903] that Welsh and Johnson Smith, two prisoners confined in the county jail in Belmont made their escape from the institution on Wednesday night by cutting through the outer brick wall of that building. The men's enjoyment of liberty, however, was brief, as on the following day they were caught in Jefferson Canyon, fifteen miles from Belmont by ex-Sheriff Tom Logan and John McCann.[40]

Although he no longer carried a badge, Tom apparently could not pass an opportunity to round up a fugitive from justice.

GROWING MORE DISSATISFIED with the new regime of elected officials, several prominent Nye County residents convened a citizens committee in early October 1903. Their purpose, as the *Bonanza* clarified, was "not to supplant county government, but to assist it, and if conducted properly would be of untold benefit to the town."

Among the committee's initial priorities was to address local sanitation issues by purchasing and distributing 500 pounds of chloride of lime. They also appointed two health inspectors charged with disinfecting all offending spaces, and began drafting a charter to incorporate Tonopah.[41]

In addition to Booth, notable members of the committee included former district attorney Tasker Oddie, future U.S. Senator Key Pittman, and future mining magnate George Wingfield, one of Tom Logan's newest business associates—and the man some believe may have had a hand in Tom's death.

Poetic Invitation:
Eagles use Verse to Summon Guests

Good eagles from your lofty heights
Look earthward as you swiftly soar,
And pausing in your downward flight
Alright at Wardner Aerie's door.
There you will meet a welcome rare,
A royal love feast will ensue
While joyful greetings fill the air
From friends and brothers tried and true.

A band of "Buzzards" have confessed
They have been erring up to date,
And now they seek our Eagle nest
Before the time has grown too late.
On each of these, strong Eagle's wings
We place with tender, loving hand
And tell of joys our Order brings
To those who wear our Eagle brand.

"Buzzards," to whom this card may come,
We send you cordial greetings, too,
Bidding you to our Eagle's home,
That you may learn what good we do
Our hearts with loving kindness burn.
Each to his brother must be true.
Perhaps when you our mottoes learn
Good Eagles we can make of you.

—Anonymous, *Tonopah Bonanza*, November 7, 1903

6

POWER AND INFLUENCE: 1904

"[George Wingfield] derived a curious pleasure from pulling [a six-shooter) on other men. Often, while he was talking to a man, he would suddenly whip out the gun and jab it in the other's stomach. He apparently did it to see the effect—most people turned white…. When Wingfield intended to get a man, he used more subtle methods than a gun."

Sally Springmeyer Zanjani, *The Unspiked Rail*, 1981

WHEN IT CAME to mining magnate George Wingfield, anything was possible. Wingfield lived life like he played poker—straight-faced, calculating, and acutely aware of any opponent's strengths and weaknesses. An undisputed self-made man, he was a unique blend of laudable benevolence and dark-hearted malice, and had an extraordinary ability to devise any number of persuasive strategies to his advantage. So masterful in his pursuits, one might conclude that from a very early age, he had felt in his bones there was no greater purpose in life than achieving wealth, influence, and power.

George Wingfield, c. 1904
(Central Nevada Historical Society,
Tonopah, NV)

Wingfield emerged from a "working childhood" less than academically inclined. Rather, having kept company with the tough-talking, liquor-breathed ranch hands on his father's Oregon ranch, he became a superb horseman, a keen shot, and a cunning gamester.[1]

Arriving in Tonopah the first week of May 1901, at the age of 25, his pockets nearly empty, the "drifter boy gambler" had shared a stagecoach with Tom Kendall, co-owner of the Tonopah Club. At that establishment and others to come, Wingfield commenced mining the gaming tables one card hand at a time. He eventually acquired joint ownership of the Tonopah Club, which was less than a stone's throw north of Logan's saloon.[2]

By 1904, Wingfield had amassed power in multiple arenas—gambling, mining, commerce, and back-room politics. His trajectory for becoming one of Nevada's most notorious political bosses was fixed and pointed toward a sky without limit. This he would accomplish by not being timid, sloppy, nor hesitant to elicit the assistance of, for instance, a well-placed lawyer, accountant, or gunslinger.

Tonopah Club, Main Street, Tonopah, NV, c. 1904 (Central Nevada Historical Society, Tonopah, NV)

As to whether Tom Logan and George Wingfield were friends or foes, their association likely hovered somewhere in between. During the summer of 1903, they partnered with several others, including legendary "Diamondfield Jack" Davis, to invest in at least ten mining claims.[3] Davis was a swaggering, middle-aged cowboy, as adept at shooting off his mouth as he was a gun. He had once been convicted of killing two sheepherders in Idaho. Doomed to hang, his life was spared when, on December 18, 1902, based on an overwhelming body of evidence proving him innocent, he was pardoned and headed to Nevada to reconstruct a life in shambles.[4]

Jackson Lee "Diamondfield Jack" Davis, *Western World*, April 1905

Following a failed attempt to jump one of Wingfield's claims, Davis persuaded him and partner Nevada Assemblyman George Nixon to grubstake him to a prospector's outfit. He succeeded in locating a number of first-rate claims for his new business associates, and soon established himself as a formidable capitalist among the elite.[5] However, his gun-toting skills did not go unnoticed, which made him perfectly suited to become one of Wingfield's first bodyguards.

The Wingfield mining claims, in which Logan invested between April and July of 1903, were located west of the Cloverdale Ranch, some 60 miles north of Tonopah. While many Wingfield properties produced with abandon, the absence of any glowing accounts beyond speculation by local newspapers indicate this district was apparently not one.*

As to any "unofficial" business that might have transpired between Sheriff Logan and Wingfield, it's almost a sure bet the two interacted on some level. Both were popular, high-performing local figures. Tom was well-known for his understated yet impenetrable commitment to law and order. Wingfield was particularly adept at bypassing those rules to craft alternatives more conducive to personal interests. Some Logan descendants speculate that in Tom's capacity as the county assessor, he might have been in collusion with Wingfield, funneling inside information on property owners in financial distress. By circumventing the county lien process, cash-laden buyers like Wingfield could acquire the property at a bargain rate or even secretly conduct a transaction on behalf of Tom to avoid accusations of impropriety.[6]

With little doubt, if united in purpose, Tom Logan and George Wingfield would have formed an ominous alliance. By the same token, if adversaries, a clash of any degree could very well tumble into a matter of life and death.

THE GREAT SMOKY Valley, northeast of Tonopah, derives its name from the dust-filled haze continually teased aloft in the basin by breeze and gale alike. No more than 15 miles wide, the valley lies between the Toiyabe and Toquima Mountains and runs some 120 miles in a north-south direction through Nye County. Numerous small cold-water streams and steaming hot springs transform the otherwise desolate landscape into a quasi-oasis for farming and ranching. Here is where Tom and Hannah Logan, sometime between 1903 and 1904, acquired the ranch that would bear their name for the next 15 years.**

---

* To date, no other records of joint business activity between Logan and Wingfield have been found.

** The Chrysler Ranch, formerly known as the old Belcher place, was not officially deeded to the Logan family until five months after Tom's death. (Nye County Recorder, Deed Book 11, pg. 151) Hannah retained control and oversaw operation until most of the children were grown and on their own, at which time she sold the ranch to Will Berg in 1919 and moved to Reno. It remains a Berg family property to this day.

An established working ranch, the property had been owned for some time by Joseph Freeman Chrysler. Shortly before his son, Robert, married in 1901, Chrysler transferred title to him. Then, when Robert died suddenly, his sister's husband, Thomas Tate, became the estate administrator. Tate and his wife, Esther, had operated a valley mail and passenger stage stop from 1886 to 1901. Tate had also served three terms as a Nye County Commissioner between 1894 and 1902. According to his daughter Myrtle (Tate) Myles, he had partnered with Frank Brotherton, a Belmont merchant, to grubstake Jim Butler's big discovery but neither man ever received any return on their investment.[7 & 8]

The 1903 Nye County tax assessment roll indicated the 160-acre spread in Smoky Valley was fully functional with a house, stable, corral, fencing, 12 work horses, 50 cattle, harnesses, and three wagons. Tate granted a quitclaim deed to his attorney Eldred Moore, which was "recorded at request of T. Logan, December, 10, 1903, at 2:00 p.m." Presumably, this was the first official step toward Tom obtaining full title in the near future.[9]

Looking southwest toward Tonopah from the Berg ranch once owned by the Logan family, 2012, Smoky Valley, NV (Logan Family Collection)

As had been their practice while living in Monitor Valley, the Logan family now divided the bulk of their time between Smoky Valley and Belmont, where the children attended school. Southwest of their ranch was the James T. Darrough place, distinguished by a stone house built by pioneers in 1863 and a cement pond fed by a bubbling hot spring. The pond is believed to have been formed with rocks from a shelter built by explorer John C. Fremont in 1844.[10]

Darrough married Laura Stebbins in 1891, and they had six sons: Jim, Jr, William, Douglas, Luther, and twins Lawrence and Raymond. A house full of boys was particularly opportune given the proximity of the Logan girls living within eyesight. As it so happened, Jim, Jr. would marry Amy Logan in 1913, and six years later, Raymond and Kate Logan tied the knot.[11]

Darrough Hot Springs (steaming to the left), Smoky Valley, NV, 1910
(Dale Darrough Rodrigues Collection)

During 1904, regional newspapers captured occasional glimpses of Tom, a man still in motion, tending investments, involved with family, and engaged in the community:

March 2, 1904, *Deseret Evening News,* **Salt Lake City, UT**: *Ex-Sheriff Tom Logan and Gus Huber of Tonopah took a lease this week on the north end of the Sandstorm [Mine].*

March 10, 1904, *Reno Evening Gazette*: *Thomas Logan, Miss Logan and Mrs. T.H. Warburton of Tonopah are staying at the Overland for a few days.*

May 28, 1904, *Tonopah Bonanza*: *Monday being Decoration Day, a meeting of the grand army veterans was held on the evening of the 22d. Captain G.R. Bradley was appointed marshal for the day with aides Dr. C .L. Hammond, Capt. J B Menardi, P. M. Bowler for the Eagles; Wesley Stewart, (Knights of the Pithias); Lem Platt, Fire Brigade; W. F. Kilker, Miners Union; Tom Logan, Odd Fellows.*

Stationery letterhead used by Frank Logan, March 22, 1904
(Logan Family Collection)

Based on the stationery letterhead Tom's brother Frank used to write a letter to his wife in Belmont on March 22, 1904, the Logan-Saylor Sample Room on Main Street in Tonopah was briefly known as The Eagle Saloon before being named The American in 1905. Now, in addition to E.E. Saylor, Tom had a new saloon business partner, Reno-based jeweler, banker, and hotel proprietor Frank Golden—the multi-millionaire, mediocre poker player who first suggested George Wingfield try his luck in Tonopah.[12 & 13]

Business pacts made during Tonopah's boom years—from mining claims to real estate deals—changed course and composition with head-spinning frequency. Of Tom's many financial relationships, one individual that prompts more than a passing glance was that of Robert F. Gilbert. Born in Leesburg, Virginia, in 1857, he counted himself among those smitten with the "Westward Ho!" Movement and arrived in Belmont at the age of 21. There he married Lida Humphrey, raised five children, and served two terms in the state assembly before being elected Nye County treasurer on the same ticket as Sheriff Cushing the fall of 1902.[14]

Said to have retained some of the best traits of a polished Virginia gentleman, Gilbert displayed characteristics more evocative of the Wild West and frontier justice when he used a double-barreled shotgun to kill Indian Dan. Apparently a familiar mischief-maker to the Belmont townsfolk, Indian Dan embarked on one tirade too many the last week of June 1904. According to the *Bonanza*, he had been drinking and running through the streets with a gun, and was "particularly desirous of ending the official and earthly career" of Gilbert. Calling him "foul names prefixed by dirty adjectives and declaring at all times that he would kill the d__n dirty ___of _____ and anyone else who attempted to interfere," Dan kept up the tirade for more than six hours until Gilbert, armed with his shot gun, confronted him thusly:

[Gilbert] stepped into the street and asked, "What is that you say?" Dan repeated his threats with more emphasis, then he dropped, filled to the neck with shot. Mr. Gilbert waited a moment to see that there was no danger of his rising and assaulting him, he then went home, deposited his gun, came down and surrendered himself to the justice of the peace, who had seen much of the day's disturbances. The justice told Gilbert to go about his business, that when he was wanted, he would let him know....

[Dan] was buried the next day with all the pomp and circumstance belonging to his class. A huge grave or hole in the ground was excavated, a large box was lowered therein, and into the box the corpse was placed, then a new pair of blankets purchased for the occasion, his spurs, riata, saddle, schaps, [sic] and all of personal belongings such as apparel and accouterments; his dog was then shot, and also three of his horses. The grave was filled, the funeral was over, and Dan prepared to enter the "happy hunting ground" with éclat. When the Indians were asked about his wife, they replied, "Oh, Dan will catch another one there."

As a result of the inquest, a Mr. Goodshaw formerly of Tonopah but lately an inmate in the county hospital, was transferred from there to the county jail being charged with selling liquor to the dead Indian. The result of the inquest was in accordance with public sentiment: justifiable homicide.[15]

Railroad Days, Tom Logan's saloon in the background, July 25, 1904, Tonopah, NV (Nevada Historical Society, Reno, NV)

Gilbert's apparent comfort in taking the law into his own hands is difficult to dismiss. No mention of Sheriff Cushing or any of his deputies appeared in the newspapers. Add to that the certainty exhibited in the court of public opinion that Gilbert was justified in killing Indian Dan, and one might conclude that 20th century due process had yet to gain a foothold in Central Nevada.*

Further underscoring that perspective, just a few weeks later in neighboring Esmeralda County, an altercation in Goldfield between W.S. Elliott and Jack Madigan—partners who had started The Butler Saloon together in Tonopah—came to fisticuffs over a gambling table. When Madigan pulled a gun, Elliott came at him, managed to seize the weapon, and after a few blows to the head, shot his former partner in the neck, "severing the jugular vein and causing death in a few minutes." Friends and onlookers reported Madigan "was looking for trouble and got what he deserved."[16]

Even Nye's D.A., Charles Richards seemed to subscribe to the somewhat arbitrary, far too emotionally-charged influence of personal opinion rather than the letter of the law. On July 30, 1904, he wrote the State Board of Pardons on behalf of one W. Thompson who had come to Tonopah in "very stringent circumstances." While in a drunken state, Thompson stole about $20 from a crap dealer's table, was caught, convicted of petit larceny, and sentenced to time in the local jail. From Richards' letter:

At the time, I felt very bitter toward him, and endeavored to obtain a severe punishment, which I did. Since then I have learned that he is not such a bad fellow and his conduct while in jail has been extraordinarily good. He is also a hard working industrious fellow when at himself and I feel that he has paid all the penalty for his crime that justice demands. I don't excuse him because he was under the influence of liquor and bad company, but the court was imbibed with the same spirit as I was at the time, and upon reconsidering the matter, in view of the facts learned since, I feel that the sentence was too severe entirely.[17]

This often blatant propensity for manipulating the course of justice on a stalwart whim attracted harsh criticism from Tonopah miner Zeb Kendall (no apparent relation to Tom Kendall). After Howard Sharp chose to settle a score by putting a bullet in the back of Kendall's brother, killing him, Zeb could barely contain his fury. When the Esmeralda County Grand Jury failed to indict Sharp, Kendall—who would later serve two terms as a state senator—unleashed his outrage against the slackened tendencies of local authorities in a letter to the *Bonanza*:

I do, however, earnestly desire that justice shall be done; that Howard Sharp be brought before a jury of his peers and tried for the crime that he is charged with; that if he is proven innocent in the judgment of a fair minded jury, that he be acquitted, and if guilty punishment be meted out to him according to his desserts. The law should take its course....

* R.F. Gilbert would encounter his own share of legal woes regarding his money-management practices in 1910 when he was sued by Nye County for recovery of public funds. *Reno Evening Gazette*, December 19, 1910.

It is a disgrace to the officers and the Court of Esmeralda County and the people of the state of Nevada, that murder goes unpunished, that a murderer cannot even be brought to the bar of justice to prove his guilt or innocence. Is there any wonder that murder stalks abroad in our fair state of Nevada…. I think the attention of the people would be aroused if they had gazed on the cold clay of someone near and dear brutally and foully murdered by a shot in the back….

I think a man should be punished for taking the life of another when he can avoid it.[18]

Throughout the region, public nuisance and crime, spawned by rampant growth and lagging leadership, was taking its toll on old-timers and newcomers alike. The official arrival of the railroad in the summer of 1904, a long-anticipated godsend to the local economy and traveling public, was a mixed blessing to local government and law enforcement. Still, there was abundant jubilation on July 25 when Tonopah clad itself in red, white and blue streamers, banners, and flags to welcome their first "iron horse."

Railroad Days, Order of the Eagles' float in front of Tom Logan's saloon, July 25, 1904, Tonopah, NV (Nevada Historical Society, Reno, NV)

The three days of festivities began with an elaborate parade of floats and marching bands, and featured foot races, drilling contests, carnival acts, baseball games, bronco busting, and a grand ball at the opera house. A reviewing stand with a large sign reading, "Formerly a Desert, Now Tonopah," stood near the intersection of Main and Brougher Streets. Tonopah's first Railroad Days culminated with a race to the top of Mt. Oddie and back, a trapeze performance on lower Main Street, and a spectacular fireworks show.[19]

As the glow of that glorious day faded in the weeks to come, fireworks of the human variety exploded at the Nye County Democratic Convention at the end of September 1904. Conflict among delegates reached such a blazing state that the party split into two factions, resulting in the formation of an Independent contingent more sympathetic to the concerns of laborers and ranchers. The Nye County Democratic ticket included local attorney William Pittman for district attorney and local assemblyman Thomas McCabe for sheriff and assessor. McCabe had recently distinguished himself as a leading proponent of moving the county seat from Belmont to Tonopah. Incumbent Sheriff Cushing was opposed to the move and set his sights on McCabe's assembly seat.[20]

Robert F. Gilbert, Nye County Assemblyman (1888 and 1896) and Treasurer, (1902-09), c. 1906 (Central Nevada Historical Society, Tonopah, NV)

Less than a week later, the Nye County Republican Party nominated Mark Averill for D.A. and, surprisingly, fielded no candidates for sheriff. Running for Tonopah constable was Alex McKenzie, one of Logan's closest associates and described by the press as "a good Republican, who believes in the maintenance of the law, and will fill the office with credit to himself and friends."[21]

As for the newly formed Independents, with whom Tom Logan chose to align, they congregated at the bowling alley next to his saloon on October 7, 1904. Calling themselves the Independent Political Club (IPC), they outlined their mission as being:

..for the purpose of good government, clean politics and to further and protect the interests of Tonopah and Nye County, and the State of Nevada: also to assist and aid those who are candidates for office, irrespective of party, to the best of our judgment. This club shall endeavor to advance socially and morally the best interests of all concerned.[22]

Optimistic underdogs, the IPC nominated incumbent D.A. Charles Richards for re-election and Tom Logan to again run for sheriff against Assemblyman McCabe. "Both good men," reported the *Bonanza* on October 8, 1904, "both will make good sheriffs and in this case the Republican voter can weigh in the balance the individual merits of each man and vote for the best, irrespective of party politics."

Implicit in the public discourse leading up to the 1904 Nye County election was a coalesced determination to somehow rise above the chaos and inequities demonstrated by law enforcement during the last two years. Even the typically partisan *Bonanza*, which had so fervently supported James Cushing for sheriff against Tom Logan in the previous election, took the high road in their coverage, referring to McCabe and Logan as "two sterling good men." McCabe, they wrote, "will make a good sheriff and is generous enough to say that if defeated it will be by a good man...and like the other Tom, [Logan] thinks it will take a good man to beat him."[23]

Even though Logan had been out of office for two years, he had remained committed to public service. In the week prior to the election, a coroner's jury of six men, with Logan as foreman, was empanelled to assess the scene of yet another murder. A badly decomposed body had been found hidden beneath a pile of rocks in a mine tunnel near Tonopah. The unidentified man, attired in quality clothing, had a leather money belt fastened around his waist, "about four inches wide, with three pockets, two of which were open and empty, and the third contained a pocket edition of Webster's dictionary. A fedora hat found near the body bore the seller's name 'The Hub, Seattle.'" The jury concluded the man was likely a foreigner. Anyone who could help identify the victim, estimated to be 35-40 years of age, was asked to view his personal effects in the custody of the coroner.[24]

Most likely, the victim was never identified and joined countless other ill-fated souls who would simply vanish without a trace from the lives of those far away who knew them. For any poet or journalist who sought to romanticize the routine work of lawmen like Pat Garrett, Bat Masterson, Allan Pinkerton, the Earps, or the heretofore lesser-known Logan brothers, they would probably be discouraged by their subjects against penning any grandiose narrative.

These men, their predecessors, and peers had witnessed some of the most horrifying and gruesome deeds one human could exact upon another. Some answered the call of duty with quiet reservation and others in more flamboyant ways, but all walked the same tightrope between obligation and impulse, life and death. However audacious or flawed, guarded or driven, those behind the badge in the Wild West flirted with the stuff of legends if for no other reason than they were the ones who stepped forward when others did not to serve a purpose bigger than themselves.

The Day's Demand

God, give us men! A time like this demands
Strong minds, great hearts, true faith and willing hands,
Men whom the lust of office does not kill;
Men whom the spoils of office cannot buy;
Men who possess opinions and a will;
Men who have honor; men who will not lie;
Men who can stand before a demagogue
And damn his treacherous flatteries without winking.
Tall men, sun-crowned, who live above the fog
In public duty and in private thinking.
For while the rabble, with their thumb-worn creeds,
Their large professions and their little deeds,
Mingle in selfish strife, lo! Freedom weeps;
Wrong rules the land, and waiting justice sleeps.

—J. G. Holland, *Pacific Monthly*, Vol. 4-6

7

RETURN TO DUTY: 1905

"A political orator is a man of verbal luxuriance, and nearly always the shallowest of sophists. There is usually little to be gained in what he says, but, to 'the groundlings,' there is deep significance in how he says it."
Earnest McGaffey, "Political 'Jaw-Smiths' and their Ways,"
The Perrysburg Journal, Wood County, Ohio, July 8, 1908

TOM LOGAN WAS again elected sheriff in the fall of 1904 by a decisive margin of 180 votes out of the nearly 1,000 cast.[1] He was the only Independent party candidate on the ballot to win and the only "old guard" Nye County official returned to service by his consituents. Apparently, Tom had succeeded in bridging from the "Old West" to the "New West." Other key victories went to William Pittman for district attorney, Tasker Oddie for state senate, and James Cushing for state assembly.

When he first became sheriff in 1899, a wagon road in Nye County was considered a luxury. Change, especially in the last two years while he was out of office, had descended on the region with unprecedented ferocity. The county now had telegraph and telephone communications, electric lights, paved sidewalks, and, according to the *Salt Lake Tribune*, "every comfort obtainable, even in a city the size of New York."[2]

Upon his return to the sheriff's desk at the Belmont courthouse in January 1905, Tom likely believed he had a fair sense of the many new responsibilities weighing on his shoulders. In truth, that colossal burden would wear heavily on the tall, affable man known for his diligence and composure. During the next 16 months, "our Tom," as he was sometimes called by the local newspaper, would find himself in a day-to-day struggle to simply keep his footing, let alone take any measureable strides.

When the State Board of Assessors held their annual meeting in Carson City the second week of January 1905, Tom was once again among the participants. Meeting transcripts suggest he was noticeably more assertive than his last appearance in 1902. He made and supported several motions backing the individual discretion of county assessors to determine property valuations on, for instance, horses, hogs, telephone and telegraph, and electric light and power lines.[3]

However, when it came to cattle and sheep, Tom spoke out against what he considered the lack of uniformity from county to county and made good on his campaign vow to support the interests of Nye County farmers and ranchers. From the *State Board of Assessor's Minutes, 1905*:

Mr. Logan: *"I notice that in the assessment of last year the stock cattle in the northern counties were assessed at $17 per head, and $15 in the four lower counties. I don't know much about the value of cattle in the northern counties, but I do know that the cattle that were assessed for $15 in Nye County last year were sold for $10 and $14... I do not believe that the difference allowed between the counties last year is enough, and I have had something like twenty years' experience in the cattle business. I notice the cattle in the northern counties are higher class. When your cattle get fat they are right handy to the cars, while our cattle never do get real fat; when they get rounded out a little we have to drive them 150 or 200 miles to market."*

Mr. Randal from Lyon County moved to reduce the valuation of cattle in Nye, Esmeralda, Lincoln and White Pine counties to $13 per head, and $15 in the other counties." The motion carried.

Mr. Logan moved that the value of sheep in Nye County be placed at $2, owing to the fact that it was so expensive to get the wool to market...admitting that Nye was good sheep country. The motion carried.[4]

Elko County Assessor J. Eggers raised concerns about there being a vast difference in the value of contract land and appealed to the chairman, Governor John Sparks, to consider "that some is worth more and some worth less, so you have to average it.... There is a difference in our county. Some I assess at $2.50 per acre, and some a great deal less." Sparks responded by clarifying the government fixed the price at $1.25 per acre and, in his opinion, that value should be uniform. Tom followed with:

Mr. Logan: *"I differ with Mr. Eggers in regard to the matter. He thinks because the lands have not been fully paid for they are not worth as much. If I sell Mr. Eggers a horse for $40 and he pays $20 down, the horse belongs to him and is worth $40. In my county I assess no lands for less than $1 per acre." After a little further discussion, the matter was left with the Assessors.*[5]

Before the assessors moved on to discuss the predictably perilous topic of raising railroad assessments, Tom moved to add goats to the list of taxable stock. The motion carried and the assessors agreed to $5 per head. Attentive to matters both big and small, leveraging his years of practical experience, it appeared Sheriff Logan had become more than an enforcer of the law and tax collector. At age 43, he was fast rising to the ranks of being a bona fide politician.

In mid-January, Tom reported the outcome of the assessors' board meeting to the local press. However, in keeping with his new-found resolve, he also had an opinion of interest to both the public and former rival, James Cushing, regarding the politically charged controversy mounting over whether or not to move the county seat from Belmont to Tonopah. On January 22, 1905, the newly founded *Tonopah Sun* ran a front page exclusive, reading in part:

Assemblyman J.G. Cushing and Barney McCann, of Nye County, are working hard to prevent the removal of the county seat from Belmont to Tonopah.

Mr. Logan states the motive of Mr. Cushing has not been learned, but that of Mr. McCann is due to his being a resident of Belmont.

According to Mr. Logan, Senator Oddie and Assemblyman Cole are doing their duty by Nye County and are using every energy to give Tonopah the county seat. It is greatly feared, however, that Cushing and McCann have the better of the fight.

The *Sun* accompanied Tom's remarks with an editorial accusing Cushing and McCann of misleading voters prior to the election by signing a petition professing support for Tonopah becoming the county seat.

Sheriff Tom Logan, c. 1904
(Nye County Sheriff's Dept., Tonopah, NV)

But now, with two of Nye County's three assemblymen opposed to the effort, other legislators were reluctant to defy their colleague's position. The *Sun* further stressed the importance of counteracting, in particular, Cushing's considerable influence and making known to the state the real sentiments of their community. In the event that the county seat did not come to Tonopah, the *Sun* assured there would be a campaign to form a new county called Butler. McCann was explicitly warned, "If he wants his constituents to be in the same county with the place that keeps up all the revenue and expenses, he would better withdraw and cease to labor against Tonopah."[6]

One week later, the *Bonanza* reported that thanks to the good work of Senators Oddie and Nixon, Assemblyman George Cole, Key Pittman, and George Wingfield, the county seat removal bill was passed unanimously by the Senate. In the lower house, Cole "turned a neat trick" when he had the bill taken out of the hands of the Nye County delegation and referred to the Judiciary Committee, which prevented Cushing and McCann from further delaying the vote. "The outlook is exceedingly bright," reported the *Bonanza*.[7]

Cushing ignited more criticism from constituents when he proposed legislation to fix a taxation value of $10 per acre on mining claims, require mine inspections, and make mining companies liable for the acts of their employees.

Perhaps indicative of the power wielded by mine operators compared to labor unions at the time, all of Cushing's bills failed to pass. "Assemblyman Cushing," wrote the *Bonanza* on February 25, 1905, "evidently doesn't stand well with his brother legislators, for they seem to take delight in consigning his pet bills to the waste basket as fast as they bob up."*

The measure to relocate the Nye County Seat eventually passed the state senate, and the first meeting of the county commissioners in Tonopah took place on May 1, 1905.[10] Tom knew firsthand the immense benefit of moving the sheriff's office and jail from the remote courthouse on the hill in Belmont to the county's crown jewel of Tonopah. Less than one month into his third term, upon learning of an apparent attempted murder in the Armagosa Valley, he had had to travel nearly 350 miles by horse and buggy in the dead of winter to acquire a warrant, make an arrest, and transport his prisoner to the Belmont jail. Having the county seat in Tonopah meant less time on the road and more time tending to business. [11 & 12]

Luckily, the victim in the Armagosa Valley case did not die, so instead of facing murder charges, the perpetrator, Thomas Shipe, was charged with "assault to kill." A middle-aged miner from California known for his propensity to brandish weapons, Shipe would be represented by a young, new attorney who had only recently come to Tonopah—Patrick McCarran, future U.S. Senator and one of the lawyers who would soon represent Tom's killer.

More than likely, it was during the Shipe trial, about six months later, that Logan and District Attorney William Pittman first encountered McCarran, none imagining how inextricably linked they would soon be for all time.

THE ONLY CHILD of Irish immigrants, future U.S. Senator, Patrick Anthony McCarran was born in Reno on August 9, 1876. His father came to America as a teenage stowaway out of Londonderry County in 1848, and his mother earned her passage as a cook in the steerage before boarding a train headed west. Two years after Patrick's birth, the family moved about 15 miles east of Reno into

---

* Neither Cushing nor McCann would again be elected to public office in Nye County. In fact, less than one year later, on April 8, 1906—ironically, the day after Sheriff Logan was killed—Cushing tendered his resignation in a letter to Governor Sparks[8] to which Sparks replied on May 8, 1906: *In view of the fact that there is no probability of an extra session of the Legislature convening before your term expires and in consideration of the great expense which would be entailed on Nye County should there be a special election to fill the vacancy which would be made by your resignation being accepted, after due thought and consideration and consultation with the Attorney General it is deemed advisable not to accept your resignation.*[9]

the Truckee River Canyon where their hardiness was tested by fire and flood, searing summers and freezing winters, and the grinding rigors of unremitting poverty. They planted orchards and immense vegetable gardens, and trucked produce such as cabbage, potatoes, and peaches by horse and wagon to nearby markets. Gradually, they built their livestock to include poultry, dairy cows, horses, hogs, and sheep, and eventually acquired nearly 2,000 acres that became known as the McCarran Ranch.[13]

Even though his parents had no formal education, they very much valued higher learning, regularly discussed world history and politics (and some poetry), and embraced the "theology and liturgy of the Catholic Church" in prayer. McCarran credited two school teachers—Hanna Lineham and Libbie Booth—for helping him develop his distinguished writing and oratorical style, as well as many of the social graces essential to his eventual political influence and dexterity.[14]

Excelling as a student and athlete, McCarran was nearly 21 when he was selected valedictorian of his Reno High School graduating class. The *Gazette*, on June 24, 1897, described the commencement ceremonies, noting, "'Footprints on the Sands of Time,' was the subject of an oration by Patrick McCarran. Mr. McCarran seems to be a young gentleman of advanced and liberal ideas, able to foretell the future by the footprints of the past...."

McCarran soon enrolled at the University of Nevada in Reno and got a job stoking university furnaces before dawn to help cover his education costs. In 1900, he joined the university's first debate team, dividing his time between studies and work at the ranch, which increased greatly after his father was injured in a fall. Unable to manage both responsibilities well, his grades declined so McCarran left the university to take charge of the ranch and tend his thriving flock of sheep. Still determined to pursue a legal career, he spent much of his free time seeking guidance from those he called the "outstanding lawyers of the day." Adhering to their advice regarding reading matter while preparing for admission to the bar, he borrowed law books from the likes of the Honorable William Woodburn of Carson City, the first native Nevadan elected to the U.S. Congress.[15 & 16]

McCarran built a solid reputation in the sheep business and, in 1902, was invited by Senator William Sharon to run for the state assembly on the Democratic Silver Party ticket, which he did and won. The next year he married a school teacher from Elko, Nevada, and set up housekeeping on Mill Street in Reno where he continued to study law while serving as a member of Nevada's 21st Legislature.[17]

The first of McCarran's four children, Margaret, was born on July 22, 1904. A few months later, after just one term in the assembly, the Democratic Party nominated him for the state senate. McCarran was characterized by the *Gazette* as "a young man of brilliant qualities and showy personality. He belongs to the 'get there' type of hustlers." A portion of his nomination acceptance speech was quoted in the article:

"Go through the records of the man whose name has been dragged through the columns of this paper…and I assure you, gentlemen, that man [Senator Newlands, a McCarran supporter] was working for the movement of irrigation in the West before TEDDY ROOSEVELT RAN HIS FOOTRACE DOWN SAN JUAN HILL."

In the various other speeches which he has made about the county, he has referred to [Assemblyman] Mr. Nixon as a "railroad hireling," "tool of the Southern Pacific," and declared that he was only the "stalking horse" for Senator Stewart, after which [McCarran] attended a meeting of the Republicans at Sparks where Mr.

Patrick Anthony McCarran, c. 1908
(Central Nevada Historical Society,
Tonopah, NV)

Nixon spoke and while enjoying the hospitality of the man he had abused, commenced circulating about among the audience passing around his card.

We present this, not as any intended reflection upon Mr. McCarran, but simply to show the rather aggressive characteristics to be reckoned with….[18]

Despite McCarran "shouting from every rostrum with stentorian lungs every sort of infamy against Mr. Nixon,"[19] Wingfield's business partner, George Nixon, defeated McCarran in his bid for the state senate. With his immediate political aspirations dashed, the flamboyant orator readjusted to concentrate on his legal career and was admitted to the bar in the summer of 1905.

His first case was to defend his own father in July 1905. The elder McCarran, known for his combustible disposition, had steadfastly waged war against the construction of telephone lines by the government on his land. Failing to receive his approval, the government eventually exercised the power of eminent domain to erect the lines. Not long after, according to the *Gazette,* McCarran, Sr. "was hauled up for cutting down government telephone poles and using the same for building a fence.... A true bill was found against him and he was mad as a hatter."[20]

Indicted by the U.S. Grand Jury, McCarran's father appeared to have no plausible defense to justify his actions. Then, on the second day of the trial, his clever attorney-son took the stand to announce the wrong man was on trial. McCarran confessed he had committed the crime for which his father had been accused. The local newspapers lamented this development, and worried that the handsome, gifted attorney had jeopardized the brilliant career before him by perjuring himself to save his father." [21]

McCarran's courtroom debut showcased many of the trademark tactics he utilized throughout his career, the least of which included an incomparable, almost hypnotic eloquence, an intense allegiance to his client, and the frequently game-changing element of surprise. Few would argue his obsession to do whatever it took to prevail in a court of law. Still, the "telephone pole" case* was a bumpy start and might have been among his motivations to leave Reno for Tonopah to open a law office.

From across the nation as well as numerous foreign countries—including England, Germany, Ireland, Scotland, Italy, Portugal, France, and China—dreamers and schemers alike converged to write a line, maybe a page, or even a full chapter in the history books that would depict one of Nevada's most vibrant and transformative periods.

Yet, the established citizenry of Tonopah were becoming protective of their city's continuing expansion, openly dissuading any who were more liability than asset to the local economy to reconsider. From the *Sun*, March 7, 1905:

ANOTHER WORD OF WARNING: The "immigration" is about to begin, but it is almost certain that its proportions have been largely magnified by the press reports. At least, this is to be hoped.

Eastern people, whose purse-strings or economic ideas cause them to await a $20 reduction in fare before coming to a mining camp, are not the sort of people to build it up. They will rove, generally, of the "marked down" sort, not the liberal, big-hearted kind that make a district. A few will be mechanics and investors.

They are welcome, and will do well, but Tonopah and Goldfield have not yet had to establish free soup kitchens, as will become necessary if an army of squeeze-penny incompetents rush in, expecting to find ready-milled nuggets on the streets.

McCarran biographer, Jerome Edwards, writes of McCarran's decision to move to Tonopah, "Everyone was in on the ground floor, everyone was a carpetbagger. McCarran had been defeated politically in Reno; Tonopah thus presented

* Documents specifying the final outcome of the "telephone pole" trial have yet to be located.

political and legal opportunity. The second reason for moving was that McCarran wanted to make money."[22]

McCarran sold his sheep, moved to Tonopah in the fall of 1905, and opened an office with B. S. Wilson on the second floor of the Broker's Exchange Building on Brougher Avenue, just one block west of Main Street.[23] McCarran's office window was viewable from the front door of Logan's saloon. From the *Bonanza*, October 24, 1905:

The law firm of McCarran and Wilson, recently established in Tonopah, is rapidly forging to the front. In the Shipe case tried this week in Judge Breen's court, this firm was associated with the able lawyer George A. Bartlett in defending Shipe, and it was a matter of comment that one of the best arguments to the jury was made by McCarran. He is a Reno boy and certainly has a bright future."

MONTHS BEFORE MCCARRAN arrived in Tonopah, newly elected Sheriff Logan and D.A. William Pittman, in a show of solidarity, teamed up to address one of the community's uppermost issues. Tom publicly pledged to stand by Pittman who, as one of his first official duties, had launched a "campaign of cleanliness" in Tonopah. Deemed the guardian of public health, Pittman swore to free the bustling city of garbage, waste paper, broken barrel staves, tin cans, and iron hoops, plus "disinfect cess-pools."[24]

Tonopah's restaurant owners and merchants responded by uniting in a concerted effort to keep their properties clean and sanitary. For those who chose not to comply, the D.A. conversely assured he would use the full strength of the public nuisance abatement statutes to punish offenders who would be held liable for damages and costs. Pittman's pronouncement was highly praised by the Tonopah Ladies' Improvement Society.[25]

Well beyond the city limits, another matter of public urgency had emerged. Too many "desert mariners" were perishing, as reported by the *Sun*:

At too frequent intervals the press reports ghastly finds on the desert. Skeletons of prospectors discovered on the plains and in the mountains. Whitened bones that denote the passing of souls under the terrible agony of thirst…. Nowhere in the world is the search after gold so active at present as in Nevada, and nowhere is the thirst terror so omnipresent. Men die because they are unable to find the springs and water holes… hidden in the gulches and arroyos.

The Sun *suggests a remedy and hopes that it will be acted upon before the present legislature adjourns. Let guideposts be placed on the desert where trails cross. They cannot*

be too numerous to insure the safety of the wayfarers of the plains. Each sign board
should plainly direct the wanderer to the nearest water station.[26]

Shortly thereafter, Nye County employed gristled frontiersman Jack Longstreet
to erect signposts* throughout the region to help guide travelers.[27]

As Tonopah endeavored with renewed zeal to establish itself among the
more modern and inviting metropolitan hubs of the west, elsewhere in the state,
old ways gasped for breath. For instance, in the community of Hazen, about
50 miles east of Reno, the last known vigilante lynching in Nevada took place
on February 27, 1905. After chronic troublemaker "Red" Wood and a cohort
robbed two men at the railroad station, angry bystanders chased them into the
sagebrush wastelands. One escaped, but Wood was captured and jailed. At 2
o'clock in the morning, a mob broke into the building. Despite pleas from the
sheriff to let the law take its course, the hell-bent men wrestled the doomed
highwayman into the night where they flung a rope over a telegraph pole and
hanged him.[28] Lawmen throughout the state could not have been more graphically reminded of their responsibilities to protect citizens and outlaws alike.

In Nye County, measures to increase law enforcement forces were well underway. The first week of February 1905, Tonopah Constable Alex McKenzie
appointed George Logan, one of Tom's brothers, as a nightwatchman. According to the *Sun*, George would "assist Jack Mungan in keeping the peace and
good order.... They are both able and competent officers, and are determined
to rid the town of all dissolute and undesirable people. A word to the wise is
sufficient, and the dissolute element is said to be wise in this specialty."[29]

Ironically, that same week, the *Sun* would also run a story about another
pair of lawmen brothers:

Verge Earp, a brother of Wyatt Earp, and one of the famous family of gunologists, is
acting as deputy sheriff in the National Club, Goldfield. Verge is a mild-looking indi-
vidual, and to outward view presents none of the characteristics that have made the
family name a familiar one in the west and in all the bonanza camps of the country,
from Mexico to Alaska.... Wyatt is no more an exponent of quick and rapid target prac-
tice. He has forsworn the green cloth and the automatic revolver, and is now dependent
upon his ability as a miner for a living as well as fame.[30]

With heightened demands on county officials, State Senator Tasker Oddie, one
of Logan's bondsmen, sponsored legislation to raise their salaries. The bill
passed in March and fixed annual pay for the Sheriff/Assessor, District Attor-
ney/Ex-officio Superintendent of Public Instruction, and Treasurer at $2,000
per year, including such fees as were allowed by law. Compensation for county

---

* Samples of Longstreet's handiwork are on display at the Central Nevada Museum in
Tonopah, NV.

commissioners was now $600 per year, plus a twenty-cent mileage allotment for traveling to and from meetings. With an average income of $5.50 per day, Logan and fellow colleagues were earning only slightly more than a union laborer. Deputies received $1,600 annually, or about $4.40 per day, which was comparable to scab labor.[31]

Although increased from the previous year, at such rates, these wages precluded even the hint of career politicians taking up residence in Nye County anytime soon. All elected officials maintained other businesses and sources of income which, depending on the circumstance, could at best foster an informed awareness, and at worst, a conflict of interest.

In the spring of 1905, Sheriff Logan's first term had to have felt like a lifetime ago instead of only six years, due in no small part to the seemingly endless list of obligations imposed upon him by the county commissioners. Take, for instance, dead horses. At a commissioners' meeting the last week of March, considerable discussion concentrated on the increasing number of "disease breeders" being discarded along the road to the pest house. Many of the carcasses were being dumped within Tonopah's town limits, reported the *Sun*:

The danger of contagion is great. The dead horses were nearly all afflicted with glanders or other tubercular diseases that could be conveyed to the human system either by the air, which is laden with germs, every wind that blows from that direction, and that is the usual course of the zephyrs, or by flies alighting on the carcasses and carrying the contagion to dwellings and restaurants.

A unanimous decision was reached that anyone who placed the bodies of dead animals within five miles of Tonopah, unless buried or burned, would be arrested.[32]

With each new demand placed on Sheriff Logan and his deputies—although likely not uttered aloud—the odds of someone dying in the line of duty crept ominously upward.

Corner of Brougher and St. Patrick, McCarran and Wilson Law Firm (upper floor),
Tonopah, NV, c. 1906 (Nevada Historical Society, Reno, NV)

To Harry Mannon

No Bard will tell the story
Of his fearless life and death—
Of the call to duty answered
By his lips with closing breath.
But, when the soul of Mannon
Took its flight from earth today.
From the fields of restless toil
A true MAN was borne away.
In the hearts and in the souls
Of his friends his story's told,
Any they prize the heritage
More than Nevada's gold.
For the gold that lies hidden
In the vaults of earth and rock
With the wreck of earth will pass—
But the soul survives the shock
When the Book of Life is read
In the light of Heaven's day
There'll be a page for Harry—
The bards have naught to say.

—H.W. Knickerbocker, *Tonopah Bonanza*, April 16, 1905

8

FIELDS OF RESTLESS TOIL: 1905

"If some people ever get to heaven they will pot hunt young angels. Next to the heavenly host of doves are an easy second in gentility, but that don't spare them from the pot hunter in this country even at nesting time. If there is no law against such wanton shooting there should be. This country is desolate enough without killing birds that cross the desert to cheer the human heart."

Beatty-Bullfrog Miner, May 20, 1905

"HARRY MANNON, DEPUTY sheriff of Nye County, is dying of three bullet wounds, gained in the discharge of his duty," reported the *Tonopah Daily Sun* on March 24, 1905. "The shooting took place last evening in Beatty. Mannon, who had been deputized for the Bullfrog district by Sheriff Logan, got on the trail of two of the highwaymen who held up five Italians in the Montezuma wood camp several nights ago."

Well-liked by all who knew him, Mannon was married and just 33. He had traveled from California only two years earlier to work the Valley View mine, and quickly established himself as a sterling citizen. Most recently, prominent businessman, H. H. Clark, had hired him to represent the Bullfrog Townsite Company. He had also earned the respect of Tom Logan, who, in the aftermath of the Shipe shooting, appointed Mannon one of his deputies to shore up law enforcement services in a district located about 85 miles south of Tonopah. The rookie deputy had arrived there only the day before.[1 & 2]

A Bullfrog merchant telephoned Clark with an eyewitness account that he relayed to the *Bonanza*: "Pitched Battle with Outlaws—Harry Mannon Lying at Death's Door as Result of Thursday's Battle, Lynching Possible:"

During the afternoon Mannon told me that he thought two of the Montezuma hold-up men were either at Gold Center or Beatty and asked me to drive him [by buggy] over to look at them…. On the Armargosa River about two miles from Gold Center, we saw two men eating lunch, and Mannon [after talking with them] soon satisfied himself that they were the parties he was after. We then went to Beatty and got Deputy Sheriff McDonald, who returned with us to where we again found the men, about two miles downriver from where we first saw them. It was there the fight occurred. The officers no sooner got out of the buggy before it started, and while it lasted it was fast and furious.

McDonald was fortunate enough in getting his man by the right arm and covering him before his gun came into play, but as the man after whom Mannon went was farther away, he had drawn his gun before he could be reached. The shooting was so fast I could not keep track of it, but I think Mannon fired once before he was hit, and I believe the man was hit. Before he could fire again a bullet had torn its way through his right arm, knocking his gun from his hand and rendering him helpless. After that he was shot twice more and fell. I jumped from the buggy and ran to his assistance, the man who had shot him, making his escape.[3]

While a posse scoured the hills where a prospector said he had come upon a hungry man "skulking in the rocks," Mannon fought to stay alive. Although wounded in his lungs and abdomen, he rallied enough for transport to the Miners' Hospital in Goldfield where he lingered for several days before dying the morning of April 5, 1905. Funeral services for the first Nye County law enforcement officer killed in the line of duty were conducted under the auspices of the Fraternal Order of the Eagles, after which his body was returned to California for internment in Alameda County.[4]

Two weeks after Mannon died, Governor John Sparks issued a proclamation offering a reward for the capture of Frank Crouch.[5] Additional contributions to the fund came from the Nye County commissioners, the governing board of Esmeralda County, and H. H. Clark. The reward totaled $1,050, but Crouch was never found.[6]

Mannon's murder was one of at least three committed in Nye County during the first few months of 1905, and the unprecedented shooting of a lawman generated widespread alarm among the vulnerable and law-abiding. Was this only an isolated incident or the harbinger of darker days to come? More specifically, was the sheriff's office up to the job? The *Bonanza* offered an astute perspective in an editorial titled, "Don't Ask Too Much:"

The task of the sheriff and his deputies here is one which can hardly be appreciated by the uninitiated and with an increase in the commission of crimes of a grave character, the public is apt to overlook many of the trials and difficulties which confront the officers in their efforts to bring the malefactors to justice. It should be borne in mind that this country is being flooded with men from all over the world, and, as it is to be expected, the great rush now in progress, brings in its train no inconsiderable criminal element. His is scattered through the districts of mining activity, and the result is shown by an increasing number of offenses against the law.

Under these conditions much may be accomplished by the hard work and untiring perseverance on the part of the officers, but there are many things which cannot, and should not, be expected. No one man, nor any six men, could reasonably be expected to clear up all the mysteries which are bound to come to the public notice.

It requires more than perseverance; more than hard work, and more than experience to cope with a situation such as confronts the officers of Nye County. It calls for the widest possible knowledge of crooks and crookdum in order that when a crime had been committed the investigating officer may, through his knowledge of what criminals are in the vicinity, their previous records, methods and a thousand and one other things, arrive at an early conclusion as to the perpetrator, his motive and other necessary points upon which to base an investigation.

This wide knowledge cannot in reason and fairness be supposed to lie in the possession of men who have not served almost a lifetime at the business of thief-taking in the service of a metropolis, and therefore, all that the people have a right to demand of the officers of this branch of the County service is business-like methods and the energetic discharge of duty to the best of their ability.[7]

Generally supportive of law enforcement, the local press still did not hesitate to use their forum to bring forward matters they deemed worthy of attention. For instance, on April 8, 1905, the *Sun* printed this inquiry, "Ask the Officers: 'Will you kindly let me know through your paper how it is that the crooked games run in tents on Main Street are allowed to exist?'"

The next day, the *Sun* responded along with a graphic illustration depicting the efforts of Sheriff Logan and Tonopah's Constable Alex McKenzie:

"This Stampede is No Fake: Grafters Find Poor Pickings Here" (*Tonopah Daily Sun*, April 9, 1905, Arthur V. Buel, Editorial Artist)

The officers have replied, and in no uncertain language. The tents have been closed, the grafters are gone and their paraphernalia has disappeared. Be it known that the leader of the skin-game outfit was one Mike Golden, probably the slickest occurrence since the famous "Soapy" Smith…. Golden and his gang have gone to Goldfield, but he will discover his Nemesis in the form of fair play and honest dealing still pursues him. It is to the credit of the officers of Tonopah that they could not be bought by this gang of thieves.[8]

As to just how daunting were the months ahead for Nye County, local undertaker and dance hall owner Charles Wonacott certainly had a superior vantage point. He reported 24 people had died in Tonopah during the month of March, which he considered a low death rate for a population of 5,000. Of those newly departed, two were killed in railroad accidents, one committed suicide, two died under operation, and four died in the hospital from unnatural causes, leaving 15 natural deaths. Of those 15, seven died from alcoholism, exposure, and neglect, leaving eight to have passed from true natural causes.[9]

Many believed Wonocott had under-reported the numbers as a way to muzzle critics who were exaggerating the dangers of living in Tonopah. Duly insulted, the 56-year-old undertaker responded by publishing a personal letter in the *Sun*, titled, "Let Fears be Calmed and Liars be Silent:"

I have deposited with the State Bank and Trust Company $100, subject to the order of any man in the state of Nevada or elsewhere that will show that the above facts are not true or that we have buried any person after sundown, except one case of smallpox which was recommended by the health officer of Tonopah as a precautionary measure.[10]

Wonacott was one of several prominent inhabitants becoming increasingly defensive following a rash of grim newspaper headlines running in northern Nevada about a "death harvest" in Tonopah due to plague and other "unusual conditions." Sheriff Logan personally met with Governor Sparks in Carson City during a trip north to deliver a wanted man he had captured into the custody of an Oregon deputy sheriff. He emphatically denied to the governor the existence of any consuming epidemic. Still, in view of what Sparks called "alarming tales" coming to him, he ordered Nevada's Secretary of Health to visit Tonopah.[11] The town fathers dispatched the following statement on April 14, 1905:

There is no quarantine nor bubonic plague here. There have been a number of cases of pneumonia of a type particularly fatal. Citizens have formed a health committee, and threw $2,000 into the hat. Committee, acting as deputy sheriffs, is enforcing cleanliness. Everybody is working together. Expect to conquer disease in a few days. Panic is not justified.[12]

The harshest indictment of Tonopah's state of health that spring came from the *Nevada State Journal* claiming it was impossible to secure information of a reliable nature from even its own Tonopah correspondent. Anecdotal accounts ranged from conservative estimates regarding the magnitude of the alleged epidemic to overwrought descriptions of a disease that can kill a man within hours of the first feverish symptom.[13]

At the Tonopah Health Committee meeting on April 15, 1905, members discussed how to respond to their detractors, most notably the *Journal*. Frank Smith, enjoying renewed social status since his acquittal for killing Walter Dunn, urged they ignore the paper with "utter contempt." *Sun* editor, Lindley Branson, favored a non-threatening communique demanding a retraction and an apology. George Wingfield supported a proposal to strike at the northern newspaper's pocketbook and ask all local news dealers to not handle, sell, or receive subscriptions for the *Journal*. All agreed it was important to broadcast their version of events to allay all the fears threatening to disrupt the abundant currency flowing in and out of Tonopah. Consequently, Wingfield and two other esteemed committee members sent an explicit telegram to the Associated Press beginning with, "Reports published all over the coast about the health conditions in Tonopah are greatly exaggerated...."[14]

For several days, a frenzied barrage of words ricocheted between Tonopah and Reno contesting the scale of the problem. Tonopah leaders accused their Reno counterparts of endeavoring to retard their progress, and Reno faithfuls charged the bonanza camp with selfishly concealing a lethal and sweeping scourge.[15] This would not be the first nor last time the two cities clashed in a sea of newsprint over bragging rights to being Nevada's premier commercial hub. In 1905, Tonopah was a worthy competitor. However, that status soon began to fade as the once-bountiful mines grew less productive, and the likes of George Wingfield moved north to Reno to conduct business. Even Tom Logan would scout Reno and Carson City properties during the coming year in anticipation of retiring his badge and moving his family to a more advantaged environment.[16]

By the end of April, the upheaval began to recede as quickly as it had advanced. A *Gazette* headline proclaimed, "Disease is Under Control," and quoted mining investor and former Reno resident, L. De Sallier, as saying, "a citizens' committee has taken radical steps to clear the place of filth and to see that the sick have proper attention with the result that the death rate has greatly decreased."[17] Those actions included a fervent plea by the *Sun's* editor to discourage rampant spitting on the sidewalks. "How does it look to you, men of Tonopah," he wrote, "to have the sidewalk a mass of corrupt saliva containing the seeds of disease?"[18]

TONOPAH'S NEW COURTHOUSE.

Front elevation of the proposed new Nye County Courthouse
(*Tonopah Bonanza*, May 20, 1905, John C. Robertson, Editorial Artist)

In its tenacious quest to modernize, Tonopah had no shortage of edicts, formal or otherwise. A mounting topic of debate was where to place the new county courthouse and jail. "It would serve some of (the commissioners) to have the courthouse located on the top of Mount Butler," quipped *Sun* editor Branson, "or as a fair reward for their apathy, to have it remain at Belmont for the next ten years or more."[19]

Between mid-April and early May, Sheriff Logan joined with county commissioners to develop a plan to erect the new courthouse and jail. Despite a robust campaign to place the structure in the center of the business district on Brougher Avenue, the gift of a free lot by the Tonopah Mining Company was too tempting an offer. Tonopah's new adorning "ornament" would be built south of town on a hilltop between Florence and Upper Main Street.[20 & 21]

Another initiative, especially since the county was now debt-free, was a campaign to divide Nye into two counties. The movement failed to gain traction as soon as it became evident Belmont would soon relinquish its county seat status to Tonopah.[22] More convenient access to district services and law enforcement was especially important to southern Nye County, which was under scrutiny for illicit liquor sales to Native Americans, and escalating lawlessness. Referring to the killing of Indian Dan by Robert Gilbert, State Prison Warden John Considine expressed concern, stating:

In consequence, many of Nevada's citizens have found it necessary to take the law into their own hands for self-protection and tragedies ensue which the outside world never hears of.... Incidents like [Gilbert and Indian Dan] are arousing general indignation among the settlers, and if they continue a vigilance committee, that has been contemplated for some time, is likely to exert its influence in a manner that will suddenly rid southern Nye county of a bad lot of Indians and an equally rascally lot of white men who are responsible for flagrant violations of the law.[23]

Vigilantism breeds its own version of anarchy, so when H. H. Clark—associate of deceased Deputy Harry Mannon—donated land in rowdy Bullfrog for a house of detention, Sheriff Logan was understandably grateful and quickly gained approval from the commissioners to construct a proper stone and steel calaboose in that camp.[24] This also came as welcome news to Deputy J.R. McDonald. He had been with Mannon when he was shot, and suddenly found himself personally responsible for protecting the one suspect he did capture from a gathering mob willing to dispossess him of his prisoner.

Of late, trouble came in all forms, from all directions. Logan and McDonald surely had to have taken time to discuss the contributing factors that led to Mannon's death, and how to prevent a similar tragedy. As members of an exclusive brotherhood, they would definitely never forget their fallen comrade, and perhaps

Sheriff Tom Logan, illustration accompanying article titled, "County Commissioners have a Strenuous Day" (*Tonopah Daily Sun*, May 3, 1905, Arthur V. Buel, Editorial Artist)

concluded there was no better way to honor Mannon's memory than by continuing to uphold their oaths to serve and protect—no matter how colossal or seemingly trivial the scope of that duty.

***Beatty-Bullfrog Miner,* May 6, 1905:** *Deputy Sheriff McDonald sent three prisoners to Tonopah on Wednesday by Deputy Constable Sexton. One Dempsey for embezzling $175 from the Miners Union at Tonopah when secretary; Jack McLaughlin and Mrs. White for taking a team and buggy from Tonopah.*

***Tonopah Bonanza,* June 17, 1905:** *Sheriff Logan, who by the way is the best Sheriff Nye County ever had, appointed J. P. Brissel a deputy, and he has been placed in charge of the County jail in Belmont, while Bert Cowan officiates as bailiff in Judge Breen's court (now in Tonopah). Mr. Brissel has many years' experience as undersheriff of Sacramento County, Cal. And Sheriff Logan could not have made a better selection.*

***Tonopah Bonanza,* June 17, 1905:** *LOST: A package of books. Return to Tom Logan and receive reward.*

***Tonopah Bonanza,* June 24, 1905:** *Sheriff Logan has received from State Controller Davis blank licenses to be used in the collection of state liquor licenses, as per chapter 228 of the 1905 statue approved March 13, 1905…. [Sheriffs] hereby made the collectors of, and authorized and required to issue and collect said licenses, and shall, upon the payment of fifty ($50) dollars, issue a retail state license to any person, firm, company or corporation engaged in selling spirituous, malt, vinous liquors in quantities less than five gallons….*

***Tonopah Daily Sun,* July 1, 1905:** *Sheriff Logan arrived in Tonopah yesterday morning from Los Angeles, having in charge Ruffin Thompson, who is charged by Jack Davis of embezzlement.*

***Tonopah Bonanza,* July 29, 1905:** *Sheriff Logan has received the dog tags and all canines without a tag after August 10 will be annihilated.*

THE WEATHER IN Tonopah on June 3, 1905, was clear and warm, perfect for laying the cornerstone for the new Nye County courthouse. The band was rousing, the camp steam whistles invigorating, and the oratory effusive. Ceremonies were conducted by the Ladies of the Eastern Star and Masonic Lodge. Grand Master Gillison talked about how the Free and Accepted Masons had been dedicating cornerstones since the time of Solomon, and "hoped that the building would be the scene of good deeds and the officers would be noble."[25]

During construction, the Third Judicial District (Lander, Eureka, and Nye Counties) Court proceedings took place in Butler Hall. Presiding Judge Peter Breen was the first of three esteemed purveyors of justice from one of Nevada's most respected pioneer families. Born in Killarney, Ireland, in 1847, he immigrated to the U.S. as a young man and worked as a painter and paperhanger before being admitted to the bar in Nevada. After twelve successful years as Eureka County District Attorney, he was elected District Judge in 1902.[26]

"Law and Justice are Now Holding Sway in Tonopah," Third Judicial District Judge Peter Breen (center) (*Tonopah Sun*, June 8, 1905, Arthur V. Buel, Editorial Artist)

The illustrious career that would unfold for Breen appeared to be well underway when he brought to order the first court session held in Tonopah at Butler Hall on June 7, 1905. Beyond the usual preliminaries incumbent on him to perform, he methodically went to work setting dates for trials, estimating the current calendar would keep him in town several weeks.[27]

The Nye County Grand Jury also convened on June 7 and submitted the following key findings and recommendations, all of which related to the sheriff's office one way or another:

Whereas, the Town of Tonopah, Nye County, Nevada, is without the proper courthouse, and without vaults for the transaction of county business and the storage of county records; the said town of Tonopah being now the county seat, and on account of the scattered and confused condition of the county records; some being now at Belmont and some at Tonopah:

We therefore, most earnestly recommend that the county commissioners see that all county records and books be removed to Tonopah as quickly as possible so that the same can be inspected at the next term of court. This recommendation is made after hearing reports from various committees appointed to investigate this subject.

We further find that the posting and keeping of county records, has so far as we are able to ascertain been sadly neglected.

We also find that the Town of Tonopah, since the advent of the railroad, has been infested with confidence men, bunco-steerers and men of questionable character; and we do earnestly recommend that proper steps be taken and support be rendered our officers to rid our town of these people.

We find upon investigation that the sheriff's office has insufficient help in the way of police protection in the Town of Tonopah, and we recommend that the sheriff be provided with at least two additional salaried deputies.[28]

Jurymen further suggested Sheriff Logan impose an automobile speed limit of three miles per hour within Tonopah's habitable limits and "rid the community" of unlicensed dogs. Grand Jury Foreman James Forman further observed that Logan had failed to conspicuously post in his office the names of all persons owing license fees in the county, and recommended:

The sheriff collect the licenses from every and all kinds of business and each and every gambling game as required by law and post the names of every person so paying and the amounts of same and the nature of the business or game for which said licenses were issued.[29]

Presumably, Sheriff Logan was heartened by the Grand Jury's acknowledgment that his office needed more resources. However, their condemnation of his inadequacies related to publicizing license fees was only the beginning of more reprimands to come.

Still, from time to time, Tom managed to indulge in the lighter side of life. For instance, he served as a member of the floor committee for the May 11, 1905, Aerie of Eagles No. 228 Calico Ball in Tonopah.[30] Later that year he was among the "distinguished and select coterie of sports and wine connoisseurs" who joined Col. Martin Brady when he introduced Pomeroy, a much-heralded vintage wine, to Nye County. From the *Sun*, July 18, 1905:

Cal Shaw spoke a catchy little piece, entitled, "Who Put Wind in Willie's Doughnut." He was cheered to the echo…. A roar of laughter went up when Bill Butler said he was the 'father of Tonopah….'

"Night that Pomeroy was Introduced in Tonopah City"
(*Tonopah Daily Sun*, July 18, 1905, Arthur V. Buel, Editorial Artist)

Sheriff Logan's presence was not asked for the purpose of preserving order. Perish the thought. He was just plain Tom at the Pomeroy's introduction to Tonopah. He spoke at length, taking as his text, "When Great Men Gather." Tom is a first rate talker. He was listened to attentively.

At one juncture during his speech, many thought he had forgotten his lines, but he got "a cue" from the billiard table and proceeded in good order.[31]

As "plain Tom" proceeded to live out the last months of his life oblivious to destiny's plan, he would toil as never before to support his family, keep order amid turmoil, and resist forces to which the strongest man has been known to succumb. And he would fall short.

The Winds

You winds that roam o'er the mountains,
That shriek thru saw-toothed range
While you hurl the snow in the gulches,
With your laughter so weird and strange.
Do you ever stop for one moment
And think of the things you do—
Or is it just one of your frolics?
How I wish you would tell me, true.

I have heard you in the summer
When your breath like the scent of a rose,
Or at evening just after sunset
As the day was nearing its close.
Like balm on my cheeks were your breezes
After the heat of the day,
And those zephyrs were, o, so gently
That high in the alpines did play.

Then again in late October
Driving the clouds filled with rain;
You tore into shreds 'mid the snow peaks
While your laugh had a plaintive strain.
I have tried hard to follow your footsteps
To learn what the songs are you sing;
What lessons you have here for us,
What are those tidings you bring.

You are old, yes old as the mountains,
But to me you will ever be young.
I am always eager to listen
To the songs that for ages you've sung.
And I often just sit and wonder
If you have no sorrow or woe;
You just travel, yes travel forever
As onward and onward you go.

With the whole wide world before you,
Alike is the land and sea.
Yet whenever I hear your voices
Chanting so wild and so free,
They tell me of far off places
Where there is no sorrow or care,
And your breezes all perfume laden
Will ever float on the air.

—James W. Whilt, Mountain Memories, 1925

9

NO APOLOGIES: 1905

"The 'soiled doves' and red light districts were as much a part of the early West as the piles of mine tailings, canvas shacks and garish saloons that dotted the landscape…. Who was she, this seductive, often rowdy woman, who started her work as the sun's last rays began to disappear? Was she a captive who was caught in the web of poverty, a victim of circumstances, or a willing participant in her profession? Most likely, she was all of the above."
Anne Seagraves, *Soiled Doves: Prostitution in the Early West*, 1994

"TO THE PUBLIC: My name is R. D. Chase, not R.D. Russell," read the suicide note published in the *Sun* on September 3, 1905. "I have a brother O. L. Chase of the O. L. Chase Mercantile Co. of Kansas City, Mo. I have a wife, Anna Chase and a little boy living in Chicago… Please notify them. God have mercy on me. Russell D. Chase (formerly of Cherokee, Iowa)."

Before pressing a gun muzzle to his head, Chase first killed a woman identified as his second wife. The two had operated a rooming house in Tonopah's red light district but met with little success. Believed to be despondent over debts, and jealous of the attention his "sporting" wife attracted, Chase chose the ultimate final solution to relieve his anguish.[1]

Wrenching tales of human tragedy were routinely interspersed with intoxicating headlines about new discoveries and the burgeoning wealth of the more prosperous. Most stories of despair didn't make news, like that of an abandoned young mother who appeared at a county commissioners meeting on September 14, 1905. After revealing she had applied to have her two infant children committed to the State Orphan Asylum in Carson City, she confessed she could not afford their travel arrangements and appealed to the commissioners for assistance. District Attorney William Pittman was authorized to deliver her children to the orphanage—surely a heartbreaking situation for all those present, which included Tom Logan, father of eight.[2]

If he had never thought seriously about his family ever having to fend for themselves, perhaps he did that day, if only for a fleeting moment. Being overly concerned with his own mortality could interfere with the snap decisions required in emergent circumstances. Yet, even then, after the dust has settled, a close call could unnerve the most secure operator. From the *Sun*, September 24, 1905, "Sheriff in Battle with Two Desperate Thugs, One Secures the Officer's Revolver, but Logan, Undaunted, Pursues Pair Capturing One:"

During a battle with two desperate thugs late Friday night, Sheriff Logan narrowly escaped being shot and one of the desperados was badly cut about the head by blows from the sheriff's revolver.

One of the men was captured, but not before a running fight and chase that took the sheriff to Goldfield. Deputy Constable Nofsinger is after the other, who escaped in the direction of Sodaville….

The plan of the couple was to rifle the Jewel and the Wigwam [in Tonopah]. In the former they terrorized the landlady threatening bodily harm if she did not give them money. She got rid of them by promising to have money for them if they would return later. The pair then proceeded to the Jewel, slipping into the place unobserved and hiding in one of the rooms, evidently with the intention of ransacking the place when the inmates retired.

While making his rounds, Sheriff Logan was attracted by the pair slinking from the place. They had evidently been frightened away. Suspecting that something was wrong from the actions of the pair the sheriff followed them, calling them to halt. When they saw that they were being followed the men turned on the sheriff and showed fight. One advanced menacingly and the sheriff drew his revolver, calling upon the man to halt. The latter kept advancing, however, and attempted to grapple with the sheriff. He was felled by a blow from the officer's gun, but came up again for more fight. A second and third time was the man knocked down, but each time got up full of fight. After being knocked down a fifth time the thug was momentarily dazed and Sheriff Logan got a grip on him, at the same time fighting off the fellow's partner.

At this juncture, young Wardell happened on the scene and went to the assistance of the sheriff. The sheriff slipped his revolver into his back pocket in order to better secure the man, who had again begun to fight. During the scuffle the other thug slipped up behind the sheriff and secured his revolver, which the thug leveled at Wardell, commanding him to let go his hold on the other desperado. Sheriff Logan started after the man with the gun, who then turned the weapon on the officer, threatening to shoot. In the shadow of a building the pair broke and ran. The train was about to put out for Goldfield and, suspecting that the pair would try to get away on it, the sheriff boarded the express car and rode to the cut-off, where the train was stopped and searched. Express Messenger Burke, armed with a shotgun, and the sheriff searched the train, finding the pair hidden underneath one of the cars. Burke grabbed one of the men and held him, but the other escaped in the darkness. Sheriff Logan proceeded with his man to Goldfield, bringing him back yesterday morning….

The revolver belonging to the sheriff was found near the depot where it had been thrown by the thugs in the fight.

Understandably humiliated, Tom may very well have contemplated whether or not he was losing his edge.* Now 44, having lived as rugged a life as only the most durable would dare undertake, his reflexes and agility may have begun to fail the unflinching resolve for which he was so well known. Still, as he would prove until his last breath, backing down from trouble was simply not in his blood.

---

* One of the few stories about Sheriff Logan to have survived from generation to generation describes a combatant who got hold of his gun and how deeply embarrassed he was about the incident.

"Past and Present," from a tribute to early Nye County Sheriff Robert Steen (1868-71) and current Sheriff Thomas Logan, *Tonopah Bonanza,* September 2, 1905: "Sheriff Logan needs no introduction to the people of Nye County, whom he has served so faithfully and well for so many years. Suffice it to say that while he is a terror to evil-doers, he is held in the highest esteem by the good people of Nye County."

Among several parallels that can be drawn between Tom's clash with the two hooligans in Tonopah's red light district and the circumstances under which he would later be killed, two are conspicuous — an establishment named the Jewel and a "terrorized landlady." The *Sun's* version of the event was not clear as to whether the frightened proprietress was affiliated with the Wigwam or the Jewel. However, at the time, the latter was listed in the Tonopah telephone directory, but not the following year (1906) after a different Jewel house opened in the new mining camp of Manhattan.[3] The likelihood that May Biggs, the woman with whom Tom was involved at the time of his death, operated both Jewel establishments is very plausible since she would later state she had come to Tonopah in early 1905.[4]

ONLY TINY FRAGMENTS have been found of May Biggs' life. Estimated to be about ten years younger than Tom, she married James Poe Biggs, age 25, on May 11, 1893, in the New Mexico Territory town of Socorro.[5] The couple eventually migrated to Cochise County (Arizona Territory) and surfaced here and there in the local newspaper—usually in an unflattering way.

The following account appeared in the July 2, 1899, edition of the *Weekly Orb* in Bisbee, Arizona, and eerily prophesized a future fracas to come for May with unsettling commonalities:

On his return from the capitol city, Constable Lewis will bring with him one Joseph Micheler, wanted here for breaking into the cabin of Charles Gerdes, last February, and stealing a gold watch, six shooter, clothes, etc. The officers have been on the watch for him for some time and while in Phoenix recently he was located by a citizen of our city, who notified the authorities there to arrest and hold him, which was done a few days ago.

Mr. Micheler is quite well-known in Bisbee, having had a shooting scrape here with a party over one, May Biggs. Mr. Micheler was shot in the arm and received a flesh wound in the abdomen. He worked in the Copper Queen mine for some time previous to the shooting.[6]

This pistol-wielding skirmish between two men connected in some way to May—still legally married at the time—was symptomatic of her inclination to entice danger. Her husband also did his share to contribute to the strife and strain of their volatile relationship. Included in the "Court Matters" section of the November 29, 1899, edition of the *Arizona Weekly Journal-Miner*, "Counsel for…James P. Biggs, charged with a murderous assault at Congress [AZ], objected to the entire jury on the grounds that the same was not summoned as provided by section 2176 and 2191 revised statutes. Objection was overruled and exceptions noted." At the end of the day, the Grand Jury dropped charges against James and allowed him to go free.

As her marriage to James degenerated, May is believed to have relocated to San Francisco where, just after the turn of the century, she joined the flow of intrepid women bound for the Alaskan gold camps. Although not absolutely verified to be the one and the same May Biggs, the following story not only fits that time period but reflects a brand of gumption consistent with the personality Nye County would soon come to know. From the *San Francisco Call*, December 4, 1902, "San Francisco Girl's Long Tramp in Arctic – Makes Her Way From an Ice-Blocked Steamship to the City of Dawson:"

Dawson, November 18, via Seattle, Dec. 3: *The last of the Yukon Fleet to navigate between White Horse and St. Michael barely escaped a tragic fate in the great ice floes of the mighty stream. After running the gauntlet 400 miles in thick ice, the steamer La France, which has the honor of being the last of the big fleet to continue in service, was forced by the elements to give up the attempt to reach Dawson…. After getting within 100 miles of Dawson the La France became blocked for the winter in Steamboat Slough…*

Ten passengers were on the La France and they had a true Arctic frontier experience in getting out of the isolated quarters at Steamboat Slough. The Slough is many miles from the overland trail and an untrodden course had to be taken. All members of the crew and the officers and passengers had to walk eighty miles to get out of the place.

Miss Gertrude Timm, a San Francisco girl, and Miss May Biggs* were in the party and bravely tramped out with the men.

May's stay in the frigid wilds of Alaska lasted less than a year before she was back in sunny Cochise County, where she filed for divorce on April 15, 1903. James did not attend the court proceedings during which May informed the judge that she and her husband of ten years had no community property and no "living issues," meaning children. The court's ruling acknowledged that James had treated May "in a cruel and inhuman manner, and for more than one year prior to the filing of the complaint herein, defendant has failed to provide plaintiff with the common necessities of life by reason of his idleness, profligacy and dissipation." May was granted a divorce decree on June 2, 1903, and wasted no time fashioning a plan to support herself.

After arriving in Tombstone during the summer of 1903, May secured a chattel mortgage loan from mercantile store owner, Paul B. Warnekos, for $279.85. She then purchased "8 beds with mattresses, springs, sheets, pillow cases, pillows, quilt for each bed, 5 dressers, 5 commodes, 24 dining room chairs." It could be construed that given the number of dining room chairs, May was running a boarding house and nothing more. However, entrepreneur that she would prove to be, May probably also vended female company for her guests.[7] Business was apparently profitable, since her loan was fully satisfied and discharged one month later, plus she invested $500 in a 20-year lease on two acres known as the Deep Down mining claim.[8 & 9]

Located 30 miles north of the Mexican border, the one-time silver boom-town and Earp brothers' domain, had long ago crested in both industry and mayhem. Still, efforts to curtail the undesirable elements frequenting Tombstone's red light districts required ongoing vigilance and became a statewide campaign. By spring 1905, numerous new city ordinances throughout the Arizona Territory were adopted, prohibiting women from frequenting saloons and, according to the *Bisbee Daily Review* on May 17, 1905, in regard to brothels, "they will not be permitted there much longer."

With tighter restrictions, a large number of "enterprising ladies" were subsequently driven northwest to Nevada, where the social boundaries were more forgiving. Since no additional property records seem to exist for May in Cochise County, she was very likely part of the flock of soiled doves that arrived in Nevada during the early 1900s. Her name occasionally appeared in the unclaimed letters section of a Reno newspaper between October of 1904 and December 1905, the same time period she reported coming to Tonopah.[10]

---

* During the murder trial of Sheriff Logan's killer, May Biggs' one-time housekeeper testified she and May had met in Dawson, AK, three years earlier.

Before going to work for May in early 1906, dancehall girl Vivian Carlton* made a name for herself in Tonopah by "battling" her way into Justice William Sawle's court on October 9, 1905. Trouble began when she and two other be-decked light-toed doxies assembled outside Riley's Dance Hall to vie for patrons inclined to have their wallets harvested. In the shadows of a waning moon, the women sought to determine a hierarchical criterion for soliciting the "easy-moneyed as they sauntered in."

For Vivian and adversaries, Bertie Kelly and Margie Rutherford, negotiations rapidly deteriorated. The *Sun* elaborated:

And to this was due the swift recourse of hair and hats, and blonde and brunette hair-sute appendages, were soon made to look like tumbled mats by dexterous and angry fingers. Bertie Kelly, versed in the art of hooks and counters, was fast winning her spurs when Watchmen McCabe and Jack Kennedy happened along and called time. Their ears had been regaled with some choice remarks, and the sound of scrimmage bore a distinct resemblance to peace disturbances, so they guided the warring "belles" bastileward.[11]

At the justice court hearing, the accused each swore she had never been in trouble before and begged for leniency. Judge Sawle's response revealed a man prone to both measured tolerance and poetic expression:

First offenses are sometimes pardonable, provided they are not too frequent. Dancing is under propitious and orderly circumstances, doubtless a delightful past-time, but when women proceed to choose each other's hair as a pavilion and to muss that unusual dancing ground up, they must expect to wind up their jig to the law's quick step, and it's a costly dance. In view of the fact that this is the first time any of these women of the toe-tripping variety have been before me, I will let you go this time with a warning that a next appearance will mean a tune that only golden sacrifice can prevent from tangling you up.[12]

The nightlife in Tonopah was running full tilt in 1905, and the competition between drinking establishments was brisk. Tom's saloon, renamed The American, adjusted accordingly:

The American saloon, formerly conducted by Thos. Logan, is now under new management, the firm being Logan & CO. Billy Butler, who don't know "Billy," has purchased an interest in this popular resort and with the genial "Tom" Logan, make a strong pair to draw to. The big time comes off tonight [July 29, 1905] and a general invitation is extended to the "boys" to be present.[13]

---

* Vivian Carlton's "professional history" was used to dampen her credibility as an eye witness to Sheriff Logan's killing.

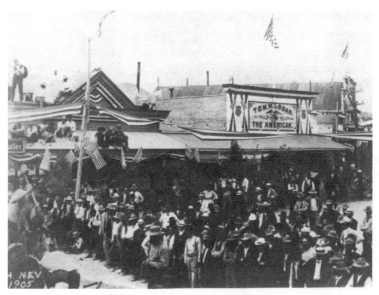

Railroad Days drilling contest in front of The American saloon,
Main and Brougher Streets, Tonopah. September, 1905
(Central Nevada Historical Society, Tonopah, NV)

In the fall of 1905, many of the power-broker "boys" were diligently working
to form a Tonopah Board of Trade in the wake of the town's recently failed attempt to incorporate. This board would address issues normally fielded by a
city council and function as advisor or critic—whichever most fitting—to the
county commissioners. Paramount priorities included increasing fire protection
services, improving sanitation, and ensuring law and order. As a means of generating more business capital, they planned to advertise to the entire world the
vast wealth of mineral resources in the area and invite investors to partake of
Tonopah's many modern assets. Well-supported by local trade unions, the board
membership included S. H. Gillette, Mark Averill, H. B. Gee, Augustus Tilden,
and Key Pittman.[14]

The prospect of incorporation produced myriad opinions as to how to allo-
cate public dollars to fund basic needs such as installing fire hydrants, sprin-
kling streets, or enforcing sanitation measures. "No money" had become too
frequent a refrain for the commissioners.[15] On August 8, 1905, they voted to
levy licenses on Tonopah businesses as a means to generate more revenue for
government operations. The new ordinance, assigned to Sheriff Logan, would
go into effect on August 21 and set forth that:

All persons, firms, associations, corporations and professional men must pay licenses.
The sheriff is to collect money quarterly and the documents are to be issued by the County
auditor and countersigned by the sheriff. Failure to pay is liable to incur a fine not to ex-
ceed $500, and in case of an arrest, the sheriff is to get one-fourth of the fine collected.[16]

More specifically, on the first Monday of February, May, August, and November of each year, Tom was now required to deliver to the county auditor a detailed accounting of all licensees issued and a balance sheet for all fees collected.[17] Additional duties imposed on the sheriff's office were not limited to the new business license ordinance. Citing an average cost of $600 a month to feed vagrant prisoners in the jail, the commissioners further ordered that Sheriff Logan use "vags" to do the work of removing garbage from public places in Tonopah. The program was intended to serve dual objectives—supplement public resources in the form of labor, plus dissuade the inmates and other itinerants from engaging in future criminal activity.[18]

On August 16, 1905, the commissioners further ordered the D.A. and Sheriff Logan to better enforce the law regarding obstruction of the streets and alleys, with particular attention given to construction sites. Specific directives were to: notify a store owner he will not be allowed to erect a staircase for his building since it would obstruct sidewalk traffic; hire and deputize a man to drive the garbage wagon; relocate the dog pound to the lot occupied by the Tonopah jail; and procure a sanitary water closet for the new jail.[19]

On the same day, the county commissioners adjourned and then promptly reconvened as a town board to devote the remainder of their time to Tonopah business. Now with a population of approximately 6,000, the town had long passed the point of installing a chief of police. Undoubtedly, Tom had input into the board appointing his friend and business partner, Constable Alex McKenzie, as Tonopah's first police chief—salary $100 per month. Like Logan, McKenzie was well-respected by those he served. A few months later, when presented with an elaborate gold badge during a spontaneous ceremony at the Tonopah Club, McKenzie humbly responded:

I certainly appreciate this token you have presented to me, not on account of its intrinsic value but because it shows your appreciation. It comes from the hands of my friends, and it shows your appreciation of my efforts as a peace officer of Tonopah. I assure you I will wear this beautiful emblem with great pride and I will always endeavor to prove worthy of your most esteemed confidence…I have tried to be impartial, just and fair to all and if I have failed, it has not been intentional.[20]

As ex-officio license collector for the city, McKenzie would also oversee the new dog pound master, 15-year-old Eugene Brown, fresh off the train from Denver and described by the *Bonanza* as "industrious, enterprising and plucky."[21]

Toward the end of October 1905, Assessor Logan, with the assistance of deputies Wm. Bryden, Wm. Cowan, and George Swasey, completed their property assessments for that year. Outside of Tonopah, the total assessment for Nye County was $483,967.81, of which $308,796 was for real property, $175,186.81 for personal property, and $306 for poll tax.* For Tonopah itself, assessments

---

* A tax levied on a person, rather than a property, as payment for the privilege of voting in a district election.

were almost double at $826,184.74 with $615,905 for real property, $210,278.75 for personal property and $603 poll tax. Total tax revenue generated for the county amounted to almost $23,000 and for Tonopah the figure was slightly more than $40,600.[22] "Tonopah's assessment this year," observed the *Sun* on October 28, 1905, "exceeds that of last year [under Cushing] by $368,376 which is certainly a credible showing. It will be noticed that the assessment has been nearly doubled by the efficient Assessor and his capable deputies."

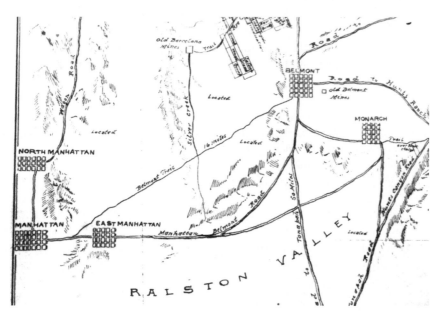

Mining Districts of the Goldfield-Tonopah Keystone Mining Co., 1906
(Nevada Historical Society, Reno, NV)

On November 8, 1905, Assessor Logan submitted his final quarterly report for the year to the county commissioners, which was reviewed and approved. Also during that meeting, Tom learned that his office in the new courthouse, which was nearing completion, would be on the ground floor, down the main hall to the right, and next to the jail.[23] The news surely heightened his anticipation toward finally being able to operate out of the majestic modern facility.

Meanwhile, as the bitter cold of winter crept down from the mountains and across the desert, freezing every water pipe in its path, demands on Tom continued flowing with the vigor of a gully wash in a rainstorm.[24] More and more, when dispatched to the outer realms of the county, he considered, as an option to his trusted mount or horse-drawn buggy, the tempting convenience of "a machine."

Labeled "devil cars" by a writer for the *Bullfrog Miner*, the arrival of the "horseless carriage" in Nye County spawned this disparaging rebuff on June 17, 1905:

It enables the rich and romantic to seek gold with speed and comfort. Day and night the noisy devil car winds its way over the sands from Goldfield, Las Vegas, and other camps to Beatty, where it drinks at the wells like a famished monster. The cloud of dust in the distance may be a simple whirlwind, or in it may be concealing the snorting auto and half a dozen, goggle-eyed passengers.

God inspired man to invent the auto to play hide and seek with the gold hidden in the desert by the Creator. He did not want the sissy boys to get it, and they don't.

Whether manufactured in hell or divinely delivered from on high, the automobile was tempting Sheriff Logan more and more as an alternate form of transportation, especially in light of the following snippet posted by the *Sun* on October 30, 1905:

"Sheriff's Team Breaks Through Entanglements:" Sheriff Logan and Chief of Police McKenzie drove to Manhattan last Friday and besides getting lost on the way had quite an adventure after arriving. Their team ran away and like Japanese fort stormers, went straight for the wire entanglements of a corral. The horses ran through two wire fences and escaped with only a few scratches.

Two weeks later, during one of the last trials conducted by Judge Breen in Belmont, proceedings ceased after a key witness took flight. Desperate to locate the fugitive, the defense team offered Sheriff Logan a reward, expenses, and an automobile to find the man. A mining disagreement, the *Finnegan v. Montgomery* case relied heavily on the testimony of Indian Johnny, the man who had presumably staked the disputed claims for Montgomery.[25] Although Johnny had been thoroughly questioned before the trial and was not considered a flight risk, general consensus was that nerves got the best of him after other Native Americans threatened to kill him if he went against Montgomery with whom they enjoyed dealing.[26]

The *Sun* described the search for Johnny as "one of the hardest chases in the history of the state." Whether or not Sheriff Logan concurred with that depiction, his personal account documented by the *Sun* on November 14, 1905, did reflect the magnitude of his personal resolve:

The evening I got word [from Police Chief McKenzie)] that Indian Johnny had been seen in Goldfield, the defendants who were so anxious to get him furnished me with transportation and told me they would give me $1,000 if I caught the Indian.

I went to Goldfield and also to the Indian Camp at Columbia and not finding him there thought that he had gone to Lida. We arrived there at 5 a.m. No one had seen him. I engaged an officer to make a search of the outside camps. I then went to Tule Canyon and from there to Pigeon Springs, then back to Lida. I got no word there and went back to Goldfield and heard there that he had been seen in Montezuma and we drove the machine there but there was no trace of him and so back we went to Goldfield, then from there to Lida valley and on to Thorps Wells and then to the Grapevine Ranch.

Here I hired a team and went down in the canyon where we met some prospectors but they had not seen anything of the Indian.

We left Grapevine yesterday at 3 o'clock and arrived here this morning. I have not had my clothes or shoes off since I left Thursday night and the only sleep I have had I got while the machine was going.

We put MacDonald's machine out of commission and they provided us with a three-seated one. The roads we traveled and the distance we covered was a most severe test for the autos.

After Sheriff Logan's futile efforts were reported to Judge Breen, he moved the trial forward without Indian Johnny.[27] Unfortunately for Tom, there would be no $1,000 reward for the father of eight whose daughters Annie, Jessie, and Joie were now enrolled in Business College in Oakland, California. Finding time for family matters had never been more difficult:

December 13, 1905

My Dear Daughters: Yours of the 11th to hand this a.m. and I hasten to reply. You will find enclosed money order for $50.00 which will last you for a few days when I will send you more. I have not time to write you in full today, but will try and finish tomorrow. If I do not write tomorrow, it will be for lack of time. All well and glad that you are the same. Will surely try to write you tomorrow.

Lovingly, Papa[28]

Although reassuring his daughters that all was well, Tom had obviously glossed over the reality that now consumed his attention day and night. The letter, swiftly written with the sweep of a fountain pen, was on Nye County stationery featuring two names: Sheriff & Assessor, Thos. W. Logan and W. H. Cowan, Deputy. Unexpectedly, Cowan had succumbed to pneumonia a month earlier on November 13, 1905. Also a native son of Nevada, Cowan left behind a wife and daughter, and "had been a public servant for a long time," reported the *Bonanza*, "and as a deputy under Sheriff Logan made a most efficient and painstaking officer."[29]

Losing his right-hand man could not have come at a worse time. Tom was only partially moved into the new courthouse office, and license fees were due January 1, the same week Tom was expected to attend the annual State Assessor's Board meeting in Carson City.[30] However, perhaps the most pressing matter at hand was a very public admonition by the Grand Jury regarding his performance as sheriff. On November 24, 1905, the following headline stretched across the front page of the *Sun*: "County Officials on the Rack: Grand Jury Recommends that Commissioners No Longer Violate the Statutes and

Reprimands Sheriff." The content of their complaint, submitted to Judge Breen, read in part:

We find that Mr. Logan, our sheriff has failed to comply with our recommendation [for monthly and quarterly reports] and we request that the county commissioners refuse to allow any bills due him until he has made these monthly and quarterly reports. The district attorney is requested to bring suit against Mr. Logan and his bondsmen should the county sustain any loss by reason of his negligence.

We have had under investigation the alleged violation of the laws relative to mainte-nance of so-called dance houses and houses of prostitution upon the main business street of Tonopah.

The grand jury unanimously condemns such flagrant violation of law and recommends that the proper officers be immediately directed to bring action against any person renting or maintaining such places and that the prosecution be carried on vigorously

We find that the sheriff's office and the assessor's offices have been running in a very loose and unsatisfactory manner.

We have also found that our sheriff has accepted money from business houses giving them a personal receipt instead of a legal license as provided by law....

We find that the sheriff should be heartily commended for the amount of revenue col-lected in the county for the Third quarter of 1905, but we are at a loss to know why he has neglected to collect licenses from the hotels and lodging houses of this county....

Owing to the lack of monthly and quarterly reports from the sheriff's office it has been impossible to make the books of the auditor, treasurer and the sheriff balance and we recommend that these officers so keep their books that at any and all time they will compare and also that they strike a balance sheet monthly.

The report addressed several other issues, such as there being too many "worth-less dogs" roaming Tonopah; the need to separate the men's and women's "apartment" at the city jail; and proposing the hospital be expanded. Perhaps recognizing Logan's deficiencies to be the result of insufficient personnel rather than incompetence, the Grand Jury acknowledged "the immense amount of work now in the sheriff's office" and heartily recommended the commissioners allow and immediately appoint a salaried deputy sheriff.[31]

The very next day, the *Sun's* headlines belonged to Tom Logan: "Logan's Sharp Retort – County Sheriff Replies to Criticisms of the Grand Jury." In a barbed letter to the Grand Jury, Tom defended his work and personal integrity with precision and uncharacteristic forcefulness. As with most conflicts of this type, no one involved held a monopoly on truth. However, no matter how dis-puted certain facts might have been, the easy-going sheriff with a spine of steel didn't hesitate to rage against what he considered to be underhanded tactics and unwarranted accusations by his detractors:

The grand jury which died last night has seen fit in its wisdom to censure the sheriff's office for what it deems in dereliction of duty. Let us see what is the charge. If I have been found guilty of either malfeasance or malfeasance in office, it was the duty of the grand jury to indict me and give me a chance to defend myself before a jury of my peers, and in failing to do this they have broken every obligation placed on them by the statutes and the oaths which each took at the time they qualified.

I have no apologies to make for conduct while in office and defy the grand jury or any-one else to justly criticize my action. To take up the charges in rotation:

First—They say that the sheriff failed to make his quarterly report as required by law, which if they had been fair, and wanted to be just, they would have seen that with the enormous increase in business in the office and the lack of additional and necessary help it was impossible for the work to be done, and if the county has suffered loss thereby, I am willing to confess judgment upon the proper proof thereof.

Second—They say "that we find the assessor's and sheriff's officers have been running in a very loose and unsatisfactory manner." In what way was this run in that manner? What are the specific instances in which this was done? You surely had some evidence or so honorably a body of citizens would not make such a charge and if you did, why not indict as was your sworn and plain duty to do? I am willing to meet the issue as between the grand jury and the people of Nye County. And I wish to state further that I was compelled to pay extra deputies out of my own pocket the sum of $900 to get the work advanced even to that state where you have seen fit to criticize me.

Third—You say "We also find that our sheriff has accepted money from business houses giving them a personal receipt instead of a legal license as required by law." Now then gentlemen, if your finding is true in that regard will you kindly tell the people of Nye County why you did not indict me? What are you men drawing your salaries for if I am the arch criminal that you would imply? And you did not indict! Were you impaneled to assassinate character? This you have evidently done. If you wanted to be fair and make an investigation you would have found that my collections were something over $80,000 and we think that is going some even if we did not get it all. As to the giving of personal receipts for licenses, I will say that it was with the consent of the county commissioners and that across the face of every receipt it was marked plainly as to what it was for, that is "for a license." This method was rendered necessary by the change in the county seat of the county and the additional fact that for some time during the pending changes part of the county officers were in Belmont and part of us here. My time being principally taken up in Tonopah and contiguous territory.

In addition, if you had taken the pains to investigate the matter you would have found that I have paid into the county treasurer and hold his receipt for the sum of $1,833.90 on this personal receipt racket that you are trying to magnify into a crime. I deem it *my duty and frankly say that it is about the only consolation that I get out of your report that you have "heartily commended the sheriff for the amount of revenue collected for the third quarter of 1905," and must say that you certainly allowed your commercialism to govern you in that commendation for in the next breath you again censure by saying that you are at a loss to know why I don't collect some more money for various purposes and so forth.*

To show you that I am all right, I want to thank you heartily, gentlemen, for the recommendation that the sheriff be allowed by the board of commissioners, a salaried deputy and that he be appointed at once and if the board of county commissioners see fit in their wisdom to follow your suggestion, I assure you of the fact that my appointment will be such that it will not only meet the approval of the next grand jury, but of the people of Nye County, generally.

Very truly, etc., Thos W. Logan, Sheriff of Nye County

If local newspapers are any indication, the conflict between Logan and the grand jury receded from public view until March 10, 1906, when a lengthy letter from businessman Frederick W. Schmalling appeared in the *Sun*. No longer a member of the grand jury that had chastised Tom, Schmalling was determined to make known to the people of Nye County his personal perspective, and this time name George Wingfield as a Logan co-conspirator.[32] A resident of Nye County for at least six years, Schmalling's treatise was extremely lengthy and reiterated in greater detail how he believed Sheriff Logan had cost the county money by filing incomplete and late financial reports, making it impossible to thoroughly audit his books.

Schmalling further maintained that Tom had never been authorized by the commissioners to use personal receipts and that he, his deputies, and bondsmen had been disrespectful and uncooperative, leaving the auditing committee "standing in the street" by never finding time to allow access to the sheriff's books. As an example of the sheriff's arbitrary practice for collecting license fees, Schmalling wrote:

Everyone who has been in Tonopah has seen the Tonopah Club, which is owned by Wingfield & Co. For the first quarter of 1905, Wingfield & Co. paid three gaming licenses which amounted to $225; the second quarter they paid four gaming licenses, amounting to $300; and for the third quarter they paid seventeen gaming licenses, which amounted to $1,275.

Continuing on to state the Tonopah Club ran just as many gambling tables the first and second quarter as they did the third, Schmalling calculated Wingfield's saloon owed the county a balance of $2,025—a claim that did not land well with "King George." The next day's headlines belonged this time to Wingfield: "Letter Writer Called a Liar." A statement from Wingfield & Company flatly denounced Schmalling's claims and suggested he was likely misinterpreting monthly numbers for quarterly payments due.[33]

Three weeks later, the new Nye County Grand Jury published their most recent findings in the March 31 edition of the *Bonanza*. Revenue collection practices and management systems were a point of focus but no single county officer was singled out for negligence or any actionable improprieties. Rather, their report noted they had first called upon Sheriff Logan to inspect his transactions covering the last quarter of 1905 and most of the first quarter for 1906. "All monies," they reported, "received by the sheriff during the foregoing period are shown to have been properly entered upon the books of his office, and were promptly delivered to the county treasurer of Nye County as the law directs."

The Jury's Public Buildings Committee had also inspected the new courthouse and ascertained that the jail, with cell room for just 32 prisoners, was already inadequate. They recommended a second floor be built and a fenced yard added to keep outsiders away from the prisoners. As to the care and feeding of those inmates, that responsibility was assigned to Sheriff Logan, along with the safekeeping of all county property, and the purchase of county supplies and services. Finally, it was suggested a long-needed safe be installed in the sheriff's office to better secure his books and collections.

The true motivation behind Schmalling's apparent personal campaign to discredit Tom Logan remains a mystery. Bad blood could have developed several years earlier when the county filed a debt judgment against him and a business partner on April 13, 1900, forcing a public auction of one of their properties. At the sheriff's sale on October 21, 1901, Schmalling did reacquire the property.[34] Or perhaps the discontented former jury member had simply taken exception to what he considered discordant numbers reported by Tom and an intentional disregard for administrative protocol.

Regardless of what drove his strident condemnation of Sheriff Logan—warranted or not—Schmalling's crusade failed to gain traction. William Booth, editor of the *Bonanza*, added his viewpoint on March 31, 1906:

The report of the grand jury filed this week makes interesting reading. The august body is composed of well-known, fair-minded citizens, and the recommendations made are entitled to great weight. It is particularly gratifying to note that the jury commends the grand work done by Sheriff Thomas W. Logan, who is a conscientious, fearless, honest official, who has the interests of the people at heart at all times. He is the right man in the right place, and the taxpayers of the county will see that he is again elected next November.

Just one short week after Booth penned this personal commendation, Sheriff Logan would be dead.

The Pessimist

There is no rose on the broad bleak earth
Worth the labor put forth to raise it,
No scarlet mouth framed in dimpled mirth
Worth the breath that it takes to praise it.

There is no song like the one that's heard
In the time of life's beginning;
No woman's love worth the empty word
That we waste in its useless winning.

There is no day with its sordid strife
Worth the serious thought we give it,
No passing hour in a careless life
Worth the trouble it takes to live it.

So pluck the rose while you chance to live,
Hold your pleasures as you may find them,
Forget, in joys that those red lips give,
The grin of the skull behind them.

—Mabel Porter Potts, *Tonopah Bonanza*, November 21, 1903

10

FINAL DAYS: SPRING, 1906

"Everything was bigger last year than it was the year before. All down the line this flourishing condition of things existed. Even the list of deaths by violence was large. The only thing so far discovered that was smaller than during previous years was the number of people who explated their crimes by paying for a life with a life…. Apparently, human life grows less and less sacred."

Reno Evening Gazette, January 3, 1906

IN JANUARY 1906, May Biggs purchased, from Daniel F. O'Brien and John. H. Myles, three vacant lots on the west end of Manhattan, Nevada, a flourishing new mining camp tucked in a Toquima Mountain ravine about 16 miles southwest of Belmont.[1] Myles was a young man known to have been grubstaked by Tom Logan.[2] O'Brien was a former actor from San Francisco now working for George Wingfield. In that capacity, he had become central to a heated legal battle involving a group of 20 high-grade "abandoned" claims he had relocated for Wingfield. When those locations were not accepted as being valid, nearly all the claims were jumped, and Wingfield was forced to get an injunction. At that time, not one pound of ore was being sacked on "Contention Hill" pending a judgment from the Nye County District Court.[3 & 4]

Early Manhattan, Nevada, c. 1905
(Central Nevada Historical Society, Tonopah, NV)

May Biggs bought mattresses and furniture for the Jewel house about to be built on her property in Manhattan. The lumber was ordered from the Tonopah

Lumber Company by Tom Logan.[5] Opinions differ as to the depth and nature of their personal relationship. Most concur the two were intimately involved and probably met sometime during 1905 after May moved to Tonopah. Some believe she was Tom's mistress and perhaps even a silent business partner. Others theorize Tom had simply been one of her clients and a soft touch for a beguiling woman with an ambitious agenda.

Although frowned upon by mainstream society, prostitution was common in 1906 and openly tolerated, if not patronized, by the more liberally inclined — some of whom happened to be married men. New boomtowns, such as Manhattan, were especially accommodating and readily attracted women like May, who had both business experience and a way with men.

Like Tonopah, Manhattan's meteoric ascent was sparked by chance. In April 1905, John and Frank Humphrey (one of Logan's mining partners) and two other "cowpunchers" stopped for lunch in Manhattan Gulch along the 30-mile route between Belmont and Smoky Valley. There, John stumbled upon an outcropping of rocks "impregnated with shining gold." News of the discovery spread with lightning speed and within a few months, more than 3,000 claims had been staked in the vicinity.[6] Among those early claims were the "American," "McKenzie Fraction," and "Totem No. 1 and No. 2," located by Tom Logan and Alex McKenzie.[7]

Situated at 7,000 feet, Manhattan's gold rush captured worldwide attention, as described by journalist Edwin W. R. Lawrence:

The naked facts, newborn of Mother Truth, concerning Manhattan seem miraculous and mythical. Never since the halcyon days of Virginia City has a camp sprung into existence which gave such instant fulfillment of mighty promise…. Manhattan literally has sprung into existence like Minerva, full-panoplied from the brow of Jove. In one bound it presses to the van of the Nevada camps, the youngest of all, but the giant chief. The gold excitement at Manhattan is undying.[8]

While newspapers near and far extolled the glittering wonders and seething bustle of the nugget-laden canyon camp, Sheriff Logan would spend the better part of the coming months trying to establish some semblance of law and order in Manhattan. Tonopah broker and future Nye County assemblyman, Cada Castolas Boak*, provided a vivid account of the "buzzsaw" atmosphere permeating the remote camp in a letter to his wife on January, 21, 1906:

A bunch of us bonded another mine for $25,000 (does that scare you?). Well, we took up the first payment, and all the papers to have signed….Well, we had spoken for a

---

* Originally from Iowa, Cada Castolas Boak organized the Tonopah Chamber of Commerce in 1924. A 50-year resident of Nye County, he served ten laudable terms in the state assembly, beginning in 1927, and was a national director of the Highway 50 Association earning the nickname, "Good Roads."

single seated buggy and a good team. When we got ready to start, we found that the liveryman had got things mixed up and gave our team to someone else. About 25 rigs left that day for Manhattan, and only one team was left in town and a man had hired that and was just starting out to drive two tenderloin girls up there. So we had to buy him off and take the rig and the girls...as soon as we struck the Manhattan foothills, we found lots of snow. It was warm and the frost coming out of the ground, and it was mud, mud, mud....

Instead of a peaceful, quiet little mining camp of perhaps 200, I found the wildest ex-citement I have ever saw anywhere...a city of 1,200 people, and coming in at the rate of 50 to 80 per day. Small town lots that sold six weeks ago from $50 to $200 are now snatched up quick for $3,000 to $5,000 each...entire streets are built up solid for blocks in the space of a few days time. Men and women walk the streets nights or spread down a blanket on a saloon, office or store front to sleep...inside of an hour while I was there, 9 wagon trains each drawn by a team of 20 horses came in, all loaded with provisions and merchandise. It is simply wonderful.[9]

Besides May Biggs, within the human stampede to Manhattan were Vivian Carlton (one-time visitor to Justice Sawle's court in Tonopah) and Pauline Leslie—two tenderloin girls bound for residency and employment at the Jewel. Like so many women of dubious virtue, harsh circumstances usually relegated them to near anonymity save for the happenstance of a noteworthy public event. Few stayed anywhere very long, frequently changed their names, and left little sign of their time on earth.

Tonopah-Manhattan Stage, from a period postcard, c. 1907 (Logan Family Collection)

May would also hire Wilson "Jimmie" Bering, a 25-year-old piano player from California. Raised in San Francisco, he had worked as a clerk from 1901 through 1905 for one of the Bay Area's pre-mier hardware stores, Dunham, Carrigan & Hayden Company.[10] Per-haps wanting to follow in his father's footsteps as a working musician or sim-ply surrendering to the temptations emanating from a booming mine camp, Jimmie left city life behind and trekked to Manhattan where more people than he probably ever imagined kept a gun handy.

New York Saturday Evening Post journalist, Barton W. Currie, would write a feature article later that year titled, "Wild West in Nevada," informing readers that Nevada had imposed a fine of $200 for carrying revolvers. However, he continued, "the lettered prohibition is looked upon as entirely in the light of a joke. You rarely see the glisten of a gun in the open, but you can see the eloquent bulge on the hip."[11]

Gunplay remained an ever-constant threat in Nye County's high-strung mining camps. An incident at the Bank saloon in Tonopah the first week of the New Year attested to how quickly a nervous trigger finger could risk disasters wholly disproportionate to the circumstances at hand. From the *Bonanza*, January 6, 1906:

An individual with a red handkerchief over his face entered the Bank saloon in the Golden Block [diagonally across from The American saloon] last evening at eleven o'-clock and took six shots at P. H. Sandlin, the night bartender.... The fellow was about 5 feet 10 inches in height and wore a black overcoat and slouch hat. The revolver was of .38 caliber and the fellow was undoubtedly an amateur. Four suspects have been arrested by Sheriff Logan and are now in jail. If the right fellow is caught he should be given short shrift at the end of a hemp rope.

The shooting apparently started when Sandlin reached for a pistol. The masked intruder panicked and began firing. The first bullet passed through a counter and the bartender's hand before lodging only skin-deep beneath the clothing stretched around his ample girth. The other projectiles struck a partition and the ceiling, but as soon as Sandlin took aim with his own pistol, the overexcited highwayman fled. A local reporter concluded the dastardly plot was foiled "due solely to the plucky attempt of Mr. Sandlin to defend his employer's property, which attempt came so near resulting in fatality for him."[12]

Since no one died at the Bank saloon, *Sun* cartoonist Arthur Buel drew an illustration depicting the scene more as a comedy of errors than a precarious brush with a man's mortality—the humor of which was likely misplaced for the victim, Sheriff Logan, and his deputies.[13]

Regrettably, the Bank saloon shooting was not an isolated incident that month in Nye County. The first week of February, a dispute at the Tonopah Club in Tonopah resulted in a liquored-up faro dealer shooting at a man who refused to loan him more money. Before the end of the month, an incensed former bartender at Manhattan's new Tonopah Club confronted the manager who had fired him. A volley of epithets led to a scuffle, at which time the disgruntled party pulled a six-shooter and shot the manager twice in the side and once in the back and leg. The victim was expected to survive, and the shooter was released on bonds after a preliminary hearing in the justice court. In March, two men in Manhattan hurled "high words" over a $60 debt and, after both were tossed out the back door of the Gold Wedge saloon, one drew a gun and killed the other. Two days later, a coroner's jury reached a verdict of justifiable homicide.[14]

"Robber Shoots Five Times at Bartender of Bank Saloon"
(*Tonopah Daily Sun*, January 6, 1906, Arthur V. Buel, Editorial Artist)

Nothing so contributed to the growing lawlessness in Manhattan as did the lethal combination of hot tempers, copious amounts of liquor, and an abundance of weapons poised for action. In less than a year, the fledgling pine-tree camp had exploded with nearly as much havoc as it had wealth. For Sheriff Logan, the pressure to erect a secure jail and ramp up law enforcement mounted with each passing day. From the *Bonanza*, January 27, 1906:

While in Manhattan last week, W. T. Cuddy, County Commissioner, and Sheriff Thomas W. Logan selected a location for a temporary jail building and made all the arrangements for construction work to be commenced at once.

A steel cell will be removed from Belmont and installed in the Manhattan jail for keeping prisoners charged with felonies until they can be removed to the more substantial jail in this city [Tonopah].

Sheriff Logan appointed Henry Nofsinger, formerly of Tonopah, to be deputy sheriff at Manhattan, and Officer Nofsinger will have charge of the jail and upon him will fall the task of maintaining order in the new camp.

While waiting for a jail, peace officers in Manhattan were forced to improvise. The common practice of chaining prisoners in custody to a wagon wheel was not practical, since the cavalcade of freight wagons didn't stop long enough to oblige. Consequently, Constable Nofsinger escorted "unrulies" down the gulch where he placed their arms around the trunk of a compliant cedar tree and cuffed their hands. After spending the night in the darkness, surrounded by the howl of nearby coyotes, and sobering up, lawbreakers were generally less likely to re-offend. "Occasionally," said Nofsinger, "one of the prisoners will get obstreperous when we take him to 'jail,' but he becomes reconciled when he finds out that he cannot pull his tree out by the roots. They are pretty docile when released."[15]

In early January, Sheriff Logan once again traveled to Carson City for the annual State Board of Assessors meeting hosted by Governor John Sparks. The night before their session, Tom joined fellow assessors in the formation of a local lodge, a fraternal organization* steeped in mythology, charity, and right-eous tomfoolery.[16]

In addition to updating property valuations ranging from work horses to railroad lines, the two-day assessors' meeting yielded positive news for Nevada: an increase in taxable properties and, with the abundant snowfall of winter, the promise of bumper crops ahead.[17] Before returning to Nye County, Tom, a half dozen other assessors, and Frank Golden were hosted by G. Waters, tax agent of the San Pedro, Los Angeles and Salt Lake Railroad for dinner at the Golden Grill. "The best that the markets of Reno afford was spread for the guests who remained at the tables for two hours."[18]

After returning from Carson City to Tonopah, Tom caught up on matters that had accumulated during his absence, one of which was fatherly obligations. He wrote the following letter on January 14, 1906, to his eldest daughter away at school with younger sisters, Jessie and Josephine, at the Polytechnic Institute in Oakland, California:

My Dear Annie: I received your letter some time ago but did not get around to answer it. I have been to Carson twice since the 1ˢᵗ of the year and running around in other places with my usual work keeps me going. I am glad you girls are getting along all right and I want you to keep at it.

I noted what you said in regard to my feeling about Lot [Annie's husband] but the day will come when you will say or think that your Father was right—I want you to tell me whether or not since he returned and how much he has told me that he sent you money

---

* E Clampus Vitus chapters, otherwise known as "Clampers," thrive throughout the Western United States to this day, blending good-humored high jinx with a mission to preserve and memorialize historical figures, events, and structures.

Nye County Sheriff's Office first occupied by Sheriff Tom Logan in 1906, c. 1912. Far left is Sheriff Ed Malley, who served from 1910 to 1913. (Nevada Historical Society, Reno, NV)

and I have my doubts about it. For several reasons that I may tell you some day when you get your eyes open.*

I know that Lot has told you a whole lot of rot that is not true. I don't want to keep this matter up, and won't say much more about it, but when he tells you all the lies that I know he does and I can prove it makes your old Father pretty sore.

Well, you said that you were anxious to continue on at school. I will say that I want you to because some day you will have to make your own living.

I sent you some more money day before yesterday, and hope you get it all right. Don't let yourself run so short that you go broke any more before you send for money, because I am liable to be so busy that I overlook sending. Tell Joie that Papa received her letter and will answer later.

With love to you all, I am Your Affectionate Father

---

* Less than five months after Tom's death, Annie would validate her father's concerns by leaving her husband. The education he insisted she acquire emboldened her to exit a failing marriage and gain respectable employment as a single woman. Taking a variety of clerical positions in the next several years, Annie eventually divorced Warburton in 1908. By 1910, she was working as a clerk at the Tonopah Post Office, boarding with family friends, John and Myrtle Myles, and had tucked away the above letter as a keepsake to carry with her always.

Annie Logan Warburton, c 1904, Tonopah, NV (Logan Family Collection)

"WINTER, WHICH WAS a hard one in this section," reported the *Bonanza* on February 10, 1906, "has passed and gone and spring is at hand. Many residents of Tonopah are preparing for prospecting trips and Nevada will be covered by tenderfeet and mining men this year as never before." For Tonopah, the certainty of an even more profitable year ahead traveled from speculator to prospector to investor to operator and all points in between:

The early morning scenes on Tonopah's main streets are well worth witnessing. As many as eight stages can be seen being loaded with human freight besides a dozen autos, many carriages with spirited horses, and from fifteen to twenty large 14-animal teams laden with freight for the outside new camps just springing into active life. Besides the different wheel carriages, no less than a thousand people can be seen hurrying in every direction doing something to help make the greatest mining section in the world.[19]

Journalist Clara Douglas published similar impressions of "what Tonopah's gold has wrought" in the February 1906 edition of *Sunset* magazine, further exalting, "The huckster's cart serve at your door; or, you may purchase, over all sorts of counters, on Brougher Avenue, anything you desire, from a head of cabbage to a modish silk gown."

Few had so closely witnessed and experienced the stupendous transformation of Nye County as had Tom and Hannah Logan. Now in their 24th year of marriage, they had steadfastly labored together to furnish both a home and secure future for their children. In Tom's absence, Hannah tirelessly worked behind the scenes. Upon her sturdy shoulders fell the colossal responsibility of tending the family hearth, feeding hungry mouths, and clothing growing bodies; and in the quiet of absolute darkness, as the last child slipped into slumber and she was alone, within her heart surely churned the distress of too many days and nights alone.

As with most wives of this era, especially those raised within the Mormon faith, she was expected to support her husband's aspirations. In turn, she hoped to also benefit from his achievements, which for Tom in 1906, were numerous and on the upswing. Even though the spark that first attracted one to the other had perhaps dimmed, Tom and Hannah Logan's union as provider and caretaker held true.

OF INCREASING CONCERN for Sheriff Logan was the tension building steam between Nye County labor unions and mine operators. From the *Nevada State Journal*, "Bloody Battle Fought at New Mining Camp: Jack Gineau is Dead, George Cole is Wounded and Murderers are in Jail at Tonopah," January 28, 1906:

In a pitched battle between non-union miners and a committee of the Tonopah Miners' Union this afternoon at Cliffords, the scene of a new strike, forty-four miles east of Tonopah, Jack Gineau, a union man, was shot through the lungs and killed and George Cole, a member of the legislature, was shot through the arm. Sheriff Logan immediately went to the scene of the shooting and placed six non-union men under arrest. The murderers, after the shooting, defied a posse of citizens and it was not until the sheriff arrived with a posse of gunfighters that they gave themselves up.

Excitement is at fever heat and the non-union miners were brought to this city this evening under escort of a strong guard. They were taken from Cliffords just in time to prevent lynching.

This incident was precipitated by union president George Cole, and his committee members, Walter Fancher and Jack Gineau, when they showed up at a new ore strike to interview miners suspected of working for less than the $5 scale. Cole made clear to those they encountered that, if that was their wage, there was no problem, but if not, they would be considered a "scab." Reportedly, the mine's owner was the first to hurl curse words at the union men. The escalating quarrel led to fisticuffs, at which time an irate miner, J. H. Hennessy, whipped out a pistol, killing Gineau and wounding Cole.[20]

Samuel Vermilyea,* from Goldfield, represented Hennessy at his murder trial and submitted a plea of self-defense.[21] Not known if or how his client might

* Samuel Vermilyea previously defended Frank Smith, acquitted in the Walter Dunn murder trial, and was also the lead counsel for the union members acquitted of any wrongdoing for the death of Chong Bing Long during anti-Chinese riots in 1904.

have been related to Wingfield associate John P. Hennessy, John H. was found guilty of manslaughter in Nye County but filed an appeal with the Nevada Supreme Court. Although that conviction was eventually upheld, he would spend the interim time out on $5,000 bail, courtesy of Wingfield partner, Tom Kendall, and J. V. Stewart. [22 & 23]

Additional resources came to the sheriff's office in February, 1906, when the county commissioners appointed Tom's brother Deputy George Logan as jail keeper at the new courthouse, and J. K. Chambers as Manhattan's first justice of the peace.[24] Local justice courts were an invaluable tool for keeping order and mostly adjudicated minor one-on-one infractions. However, the first week of March 1906, the justice assigned to Berlin, located in the northwestern corner of Nye County, had to send for reinforcements.

Populated by mostly Portuguese, Italian, and Basque workers, Berlin was a single-company mining camp. When management began exclusively importing Basque men to replace Portuguese employees, resentment festered. At one point, discharged miners corralled the mine foreman and beat him severely enough to drive him out of the area. Fearing more trouble was brewing, the Berlin justice of the peace wired Sheriff Logan for emergency assistance. Tom responded by first gathering a contingent of deputies to accompany him to the camp:[25]

The big White Steamer [automobile] that carried the deputies in the mad dash to Berlin is back in Tonopah again and the story of that ride and the exciting events which followed is dramatic and thrilling, indeed, as told by J. W. Johnson, the man who held the wheel over all the long way.

When Sheriff Logan received the call for aid from Berlin on March 1, he telephoned at once from Austin to H. T. McKnight, manager of the Desert Auto Company, who, with commendable promptness and zeal, rushed Johnson and the big car to the courthouse. There Thomas Murphy and A. Gilzean were sworn in as deputy sheriffs and piling into the auto they were off for Manhattan, lurching and pounding through mud and chuck holes. Manhattan reached, Scott Hickey and Hugh Willis were added to the valiant little force and [joined by Tom] they early next morning, started for Berlin.

Johnson says that the road from Cloverdale to Berlin was the worst he ever encountered, broken by steep pitches and rocky defiles and filled with mud and snow. Through the night they pounded along with lights out as the water in the gas lamps was frozen.

On reaching Berlin they got out of the car on the edge of town and, revolvers in hand, they scattered through the streets, holding up every one they met and driving the excited men before them into the big store building. In almost no time forty frightened Basques had been rounded up and a pile of guns ranging from .22 to .45 caliber were in the deputies possession.[26]

Tom informed the *Sun* that their "arrival on scene was very opportune and that serious trouble was narrowly averted." Twenty-seven men involved in the conflict were arrested and tried before the justice of the peace who dispensed heavy fines all around. Those who could pay were ordered to leave camp, while the remainder stayed in custody until they could. Not just management, but the entire camp had learned its lesson and no further incidents related to issues associated with "cheap foreign labor" occurred under Sheriff Logan's watch.[27]

Accounts, logged by the *Bonanza* of Tom's comings and goings during his final days, conveyed a continuing measure of confidence in Nye's seemingly indefatigable sheriff as he traversed the county on one mission or another:

February 10, 1906: *Nye County's most efficient Sheriff Thomas W. Logan left for Bullfrog Weds. on official business.*

March 3, 1906: *Deputy Assessor Wm. S. Bryden commenced the work of assessing the property of Tonopah for the year 1906 last Monday. Mr. Bryden is a very capable and painstaking official and Assessor Thomas W. Logan is certainly to be congratulated on having his services.*

March 16, 1906: *Sheriff Logan was instructed [by county commissioners] to procure "uniforms" for the prisoners in the county jail. County Commissioner Cuddy was given power to purchase steel bars to be placed at the windows of the jail to prevent outsiders from passing drugs and other things into the prisoners. Assessor Logan was requested to turn in all plats of townsites, showing lots and their owners, when he turns in the assessment roll next fall.*

Conspicuously absent from the headlines that March, was an unfolding drama between George Wingfield and his common-law wife, May Baric. Maintaining that they had been together for more than three years, Baric filed for divorce and spousal support on March 2, 1906. She was represented by a team of four attorneys, one of whom was Tonopah newcomer, Patrick McCarran. Wingfield retained the services of the preeminent corporate law firm of Campbell, Metson and Brown, who had law offices in Tonopah, Goldfield, Rhyolite, and San Francisco. Baric's claims of abuse by the man who was well on his way to ruling the Silver State were scathing and foretold of a reign that would indeed be riddled with trickery and violence. Given the severity of the following excerpts from her voluminous complaint, it is hard to imagine Tom Logan was not at least aware of the strife in the Wingfield household:

March 18, 1905, page 2: *...said defendant without reasonable, probable or any cause, and while in a rage of temper beat the said plaintiff over the head with the butt end of a pistol...at said time said abuse was inflicted, was of so severe a character and nature that plaintiff herein bears the scars of said abuse to this day....*

March 18, 1905, page 5: *…at the same time defendant well knew that he was suffering with a severe attack of a loathsome and infectious disease, to-wit: Syphilis…and shortly thereafter (plaintiff) was in such a physical condition from the ravages of said disease that it was necessary for her to receive constant attendance and for many months the services of one to two nurses both day and night….**

February 17, 1906, page 7-9: *…defendant telephoned requesting plaintiff to come to his room in the Nixon Building in Goldfield, that he wished to speak to her on matters pertaining to the domestic relations…he had made up his mind to take her back into his heart and install her in the home which he, the defendant, had built for plaintiff in the town of Tonopah…. [Then] he had changed his mind…she had no recourse against him, for the reason that he was a man of high political standing, and that there were no lawyers who would take her case, and that if they did take her case he could buy them…and knew the judge [Peter Breen] that presided over the Third Judicial District Court and that said Judge did not dare under any circumstances to render a judgment against him.*

Wingfield answered Baric's claims by categorically denying any form of marriage, cohabitation, abuse, adultery, promise to take her back, or financial responsibility for her wellbeing.[28] His preeminent biographer, Elizabeth Raymond, contended Baric's suit should not be dismissed as a "gold-digger's harassment of a wealthy man." She further acknowledged there had to have been some truth to Baric's assertions regarding the far-reaching power of Wingfield's influence—one being the fact that there was not one mention of her otherwise incendiary suit in the newspapers of either Tonopah or Goldfield. "No newspaper editor in 1906," wrote Raymond, "could have risked alienating a man already being heralded as Nevada's Napoleon."[29]

The Baric case was very likely the first known public engagement between Wingfield and McCarran, whose lives were to be forever entangled and, however briefly, unequivocally connected to Sheriff Tom Logan.**

---

* *Tonopah Bonanza*, February 4, 1905, reported George Wingfield was on the "road to recovery" after being quite ill in Carson City.

** The trial of Sheriff Logan's killer stalled Baric's case. Only after Walter Barieau's acquittal did Baric's case reach the court, at which time all allegations and requested relief was denied, and she was ordered to pay Wingfield's legal fees.

Seated across from Patrick McCarran (far left) is George Wingfield and, next to him, one of his attorneys, Hugh Brown; "Diamondfield" Jack Davis is facing Wingfield. c. 1906 (Central Nevada Historical Society, Tonopah, NV)

IN THE LAST known letter written to his three daughters, Tom's concern for the wellbeing of his family in the turbulent whirlwind of official duties was undeniable. Despite any delinquencies his killer's defense team would exploit at trial time, his encouraging words revealed a man guided by the laudable principles residing in his heart and soul.

My Dear Daughters,

No doubt you think your Father has forgotten you, but I have not. I have been away far from home for a long time, after jurors and witnesses. This County is getting so lively now that it keeps me going day and night. I received Jessie's letter this a.m. and two or three from Annie after I came home. Do not get disheartened but stay at school all of you. I am trying to shape up for the rest of the family to come down [to Oakland, California] by the middle of next month, although they don't know it, as I expect $500 by the 10th of April and if it comes and will, I will give it to your mother to go and spend, and give her a chance to see something. Do not say anything to her about it because sometimes these things fall through but I don't think that this will.

Annie, it would be hard for you to get anything to do here as there are so many coming in looking for all of these jobs. I want you to stay where you are and go to school. Lot [Annie's husband] is doing nothing no matter what he writes you or tells you what his chances are and I know what I am talking about. If everything turns out all right, I may come down with the folks to see you. Be good girls and do not worry about me. We will

Jessie Logan, c. 1908, (Logan Family Collection)   Josephine (Joie) Logan, c. 1908, (Logan Family Collection)

come out all right—before this summer is over your Father has some chances to make money that he never had before. I enclose $50 and will send more before long.

With all kinds of <u>love</u> to you <u>all</u>, I am your affectionate Papa

The 50-mile route from Tonopah to Manhattan meanders over vast and gently-sloped desert land before dipping into the Great Smoky Valley. Travelers head due north then, midway, turn eastward into the foothills of the imposing Toquima Mountains before snaking upward into the Manhattan gulch. The Logan ranch lies about 30 miles further up the basin. Nye County native, Olephia Nay King, described the area, writing:

I'd seen patches where the Indian pinks an' the lupine an' little white desert flowers, or mountain flowers, were growin' together. See the colors red, white and blue all together. We always stopped, an' we took interest in those things. An' the beautiful mountains, an' the mahogany-filled basins, an' quaking aspens…. They just turn the most beautiful colors! You'd have to stop an' look at them. They're so beautiful. To some people, things like that might not mean very much but we always liked to watch the sunsets, and the sunrises.[30]

"Tonopah Fads and Fancies," upper right notation pokes fun at Tom Logan's badly bleached hat. (*Tonopah Daily Sun*, April 4, 1906, Arthur V. Buel, Editorial Artist)

Any number of business or personal matters had beckoned Tom Logan up the hill to Manhattan the first week of April 1906. He had mining claims in the district, a jail under construction, annual property assessment duties…and a place to hang his trail-weary hat at the Jewel.

Night

The day is done, and the darkness
Falls from the wings of Night,
As a feather is wafted downward
From an eagle in his flight.

I see the lights of the village
Gleam through the rain and the mist,
And a feeling of sadness comes o'er me
That my soul cannot resist:

A feeling of sadness and longing,
That is not akin to pain,
And resembles sorrow only
As the mist resembles the rain.

Come, read to me some poem,
Some simple and heartfelt lay,
That shall soothe this restless feeling,
And banish the thoughts of day.

Not from the grand old masters,
Not from the bards sublime,
Whose distant footsteps echo
Through the corridors of Time,

For, like strains of martial music,
Their mighty thoughts suggest
Life's endless toil and endeavor;
And tonight I long for rest.

Read from some humbler poet,
Whose songs gushed from his heart,
As showers from the clouds of summer,
Or tears from the eyelids start;

Who, through long days of labor,
And nights devoid of ease,
Still heard in his soul the music
Of wonderful melodies.

Such songs have a power to quiet
The restless pulse of care,
And comes like the benediction
That follows after prayer.

Then read from the treasured volume
The poem of thy choice,
And lend to the rhyme of the poet
The beauty of thy voice.

And the night shall be filled with music,
And the cares, that infest the day,
Shall fold their tents, like the Arabs,
And as silently pass away.

—Henry Longfellow,
The Weekly Jeffersonian, August 6, 1857

11

BLOODSHED AT THE JEWEL: APRIL 7, 1906

*"We all know the evils of gambling; how it dissatisfies society in its daily oc-
cupations, absorbs thought, dissipates energy, and renders men unfit for that
steady application and reasonable economy which alone make a community
prosperous. It destroys the finer qualities both of mind and feeling; it makes
men moody and nervous, makes them live a life of extremes, now exhilarated
by success, now despondent through failure. What folly!"*

Hubert Howe Bancroft,
The Works of Hubert Howe Bancroft: California inter pocula, 1888

WALTER AMPHILOQUE BARIEAU had been a gambler most of his life. The
night before he killed Tom Logan, he and an eccentric attorney friend, Volney
Hoggatt, made their way to the Jewel, located in lower Manhattan at the north end
of Dexter Street. Established patrons of red light districts from Denver to Nome,
they were likely as comfortable in May Biggs' parlor as they were their own
homes—if not more so. Here, cards, liquor, cigars, perfumed women, and tinkling
piano keys prevailed, and the merriment frequently continued far past midnight.

April 6, 1906, was a Friday. By the time May bid farewell to the last of her
guests, it was the next day and nearly dawn. Her employees, Vivian Carlton,
Pauline Leslie, and Jimmie Bering had retired to their personal quarters. Also
lodged at the Jewel, was Wingfield operative, Daniel O'Brien, one of the two
men who had sold the Jewel lots to May just three months earlier.

Sheriff Logan had apparently already retired to one of the front rooms. His
trip to Manhattan that week had been a perilous one. According to others who
had traveled that route:

*Logan was mixed up in an accident. His team ran away with him and in stopping them
he was badly hurt. He received several cuts on the head, and his hands were so badly
lacerated as to require bandages.... Logan was so badly handicapped by them that he
could not have handled a revolver with speed or accuracy.*[1]

As she checked for dawdlers in the house the morning of April 7, 1906, May
discovered Barieau in the back parlor stretched out on a couch. In May's words:

*Well, about five o'clock this morning I went into the back parlor. Several of the boys
had already left and [Barieau] was the only one there. I asked him to go. He said he
did not want to go until daylight. I told him it was daylight then. At first I said hurry
up as there was a hack at the door and I thought he might ride, and he kind of raised
up and then he said, "No, I'm not going."*

I said he should not spoil the fun that they had by keeping me up any longer, or words to that effect. So he got up and when I started out of the door, he went back. His hat was on the table. I thought he would come out for sure. He told me to mind my own business. I did not think he was going to go. I spoke to him again and he took me by the wrists in a rough way. Then when he took hold of my wrists I went down on one knee and then I screamed. I thought he was going to hit me.[2]

BORN TO AMPHILOQUE and Mary Vignault Barieau on October 29, 1869, in Nova Scotia, William Amphiloque Barieau, who later called himself "Walter," was their third child. Of French descent, the young family settled in Boston, Massachusetts.[3] During the summer of 1872, before Walter turned age three, his family suffered an unthinkable tragedy:

"The Merrimac Street Wife Murder," A jury summoned by Coroner Foye held an inquest to-day [sic] in the Truant office upon the death of Mary Barieau, who died Monday evening at her residence on Merrimac Street. It is believed from the blows and kicks and general brutal treatment of her husband, who is now in custody.[4]

One of several witnesses for the state, Mary's next-door neighbor described how two weeks earlier she had heard a scuffle and screams, and went into the house to investigate. There she found Mary on a lounge with her angry husband pressing a knee into her abdomen and his hands upon her throat. She shouted, "You are killing her!" and he replied, "I mean to kill her," but was soon persuaded to let her go.[5]

The Boston Globe reported on July 19, 1872, "From testimony it appears that the murder was one of the most wicked ever committed in this city." An entry in *The New York Times* that same week stated Mary had been "killed by the brutality of her husband." The Boston death record listed cause of death to be "Abuse/Miscarriage," and Walter's father was charged with murder.

Less than four months later and after just two hours of deliberation, the jury foreman announced to the Supreme Judicial Court of Suffolk County, Massachusetts, that they had found the defendant "not guilty." *The Boston Globe* reported on November 2, 1872:

On behalf of the prisoner, the following witnesses have testified: Susan B. Stickney, that she nursed the deceased, and that the sickness was not unusual; saw no trouble between prisoner and wife. Mrs. Sarah Ormsby, the cook, and Joseph Johnson, the barkeeper, that the deceased was struck by her nephew, John Marshall, with a boot; J.G. Chase, that he had seen her drunk and dirty. John Mulcahy, that he saw her after she fell down stairs, and he was positive the prisoner was out of the house at the time. Hubert Teisser and ten others that the prisoner was of good character....

When [the prosecutor] had concluded, the prisoner was informed by Judge Gray that he could now address the jury in his own behalf if he chose to do so, but that no prejudice or presumption would result from his declining to speak. In response to His Honor's remark, the prisoner availed himself of the privilege, and addressed the jury at some length....He concluded his speech with the words: "I know before God that I am an innocent man, and should I meet my wife in heaven to-night [sic], I should meet her without remorse. I leave the case with you now, gentlemen of the jury, with the hope of justice at your hands."

For the three children whose father many believed had a hand in his wife's death, the wounds on their impressionable young hearts had to have cut deep. One year later, Amphiloque, now 29, re-married 18-year-old Mary Moen on November 29, 1873. She would bear him one child every other year for the next 24 years. In 1876, the growing family moved from Boston to Fresno, California, and by 1879 Amphiloque had become a naturalized U.S. citizen.* A master saddle and harness maker, he took up farming and expanded his harness shop to a buggy service station and then to a general merchandise store, earning enough spare capital to invest in the area's emerging oil fields.[6]

Amphiloque's relationship with Walter was strained and combustible. That tension was compounded by his second wife's bias against her three step-children, who reportedly slept in a modified chicken coop at the farm because the main house was full. At the age of fourteen, Walter, a one-time honor roll student, left home for good to begin his long affiliation with the gambling industry.[8]

By the age of 23, he was living in Sacramento, California, and was well-known to both the local sporting circuit and law enforcement. The first week of May, 1893, Barieau was among six persons arrested for running an illegal craps game at The Peerless saloon.[9] On another occasion, he was brought into police court charged with stealing a woman's jewelry, but the case against him was dropped.[10]

William (Walter) Amphiloque Barieau, c. 1895 (Logan Family Collection)

During the summer of 1893, Walter asked 17-year-old Margaret Young from Liverpool, England, to marry him. When her parents refused to approve the union, and Sacramento County officials would not issue a marriage license, the couple eloped to nearby Colusa County. The *Sacramento Daily Union* reported on July 1, 1893:

"Married in Colusa: Walter Barieau and Miss Maggie Young's Short Journey"

There has been considerable gossip going on since Thursday concerning a runaway match, the principals in which were Walter Barieau and Miss Maggie Young.

The former is a young man prominent in "sporting" circles, while the latter is a music teacher. They had been engaged for some time, but Miss Young's parents opposed the match, and the lovers fled to Colusa County, where they were married on Thursday by Rev. Mr. Eastman, pastor of the Presbyterian Church of that place.

The newly married couple returned to Sacramento yesterday, and are living at the residence of Mr. and Mrs. John W. Clough, corner of Seventh and M streets.

For Barieau, like most tenacious gamblers of the day, life was beset by high risk, dubious temptations, and inevitable scrapes with the law. Wins and losses transpired with unpredictable frequency, and Barieau had his share of losing streaks—in one form or another. He attracted considerable attention the end of February, 1895, when he complained to Sacramento authorities about an unpaid debt:

The Chinamen who run the lottery business in this city for Louie Moon, the Weaverville boss, have refused to pay Barieau and Butler* the $5,000 they won the other night, or any portion of it. In adopting this course they are unintentionally but very effectively doing the community much good, for it will be the surest means of breaking up their lottery business.[11]

Amid conflicting accounts of who owed whom what, one course of action Barieau considered was to attach the lottery operator's private property. However, since the dispute arose out of an illegal transaction, even that option was not viable.[12] Two days later, a *Union* headline indicated little hope that Barieau would recover his wagers: "Two Lottery Joints Broken Up: Successful Raids Made by Determined Policemen." One of the dens, reported to have been frequented by Barieau, was located behind a popular cigar stand. Rigged with electric wires and signals, spring doors, secret panels, and a disappearing floor, the elaborate configuration was designed to both evade detection and provide a secure environment for customers who tunneled their way to "the mystic shrine where lottery players worshipped the Mongolian golden calf."[13]

---

* No known relation to Jim Butler, "Father of Tonopah."

Failing to collect on his ill begotten lottery winnings and next employed as a saloonkeeper for the Pullman, Barieau's financial woes multiplied. The Sacramento Superior Court declared him an insolvent debtor with unpaid sums totaling just over $2,000. A list of more than two dozen businesses and individuals to whom he owed money was published by the *Union* on March 11, 1895.

Partial relief came to Barieau, now with a baby on the way, the next week in police court when Justice Henry acquitted him of selling saloon fixtures he did not own to someone else. Although discharged, a contempt case filed against Bareiau was continued until the next week.[14] That charge stemmed from the following incident:

Constable Faris had quite a scrimmage with the Barieau household at 1020 N Street on Monday afternoon, when he attempted to take possession of some furniture in the house, which was attached by Ingram & Bird.

The constable put Thomas L. Acock in charge of the property as keeper, but Barieau and his wife refused to recognize Faris' authority in the matter. They locked Acock out and refused to give up possession of the furniture until 4 o'clock.

Faris waited until that time, and in the meantime Barieau went away. No action was taken until 5 o'clock, when Faris again demanded that Mrs. Barieau admit him, which she refused to do. He then broke in a window, crawled into the house and unlocked the door. A truckman was at hand, and the property was carried off.

By this time Barieau returned, and he was wrathy. He saw a pistol which belonged to him in possession of Faris, and he told the officer that if he was present when he broke into the house the latter would have paid dearly for his raid.[15]

Rapidly wearing out his welcome in Sacramento, and not long after his only child, Edith, was born on October 3, 1895, Barieau moved his family to Stockton, about 50 miles south of Sacramento. Before the next year came to a close, he had again agitated local authorities. From the December 5, 1896 *Union:*

"Barieau's Bad Break, Likely to Lose His Saloon License over in Stockton."

[Barieau] not only didn't get his $3,000 from the Chinamen whose game he had beaten, but he was sold out of his saloon business, got into trouble with his creditors and had to leave the city. The Chinamen declared that Barieau's winning lottery ticket was the result of a conspiracy with someone in their employ, and having a strong pull with certain political managers, they stood pat on their refusal and caused Barieau to be deprived of some money making privileges he had been enjoying in connection with his saloon.

Lately, Barieau has been running a saloon over in Stockton, and now he is in trouble there. He interfered the other day to prevent the police from arresting a man in his place without producing a warrant, and now the chief of police has requested the city council to cancel Barieau's license.

Not long after that altercation, Barieau left California for Alaska, and then chased Lady Luck to Denver, Colorado, before moving to Nevada sometime in 1903. Settling in flourishing Goldfield, the gallivanting nomad forever in pursuit of the next big win found work as a faro dealer.[16] Somewhere between Alaska and Nye County, he befriended Volney Hoggatt—the man with whom he entered May Biggs' establishment the evening of April 6, 1906.

An attorney, promoter, and mine operator, Hoggatt was "big and broad of frame, paced with nervous energy that is at times disconcerting, and full of youthful enthusiasms that defy his years."[17]

Born in Ames, Iowa, in 1860, Hoggatt graduated from Iowa State College and taught at a Native American reservation before studying law in a South Dakota law firm. From there he drifted southward, where he served as the first Mayor of Guthrie, Oklahoma, from 1889 to 1895. Moving on to New Orleans, he befriended a lottery operator named Fred Bonfils, who would soon become one of the publishers of the *Denver Post*.

Years later, Bonfils would hire his longtime friend as a columnist, despite his revulsion to Hoggatt's compulsive habit of slipping his false teeth through his lips and barking like a dog.[18]

While in Texas, the jocular opportunist from Iowa fell in with Tex Rickard, a recently widowed cowpuncher and future world-renowned boxing promoter.[19] The two, along with Hoggatt's wife, joined the gold rush to Alaska in the late 1890s. There, working between Nome and Valdez, Hoggatt served as a U.S. district attorney and livened up the dreary-cold environment by founding the Ornery Men's Club* in Rickard's saloon, The Northern.

Volney Hoggatt, (2nd from right) in Valdez, AK, c. 1903 (Alaska State Library, Anchorage, AK)

---

* Established in 1900, the Ornery Men's Club membership grew to an astounding 400,000 nationwide by 1932, claiming within its ranks, besides Rickard, Senators Key Pittman, Huey Long, Lawrence Phipps, California Governor James Rolph, Oklahoma Governor "Alfalfa Bill" Murray, U.S. Vice President John Garner, the entire Anti-Saloon League, and Albert Pink, legal counsel for Al Capone.[20] Described by the Huntington, Pennsylvania, *Daily News* on April 30, 1932: *[The Club] welcomes all men who wear a watch chain across their vests with a peach seed carved in the shape of a basket and bearing a lover's bow knot across the middle. Likewise, the man who invariably shows off the wife's picture and says: "She's not much for looks but she's dependable."*

Besides the lure of Manhattan's resort district in the spring of 1906, any number of fast and furious mine deals were attracting world-class investors, such as: American steel magnate, Charles Schwab; longtime London Exploration Company mine inspector, E. E. Stuart; and Guggenheim's expert, W. W. Adams. The Great Silver Group, composed of San Francisco attorney, C.F. Humphrey, Goldfield businessman, C. F. Kapp, and Volney Hoggatt were in the process of purchasing several claims "involving a million dollars."[21] Actively engaged in the mining business in Bullfrog and Manhattan for at least a year, Hoggatt also helped organize the Manhattan Electric Light, Power and Telephone Company. [22 & 23]

Before pairing up for their fateful soirée to the Jewel, Hoggatt and Barieau may very well have first met in Alaska where Rickard, who had come to Nevada in 1903, now ran The Northern saloon in Goldfield. Old-timers would someday claim that "the greatest gambling plays ever witnessed on the desert" took place in that saloon — where bets as much as $10,000 could rest on the turn of a card. A 24-hour operation at its height, with eight bartenders and up to 24 dealers per shift, Rickard's establishment was probably affiliated with The Northern in Tonopah opened in 1904 by his friend Wyatt Earp.[24] A third Northern was established in Manhattan in 1905.

Gambling tables, from posh gaming parlors to drafty canvas tents, were prevalent throughout the region if not epidemic in proportion. Experienced dealers like Barieau had to have reveled in the heady extravagance of those ever-driven to compound whatever wealth they had accumulated. Yet, as time would tell, Barieau would lose more than he won.[25]

However huge, wide open, and unpopulated the West was in 1906, those in the mining and gambling circles tended to concentrate along the nearly 4,000-mile corridor between Nome and Goldfield. Clustered around the high-rollers were countless "accomplices" instrumental in their success. From Wingfield go-betweens like Daniel O'Brien to Walter Barieau, a self-professed bodyguard for Hoggatt, these obliging operatives occasionally thrived, but mostly scraped and scrapped until their dying day. For restless gamesters like Barieau, there was always another game, another town, or another person with long coattails and gilded prospects with whom to align. On April 6, 1906, for Barieau, those coattails belonged to Volney Hoggatt.

FATIGUED FROM THE preceding hours of carousing with Hoggatt and company, Walter Barieau wanted to sleep it off in the rear parlor of the Jewel. When May objected and urged him to leave, he grabbed hold of her wrists with such force that she buckled to one knee. Her sudden cry for help reached Tom's room.

Dressed in a blue silk nightshirt and unarmed, he hastened to the scene, and upon arrival, asked, "What is all this?"[26] May described what happened next:

I was sorry I had hollowed [sic]. In just a moment Mr. Logan come in.* He let go of my wrists. I picked up his hat, so then he got up like as if he was going to start. I was just a little ahead of him. I went right on. I thought he would go out. I went out the door and I put his hat on his head then he walked right out and turned around and reached on his side and he picked up his over coat. I was back of the door. Mr. Logan and I thought he was going to pull his gun. I cried, "He's going to shoot!" I started to run for the door. I heard the glass. I went to get Mr. Logan's gun, for Mr. Barieau had shot and I was afraid he would shoot someone. By this time he was a little off of the side walk down from the door. Jim come right in after me to get Mr. Logan's gun and I handed it to him. In just a second after Jim started out there were a couple more shots being fired.[27]

Minutes later, the tall man, who had collared countless rabble-rousers to keep the peace, would lie bleeding to death from five bullet wounds inflicted on him by a common gambler. Had Barieau not had a six-shooter handy, Sheriff Logan would not have fallen victim to what he had seen too frequently and wanted so much to prevent—a senseless death.

Just the week before, Tom had informed a representative of the *Manhattan Mail* that he and District Attorney William Pittman attributed most of the shooting affrays in the district to the rampant practice of carrying concealed weapons. They wanted the county commissioners to require a special permit to do so and, if violated, the offender would be jailed. As instilled in him so long ago by his father and re-enforced by years of law enforcement work, Tom emphasized to the *Mail* that "in a mix-up it's the man who has a gun in his pocket with no special purpose who gets into trouble and causes trouble for others." From the *Bonanza*:

When Logan outlined this policy he was on the right track. He met his death a week later because a man who had no business with a gun, carried one in his pocket. The fellow who carried the gun, and who now must answer for Tom Logan's life, is no doubt the sorriest man on earth and has wished from the depth of his heart that he had not carried a gun.[28]

---

* During his murder trial, Barieau claimed he had never met Sheriff Logan and did not know it was him coming to May's aid after she screamed.

LESS THAN TWELVE hours after Tom was pronounced dead at 8:10 a.m. on April 7, 1906, a coroner's jury of twelve men convened an inquest in the Manhattan justice court at 7 p.m. Justice J.K. Chambers presided, District Attorney William Pittman and Wayne Floweree appeared on behalf of the state, and Volney Hoggatt represented Barieau.[29] Mrs. Etta Hoffman transcribed the proceedings and would later reveal her frustration with Hoggatt for his frequent interruptions and being in a badly intoxicated state.[30]

The newly founded *Manhattan News* summarized witness statements in its evening edition on April 7, 1906, beneath a bold-lettered headline that read, "Sheriff Logan Most Cruelly Murdered:"

This morning the neighborhood in the vicinity of the Jewel, a house of ill fame, was awakened by [six] piercing shots, which rang out clear and loud on the morning breeze, followed by the screams of a woman. Upon arising the people in that vicinity witnessed a struggle between two men, both of whom were wet with human gore....

An eye witness states that the mortally wounded sheriff prevented a double tragedy in a manner that showed the temperament of the man who crossed the great divide. After (Jimmie) Bering got Logan's gun he returned and leveled it at the accused and would have pulled the trigger but for the sheriff who waved Bering away and told him not to shoot....

[Deputy] Scott Hickey testified to having arrived upon the scene of the shooting while Logan and the man under arrest accused of the murder were on the ground. Logan, he declared, was holding Barieau down on the ground, having hold of his hands, in which the latter grasped a revolver. Hickey told of having taken the gun from Barieau and arresting him. He testified that the accused stated he "would not take the worst of it."

Word of Sheriff Logan's death traveled like wild fire throughout the West. In Nye County, newspapers hurried to gather any detail about the incident and those involved. Deciphering fact from fiction or truth from rumor put editors to the test. The *Bonanza* described Barieau as a "low Creole gambler" and an "absinthe fiend" who at one time ran a roulette wheel in the Tonopah Club. He was also said to have attempted to clean out a saloon in Bullfrog the previous year with a dirk knife and might have succeeded if a Nome mining man named Dyer had not taken three shots at him:

Unfortunately, Dyer's aim was bad, or the low creature would have met his death at that time. He is known as a general all-around bad man and several weeks ago was chained to a tree in Manhattan by Officer Nofsinger, who had arrested him for drunkenness and disturbing the peace. There is no jail in Manhattan and there was nothing else to do with him."[31]

Eyewitness testimony from the coroner's hearing appear to be the most accurate and uninfluenced accounts of the shooting. At that hearing, Barieau made no plea and provided no statement. The first person to testify was Dr. George S. Von Wedelstaedt, one of the three doctors who had fought to save Tom's life. From Chicago, he is credited with being the earliest physician and surgeon to practice in Goldfield. Less than a year earlier, his office was among several lost to a devastating fire and he had only recently opened a practice in Manhattan.[32]

[District Attorney] William Pittman: *You were called to attend Mr. Logan?*

Dr. George S. Von Wedelstaedt: *Yes, I was called early this morning to attend Mr. Logan, along about six forty five.*

Pittman: *Where did you find Mr. Logan?*

Von Wedelstaedt: *I found him at the Jewel.*

Pittman: *What was the result of your call?*

Von Wedelstaedt: *I found that he had been shot several times, and that he was suffering with gunshot wounds.*

Pittman: *Just state what wounds you found.*

Von Wedelstaedt: *One shot struck the right cheek bone, glanced and emerged about three inches below the entrance; I found another about three inches below the middle of the collar bone about three or four inches below to the right of the right nipple; I found another which penetrated about four inches below the head of the right femur on the outer side and emerging a little below the groin; the fourth shot entered about the middle third of the left thigh; the fifth sound was similarly located on the right side of the leg.*

Pittman: *Did you extract any bullets?*

Von Wedelstaedt: *No, sir, I did not.*

Pittman: *Were you present during the autopsy?*

Von Wedelstaedt: *I was.*

Pittman: *Will you please state what was the cause of Mr. Logan's death.*

(Defense counsel] Volney Hoggatt: *I object to that question because he is not asked a question about the man's qualification.*

[Justice of the Peace) J. K. Chambers: *I overrule the objection.*

Von Wedelstaedt: *Mr. Logan died from a hemorrhage.*

Pittman: *What caused the hemorrhage?*

Von Wedelstaedt: *The hemorrhage was caused by the severing of the superficial femoral artery.*

Pittman: *What caused the severing of that artery?*

Von Wedelstaedt: *From the appearances, it was produced by a gun bullet.*

Pittman: *What makes you think it was a gunshot wound?*

Hoggatt: *I object to that question.*

Chambers: *I overrule the objection.*

Von Wedelstaedt: *From its appearance.*

Pittman: *Were you present?*

Von Wedelstaedt: *I was present.*

Pittman: *About what time did he die?*

Von Wedelstaedt: *He died about eight ten this morning.*[33]

Next to testify was Pauline Leslie, who stated she had been living at the Jewel for about six weeks and was in the backyard when she heard the gunfire. Upon rounding the corner of the house, she saw Sheriff Logan on the ground with two other men. He was in his night shirt and bleeding. When Pittman asked Pauline if she had heard any remarks between Barieau and anyone else, she replied: "I did not hear anything. (Barieau) was in another room and I could not hear any words at all. We were all tired and it was late."

[Justice of the Peace] J. K. Chambers: *At any time did you see a pistol in Mr. Logan's hands?*

Pauline Leslie: *No, sir, I did not.*

Chambers: *Would you have seen one if he had?*

Pauline: *Yes, sir.*

Chambers: *Were you in a position so you could see?*

Pauline: *Yes, sir, I was.*

[Defense counsel] Volney Hoggatt: *When did you see this trouble?*

Pauline: *I saw this trouble after the shots were fired.*

Hoggatt: *In what position was Mr. Logan when you saw him?*

Pauline: *Mr. Logan was leaning over.*

Hoggatt: *Who was on top?*

Pauline: *Mr. Logan was leaning over the defendant. The piano player was down on his knees. They were in a scuffle over the revolver.*

Hoggatt: *When you saw that difficulty where was Mr. Logan?*

Pauline: *Mr. Logan was on top of him, that he was bending over him.*

Hoggatt: *Do you know the piano player?*

Pauline: *Yes, sir.*

Hoggatt: *Did you see him?*

Pauline: *YES, SIR.*

Hoggatt: *Did he have a gun?*

Pauline: *I do not know?*

[District Attorney] Pittman: *When?*

Hoggatt: *That night?*

Pauline: *I did not see the piano player have any gun.*

Hoggatt: *What was he doing?*

Pauline: *He was helping Mr. Logan, he was assisting Mr. Logan. Mr. Logan was bending over this man. I saw the piano player and when I first saw him he was down on his knees. The three men were down on the ground. They seemed to be scuffling, as far as I can see, the defendant was underneath and Mr. Logan was on top.*

Hoggatt: *What was the piano player doing when you saw him?*

Pauline: *He was trying to take the gun out of the defendant's hands.*

Hoggatt: *Where was Mr. Barieau during this time?*

Pauline: *He was between those two.*

Hoggatt: *Was the piano player trying to take the gun away from the defendant?*

Pauline: *From what I could see.*

Hoggatt: *Are you positive this is right?*

Pauline: *From where I was standing, I could not see very well, but it was an automatic gun.*

Hoggatt: *Where did you first learn about an automatic gun?*

Pauline: *I know them when I see them.*[34]

Despite several other attempts, Hoggatt failed to erode Pauline's recollection as to who was holding the pistol when she saw Logan and Barieau on the ground. Vivian Carlton next shared her version of events:

Vivian Carlton: *I had gone to my room and in about half an hour, I heard Miss May trying to get someone out of the hall. She asked him several times to go. Pretty soon, I heard her hollow [sic]. In a little while there seemed to be trouble. May hollowed [sic], "Help." I ran out. A revolver went off four or five times. I saw Mr. Logan, he was on top and there was blood all over him.*[35]

Vivian also told the court that she did not see a gun in Logan's hands. Jewel boarder, Daniel O'Brien, agreed with her:

Daniel O'Brien: *Well, I heard Miss Biggs trying to coax him to go for about fifteen or twenty minutes. He did not seem to want to. Finally, I think in some way he had got hold of her for she gave a yell, right after that I heard a little scuffling in the hall. That was all there was of it for a minute or so, then I heard a shot. Then right after that, I heard four more shots coming quickly. They commenced to hollow [sic]. I jumped up and looked out the window and saw one man on top of the other. I ran out and Mr. Logan was over on top of this other man. Jimmie was pounding him over the head with a gun. I told him to stop. Someone took the gun away from Jimmie and I took hold of Mr. Logan and started to pack him into the house and Scott Hickey took the other man… There was blood all over the place.*[36]

Hoggatt's determination to extricate his client from any criminal wrongdoing required he argue a case of self-defense. That intent was implicit in his examination of piano player, Jimmie Bering:

(District Attorney) William Pittman: *Please state your knowledge of what you saw and heard.*

Jimmie Bering: *As soon as he got in the street, he reached in his pocket for his gun. Mr. Logan said, "Don't pull that gun." The man started to pull the gun and Mr. Logan and I both started for the man. At the first shot, I ran in the house and Mr. Logan ran toward the man. There were four or five more shots fired while I was in the house. When I come out, this man was on the ground and Mr. Logan on top of him.*

Pittman: *What did you do then?*

Jimmie: *I come with Mr. Logan's gun. I saw Mr. Logan covered in blood. I was excited. I thought he was going to die right then. I was going to shoot [Barieau]. Mr. Logan said, "Don't shoot him." I let the hammer down on the gun and tried to get the gun away from Mr. Barieau. Just then I struck Mr. Barieau in the head.*

Pittman: *What did you do?*

Jimmie: *Hickey come right then and took the weapon away from this gentleman and I run for the doctor.*

[Defense counsel] Volney Hoggatt: *Mr. Logan was pushing and shoving Mr. Barieau out of the house?*

Jimmie: *Yes, sir, out of the front door.*

Hoggatt: *Where did you get this gun?*

Jimmie: *May Biggs handed the gun to me.*

Hoggatt: *When and where?*

Jimmie: *In the front bedroom, right after the first shot.*

Hoggatt: *That was before anybody was shot?*

Jimmie: *That was after the first shot.*

Hoggatt: *Where was the first shot fired?*

Jimmie: *The first shot was fired from the street at the door. I had to cross over the hall-way into the room where Miss Biggs was to get the gun.*[37]

Besides Jimmie, the star witness for the state was May Biggs—admittedly a woman of questionable reputation and, being intimately involved with Logan, perhaps lacking reliable objectivity. Determined to discredit May, Hoggatt zealously sought to expose inconsistencies in her testimony:

[Defense counsel] Volney Hoggatt: *And after you went and talked with Walter and he said he wanted to stay till daylight and then after he did not go you went and told Mr. Logan that you could not get him out?*

May Biggs: *I did not. I did not go out of the back parlor until I preceded him to the door....*

Hoggatt: *What did Mr. Logan ask you?*

May: *Well, I don't remember. I do not remember what was being done. This gentleman would not go. I took his hat and started for the door. He got up and sort of started. There was some conversation. I was out in the hall.*

Hoggatt: *Do you mean to say that Logan did not say anything to the defendant. I just want to know the facts. Were you there through all the difficulty?*

May: *I was right in the house.*

Hoggatt: *Where did the shooting occur?*

May: *Well, the gentleman who did the shooting was outside of the door.*

Hoggatt: *Did you see him reach for his gun?*

May: *Yes, I saw him reach for his gun. He just backed off the sidewalk and backed up about two steps. Then when I saw the gun, I said, "He is going to shoot." I started and ran into the front parlor. This parlor coming into the house is on the left hand side, as I come into the house, he went through the front door.*

Hoggatt: *Who hit Mr. Barieau over the head?*

May: *The piano player hit him three or four times.*

Hoggatt: *What caused him, the piano player, to hit him over the head?*

May: *I do not know what caused him to do it. He had been shooting then he began beating him. He had a gun in his hand. I suppose it was the same gun he had been shooting.*

Hoggatt: *When did they do this beating of the defendant over the head?*

[District Attorney] William Pittman: *Do not use the word "they."*

Hoggatt: *When did this beating commence?*

May: *The first I saw was when Jimmie took the gun and run out after him. I did not see when Mr. Logan was down on the ground. When Jimmie ran out, I thought he was going to shoot. I ran right out when I did not hear any shot. I said, "They are shooting Logan."*

Hoggatt: *Listen to this question: Did Mr. Barieau commence shooting before or after he was hit by someone?*

May: *I never saw him hit by anyone.*

Hoggatt: *Then he commenced shooting before anyone hit him?*

May: *That was before I saw anybody hit him. When Jimmie hit him he did it with the gun I had given him.*

Hoggatt: *Where did you get the gun?*

May: *I ran in and got the gun for the piano player and told him to give it to Mr. Logan and I give the gun to the piano player. He had shot once through the glass door then.*

Hoggatt: *Who was he shooting at?*

May: *I saw him pull the gun. Mr. Logan was right there in the front door and the shot went through the glass door.*

Hoggatt: *Well now, we have got along in this testimony, this far only you wanted to close up. Were you personally present at the time or until after he had got out of the door and you called Mr. Logan the sheriff and told him this man would not go out?*

May: *No, sir. I did not, for I did not expect to have to call anyone….*[38]

Question after question, answer after answer, Hoggatt endeavored to stir up any flaw or discrepancy glaring enough to collapse the seemingly iron-clad conclusion that his client was guilty of cold-blooded murder. Had Walter Barieau acted in self-defense, or had he simply and thoughtlessly retaliated against someone who had rankled his bad side? Or perhaps, as some believe, had Barieau lingered at the Jewel trying to muster the gumption to do what he had been sent to do—kill Tom Logan?

Regardless of why Barieau fired five bullets into a man backing away from him, the enormous consequences of his actions began to consume him, one raw nerve at a time:

"Barieau Falls Into Fit:" And while the testimony rolled from the lips of witnesses, and while the gruesome story chilled the hearts of those who heard, Walter Barieau, sitting under the shadow of the gallows, writhed and twisted in a very agony of penitence. Frothing at the mouth like a wild animal, eyes rolling in frenzy, limbs stiff, and stark with the fright that was within him, Barieau with a wild, inarticulate cry fell to the floor in a fit.

The dignity of the court was forgotten, the awful solemnity of the moment unheeded, and in a few minutes the room was ringing with the cries of horror-stricken, sickened men and women, who morbidity jostled each other to witness the poor wretch roll in agony.

In a few minutes, however, Barieau revived, but his twitching limbs and twisted features gave witness to the horror and contrition which bore down his very soul.[39]

As the second day of the coroner's inquest drew to a close, Justice Chambers reminded Hoggatt that his client had the right to make any statement of facts or circumstances regarding the case, and could also bring in his own witnesses. They declined.[40]

Pittman and Chambers sought to, once and for all, solidify the foundation upon which the jury could confidently indict Barieau for the "unlawful, felonious, willful, and deliberate" murder of another human being.[41] Again, they questioned May:

Pittman: *You said in your cross examination when Jimmie had the gun that Mr. Logan told him not to shoot.*

May: *Mr. Logan said, "Don't." That was when I give Jimmie the gun and Mr. Logan was right there. He was stooping over. He was just backing up and Jimmie had begun beating him, that is the defendant.*

Pittman: *Did Mr. Logan say anything after he was shot?*

May: *All the shots had been fired and Mr. Logan said, "Don't." When I run out all three of them were down and Mr. Logan was on him.*

Chambers: *From what you call the back parlor, how far is it to this room where Mr. Logan was?*

May: *I was in the back parlor with this gentleman. I expect twenty or thirty or forty feet, perhaps forty feet. Each room is twelve feet.*

Chambers: *Is there a hall between the rooms?*

May: *Yes, sir.*

Chambers: *There are rooms on either side of the hallway?*

May: *Yes, sir.*

Chambers: *Well, now after the gentleman got up to go out you walked the hallway ahead of them?*

May: *Yes, sir, I did.*

Chambers: *Were these parties scuffling or doing anything?*

May: *Once I looked around and they seemed to be all right. I was glad he was coming out and not saying anything more.*

Chambers: *Do you know if Mr. Logan was saying anything to him?*

May: *I do not remember any talking taking place at all.*

Chambers: *When he got to the door, what did Mr. Logan do?*

May: *When this gentleman got to the door, I handed him his hat and he went out peaceable.*

Chambers: *What occasion was there for Mr. Logan to go out of the door?*

May: *The object was to get this man out of the house. Then I saw how things were. I said, "Come on, he is going to shoot."*

Chambers: *How far from the door was he when he shot?*

May: *I should think about ten feet from the door.*

Chambers: *Was he on the porch?*

May: *No, he was not on the porch. Mr. Logan was in the door standing a little inside.*

Chambers: *Is that the time the first shot was fired?*

May: *Yes, sir.*

Chambers: *I understand you to testify that this door was a glass door and that the shot went through the door and wall into another room?*

May: *Yes, sir.*

Chambers: *This happened at the time Mr. Logan was in the door?*

May: *Yes, Mr. Logan was in the hall door.*

Chambers: *Then did Mr. Logan try to get a pistol?*

May: *He ran right out of the house.*

Chambers: *I want to ask you this and I want you to be positive. Are you sure at this time that Mr. Logan did not have a pistol?*

May: *No, sir, he did not have a gun.*

Chambers: *Where was his pistol at this time?*

May: *It was in the room in what he carries it in.*

Chambers: *I understand you to say that you told this boy to get Mr. Logan's pistol?*

May: *I told Jimmie to get it and to give it to me as I knew he did not have a gun.*

Chambers: *You told him to go and get that pistol?*

May: *I ran to get Mr. Logan's gun. This gentleman had already shot.*

Hoggatt: *How did you know?*

May: *Because I will tell you he was sleeping with me and he was in the room before I was in bed. I was not undressed.*

Hoggatt: *What objective did the deceased have on going out?*

Pittman: *She has already answered that question about twelve times. She has told the facts.*

May: *He went out like an officer would.*[42]

A Tribute to Our Martyr of Duty

Half mast, tenderly, the colors of my country
To caress the bier that bears his blest repose,
The form of him, who in Nevada's service

Has purchased new adornment with the close of life.
The jewel rare he places shall glittering shine
Her fair, white brow above;
So wreath your folds in waves of matchless beauty.
Nevada's offering in immortelles of love.

Ambition waved before him her rainbow pennon,
Strength clothed his form in power sublime;
Hope showed the future fields where awaited glory
With crown and sceptre to be his in time.
Love drew a veil o'er all his high advantage
And pointed where the dueling gamblers stay.

While honor breathed the awful words "The Duty,"
His warlike soul responded "I obey."
To check the feud that o'er pelf is started;
And in the struggle, the shots that went astray
In his attempt to quiet the rough gamblers.
He bleeding, fell and breathed his life away.

Come, soldier, ye who trod the fatal field,
With hardly any worry, grief or fear;
Come, poet, ye who drink from inspiration,
A theme like this has power the soul to cheer;
Come statesman, ye who lives a life so nobly;

Come, youth, in search of pattern for the man;
Leave slaughtered self in resolution holy,
Here the bier of Sheriff Thomas W. Logan.

—Jay Cole, *Tonopah Sun*, April 9, 1906

12

BENEATH SMILING FLOWERS: APRIL–JUNE 1906

Yet, [death] is not a final parting. The Fraternal Order of Eagles teaches that we shall meet again, and that the tender associations of life are broken only to be reunited. Whether we look into the living eyes of those we love or gaze upon the placid faces of our dead, love divine comforts us with the blessed assurance that this relation is eternal.

An excerpt from "The Final Tribute to Deceased Members
of the Local Aeries of The Fraternal Order of Eagles"

HANNAH LOGAN'S WORST fears had come true. Her seemingly indestructible husband had provoked fate one too many times and though reeling with grief, she was likely not surprised that some moth-eaten soul had killed her husband.

A messenger was sent to deliver the horrifying news to Hannah in Belmont. Once in town, he hemmed and hawed, trying to build the courage to find the sheriff's wife but chose instead to tell others and then hurried on his way. When word did reach Hannah, she immediately hitched up the buckboard and "was holding up real well," wrote one of her granddaughters in 1985, "until she went past one house where the woman came running out and said, 'Oh, Mrs. Logan, oh, Mrs. Logan…' and Gram went into pieces."[1]

Making her way over the long, rutted road to Tonopah, Hannah probably knew very little about the circumstances surrounding Tom's death. Whether traveling alone or with a consoling companion, she at least had those few hours to dwell in a merciful state of anguished bliss unencumbered by the scandal about to erupt.

On this darkest of days, Hannah Mariah Hamblin Logan became a widow and the new family provider. Tom did not have a will, and the deluge of responsibilities tumbling her way may have been so overpowering she had scant time to fret or panic. There was family to notify, a funeral to plan, business matters to sort, and sobbing children to comfort—three of whom, enveloped by sadness, would soon board a train in Oakland, California, to come home for the most devastating reason imaginable: Papa was dead.

Decades later, Tom's daughter Hazel told her daughter, Fern, about the last time she saw her father. He had just climbed into his buggy and was about to drive away when an overwhelming sense of dread invaded her heart – a forewarning that she would never see him again. Hazel, age 14, begged him not to go but he promised he would be back soon. Inconsolable, she ran alongside the buggy until she lost her breath, had to stop, and could only watch him through her tears fade out of sight. "His death," Fern said, "was a psychic shock to the family."[2]

THE WESTERN UNION TELEGRAPH COMPANY.
INCORPORATED
23,000 OFFICES IN AMERICA.   CABLE SERVICE TO ALL THE WORLD.

This Company TRANSMITS and DELIVERS messages only on conditions limiting its liability, which have been assented to by the sender of the following message. Errors can be guarded against only by repeating a message back to the sending station for comparison, and the Company will not hold itself liable for errors or delays in transmission or delivery of Unrepeated Messages, beyond the amount of tolls paid thereon, nor in any case where the claim is not presented in writing within sixty days after the message is filed with the Company for transmission.
This is an UNREPEATED MESSAGE, and is delivered by request of the sender, under the conditions named above.
ROBERT C. CLOWRY, President and General Manager.

NUMBER	SENT BY	REC'D BY		CHECK

RECEIVED at *Big pine Cal* __4/7__ 190 6

Dated *Tonopah Nev.* 4/7

To *Frank Logan*
Big pine, Cal.
Come at once Tom has just died
Sig. Geo. Logan

"Come at once – Tom has just died." Telegram sent by George Logan to brother
Frank living in Big Pine, CA (Logan Family Collection)

"[Sheriff Logan] was a person of quiet disposition and had made a strong peace officer," *wrote* the *Gazette*. "He had figured in several shooting escapades but had always acquitted himself honorably in the discharge of his duties. His death has occasioned universal regret."[3] The entire front page of the *Sun's* April 7, 1906, evening edition was dedicated to the torrent of information inundating Nye County about the senseless death of their sheriff. The following tribute appeared on the editorial page:

Hazel Margaret Logan,
c. 1910
(Logan Family Collection)

THOMAS W. LOGAN

A brave man has been laid low in the performance of his duty. All Nye County mourns over the loss of one who was universally loved for his loveable traits and the greatest of those being his bravery.

Thomas W. Logan was a naturally constituted man for the office he held. He was without braggadocio. He never talked of his bravery or threatened. He merely performed his duty as it came to him to do and did it with conscientiousness and mere as a matter of course.

When the most dangerous men were in the act of committing their crimes, instead of girding himself with weapons for a street parade and doing what some sheriffs do to attract attention, Tom Logan was a one of the quietest men in the whole camp and always did his duty quietly and well. He would look down the barrel of a loaded gun without a quiver and he never thought anything of it.

As another side of Logan's character, he was absolutely honest and honorable. He had no insatiate love for money, and ill-gotten money to him was so repulsive that his worst enemy never would have accused him of touching it. He was an honest man because it was born in him. He had no more desire or temptation to be otherwise than he had to know what fear was.

A model sheriff, a good citizen, Sheriff Logan was a man who was a benefit to the world in which he lived.

"Martyr to Duty" [upper right illustration is an inaccurate image of how Logan was killed] (*Tonopah Daily Sun*, April 7, 1906, Arthur V. Buel, Editorial Artist)

Talk of a lynching rippled through the community as citizens voiced their objections against the noxious scourge of the gambling element.[4] A joint letter from a host of prominent citizens, including Jim Butler and Tex Rickard, was sent to the *Sun* deploring the cold-blooded killing of Sheriff Logan and expressing their trust that "swift justice be meted out to the perpetrator."[5]

Two days after the killing, sheriff deputies Hickey and Nofsinger procured an automobile and, taking a less traveled route between Manhattan and Tonopah, drove Barieau at top speed to the new courthouse. They reported that Bareiau had settled down considerably. He didn't talk about anything but his injuries and seemed unconcerned about both his awful deed and what the law may have in store for him.[6]

The night before Barieau was jailed in Tonopah, Sheriff Logan's bullet-riddled body had been brought to Undertaker Wonacott's establishment where it would lie in state. From the *Sun*, April 9, 1906:

All day long weeping women and sad-eyed men snatched a moment from the busy rush to stand mourning at the still form of the man they knew and loved.

Over the coffin a profusion of bright flowers were heaped, and the calm face beneath seemed to have caught something of the spirit of rest and peace. The expression on the still features is one of quiet and content, making the onlooker wonder and stand awe-stricken in the presence of death.

Heaps of Flowers: Hour by hour the fragrant heap grew as men, women and even children added their tokens to the bright flowers that told of the grasp Logan held on the hearts of his fellows.

On the streets men ceased their talk and stood in sympathetic silence as the tall brother [probably George]…leading the sorrow-laden woman who was his wife. With them trailed [the children], the [youngest] hardly large enough to realize the awful blow that had fallen upon the family, and wide-eyed the little tots looked into the faces of their elders, and reading grief and sorrow there, wondered what it all meant.

On the dome of the courthouse, the national emblem drooped at half-mast, as it did since the sad message came from Manhattan. In the county offices, what work the business of the people required was done with half-hearted energy, for the men who serve the county thought of their dead co-worker and the grief-stricken family.

Through the night solemn watch was kept beside the bier and thus guarded the body that will lie until the time comes for its return to earth."

When Tom was killed, his brother, Frank, was living in Big Pine, California, with his wife, Georgiana. Frank hastened to Tonopah and, upon his arrival, asked one of Georgiana's resident cousins to write home with the latest news:

"Remains of Sheriff in State—Murderer in County Jail" (*Tonopah Daily Sun*, April 9, 1906, Arthur V. Buel, Editorial Artist)

My Dear Georgie: Frank asked me to write you a few lines to let you know how they are all getting along. They are quite well considering all they have gone thru and bear up real well thru their dreadful sorrow. Mr. Logan looks real natural and is keeping lovely…Think he will have a lovely funeral as there are large preparations being made.

Oh! Georgie Dearest you cannot imagine how I sympathize with you all and how my heart aches for you one and all. If I could only comfort you in some way but my words fail me here but I feel that they all know how I sympathize with them for I take their trouble as if it were someone belonging to me.[7]

IRONICALLY, TOM LOGAN died the day after the first anniversary of Deputy Harry Mannon's death. Interspersed with news related to Tom's funeral were updates on the new inmate at the county jail. Rumors rumbled for days about various schemes to extract the prisoner and "execute summary vengeance," but no such event materialized. In another twist of irony, Tom's brother, Deputy George Logan, was the jail supervisor, although it is not known whether or not he had any contact with Barieau. Heavily guarded with restricted access, the accused was again described by the *Sun* four days after the murder as "cool and unconcerned:"

Only once since he was brought in from Manhattan, since his collapse in the courtroom of his preliminary hearing, has he shown any sign of emotion, say the men who guard him.

That single exception to his calm assurance was when his sorrowing wife flung herself against the bars and wept bitterly yesterday evening. Then, and only then, did this man of iron give way to his feelings, and the tears sprang to his eyes as he looked on his dear ones.

Of his trouble Barieau will not talk, but on any other subject he is very voluble....“For one entire winter I wandered about the wilds of Alaska, and in that time I saw almost every part of that country. I went there in 1898. During my stay I suppose I experienced about every hardship that the prospector knows. It is no country for a man to stay in. For fully nine months out of the year there is nothing that one can do but eat and sleep and occasionally go hunting.

“It was nearly two and a half years ago that I first came to this country when the Gold- field excitement started. Ever since then my family has lived there....I have nothing to make public now, the whole thing will come out at the time of the trial.” [8]

Barieau further confided to the *Sun* that he had not asked for local counsel but expected his wife, Margaret, to secure an attorney from Goldfield or Bullfrog, likely referring to Volney Hoggatt.

The day before the shooting, Margaret Barieau had received a letter from her husband informing her that he had secured a cottage for them in Manhattan, had a job at the Monarch saloon, and wanted her to come at once. According to the *Goldfield Daily Sun,* Barieau was a former employee at The Northern saloon in Goldfield and:

It was understood that he was a bad man with a gun, but as he had never shot anybody the probability is that he was more bluff than anything else. One who had known him for years asserted this morning that he was never known to harm a man, notwithstanding the fact that he was at times a heavy drinker and very loud of lung and there it ended. [9]

WALTER BERIEAU, MURDERER OF SHERIFF LOGAN, IN HIS CELL.

"Walter Barieau, murderer of Sheriff Logan, in his Cell"
(*Tonopah Daily Sun*, April 10, 1906, Arthur V. Buel, Editorial Artist)

The *Goldfield Sun* sent a reporter to Mrs. Barieau's house on Tuesday, April 10, 1906. In response to his knock on the door:

…a sweet-faced little girl of eleven years opened it and at the same time the heartbroken mother appeared, her eyes inflamed and still sobbing over the predicament of her husband.

The reporter was pleasantly received and she showed a willingness to be interviewed. Asked as to whether she had employed counsel to defend her husband, she replied that Judge Hoggatt of Manhattan had been the only counsel he retained.

Of course she laid all of the blame upon the sheriff, who, she claimed, had pounded the head of her husband with a gun until he was half crazed and in this frame shot to defend himself.

She is a frail appearing little blonde woman, modest demeanor and bears strong evidence of having been well and respectably reared.

The home is on the corner of Fourth and Myers Street, one of the neatest little residences in the city and very neatly furnished.

"I am going back to Tonopah in the morning," she said, "for I must be near Walt. I want to be where I can see him every day."[10]

Ironically, despite Volney Hoggatt's erstwhile readiness to represent Barieau at the coroner's hearing, he would not reappear in any further proceedings. What distanced him from the case is anyone's guess. That mystery would only deepen when, at trial time, Hoggatt would be the only subpoenaed witness Deputy Hickey reported could not be found in Nye County.[11]

Based on a series of accounts published by newspapers from Sacramento to Manhattan, the longer Barieau was confined to his cell, the more unbalanced he became. The most graphic description of his episodic insanity appeared in the *Gazette*, "Logan Slayer May be Insane," April 17, 1906:

Tonopah, Nev., April 17 — Unless he is a rare actor and is feigning insanity in a manner so real that he is able to completely deceive the county physician, Walter Barieau, the gambler that shot and killed Sheriff Tom Logan, is crazy. For several days he has evinced every symptom of a deranged mind. He has refused food for several days and the jail authorities say the man is terribly worn.

At times he is troubled with fancied swarms of flies and insects of all sorts, which he pictures circling about him, and again he imagines that he is covered with a myriad of crawling ants, and springing from his bed, will grovel on the floor in his efforts to rid himself of them.

At other times he pleads with the keepers to allow him to go out for a moment as he has an important engagement that he must keep and he is constantly complaining that his tongue is bothering him, that it has fallen out of his mouth, and that he cannot find it.

Even in the presence of his wife his wild actions continue, and it has been necessary to keep a man in the cell with him at night, and even to tie him down to prevent his injuring himself in his staggering rambles about the cells.

Beats His Head On Bars: Several times he has flung himself against the walls and bars with such force that he was stunned for some time afterward, and his eyes glow like live coals in his head. The men who watch him are feeling the strain and they are convinced that the confinement and morbid reflections, coupled with his enforced abstinence from some drug to the use of which he had been accustomed, has completely upset his mind. They say that his talk, when he talks at all, is wild and disjointed, and that he is so weak from his ravings that he is hardly able to carry himself erect.

Dr. Cunningham, county health officer, was called to look at the man this morning, but he was very noncommittal on the subject, merely saying Barieau is a very sick man....People who knew him in other camps say that Barieau has always been a little deranged, and are certain that the man is not faking."

What possible explanation might there have been for Barieau's frantic behavior? Was he tormented by regret and images of a hangman's noose when he closed his eyes at night? Was he an alcoholic suffering through fits of withdrawal? Did he feel justified in defending himself against a man he thought was about to kill him but thought no one would ever believe him? Had he purposefully lingered at the Jewel waiting for an opportunity to kill Logan and, now, was about to take the fall for whomever had employed him? Regardless of what made him open fire on Tom Logan, Walter Barieau was a tortured man caught in the excruciating throes of contemplating life in prison or, even worse, the end of his own life.

AS PREPARATIONS NEARED completion for Sheriff Logan's funeral, the magnitude of his loss ebbed and flowed in downcast conversations throughout the region. An associate in Manhattan related how the sheriff was planning to travel to Carson City the end of the month "for the purpose of purchasing a home for his family so that his children might have the benefit of the educational opportunities in that city."[12] In Esmeralda County, where nearly 30,000 people now lived in Goldfield, the *Goldfield Review* reiterated his immense popularity "with the masses and in the elective line could have had anything he wanted."[13] The *Bonanza* summarized:

He believed that public office is a public trust and not a private snap, and it was his aim and endeavor at all times to serve the people of the county faithfully and honestly. Though big-hearted and gentle in his ways, he knew not the meaning of the word fear. He was a firm believer in justice and right and was always a friend of the poor and oppressed. Many a story of some kindly act, some charitable deed performed by Tom Logan, has been told during the past few days, with a tear in the eye of he who told it.[14]

Carriages with family and friends, funeral of Sheriff Logan, April 12, 1906,
Photo by H. T. Shaw, Tonopah, NV (Logan Family Collection)

Every mine in the district ceased operation during Tom Logan's funeral on April
12, 1906. Flags flew at half-mast. Colorful sprays of flowers arrived by train.
Schools were closed so children could join the crowds lining Main and
Brougher Streets to watch the long procession slowly pass by. A stray dog or
two wandered freely in and out of the scene. Tears welled, and the sun, riding
high in the clear blue sky, seemed to cast shadows that were longer than usual
the day Sheriff Logan was buried.

The funeral may have very well been the largest such event in the history of
Nevada to that date and was thoughtfully chronicled on April 14 by the *Bonanza*:

*All that was mortal of the brave Thomas W. Logan was laid to rest in the Tonopah
cemetery in the presence of thousands of mourning friends.*

*The body had lain in state in the Opera House from an early hour Thursday forenoon,
and sorrowing friends took advantage of the opportunity to place floral tributes about
the bier.*

*Long before the house set for the funeral services, the big hall was filled to overflowing
and those who could not gain admittance thronged the nearby streets.*

The services were very impressive, the Odd Fellows having charge. Noble Grand, C. G. Hansen, Vice-Grand John White, Deputy District Grand Master George Swasey, Warden R.B. Davis and Conductor W.W. Stuck officiated. A quartette composed of Mrs. William Grimes, Mrs. Wylie, Dr. Victors and King, rendered sweet sacred music.

C.H. McIntosh delivered an address that was couched in appropriate language, and his many touching allusions to the noble manly qualities of the dead sheriff brought tears to the eyes of his hearers.

At the conclusion of the services, the procession was formed, led by the Tonopah band and moved down Brougher Avenue to Main Street and thence to the cemetery. The casket rested on the hook and ladder truck and the fire department with Chief Jack McKenzie at its head acted as a guard of honor. The pall-bearers were R. F. Gilbert, W. J. Sinclair, and W. J. Douglas, representing the Odd Fellows, and George Cole, Curley Graham and Bob Govan, representing the Eagles.

Upon the cortege reaching the little plot in the cemetery, which is to the last resting place of the beloved Tom Logan, Tonopah Aerie of Eagles assumed charge and conducted the final ceremonies. Judge Sawle, President of the Aerie, Chaplain Walker and the other officers of the aerie read the impressive funeral service of the order in the presence of thousands of sympathizing friends, who stood with heads bared and tears in their eyes.

The funeral cortege was one of the longest ever seen in Tonopah or, as a matter of fact, in Nevada. Business was at a standstill, every store and every office closing their doors as a mark of respect to the dead official, who had done more than any other man to give Tonopah the proud distinction of being the most peaceable, law abiding mining camp on the face of the earth.

Tom Logan was a faithful public servant. He had the interests of Nye County at heart at all times and died a martyr to duty. May he rest in peace."

Tom Logan's "wilderness of smiling flowers" upon his grave, April 12, 1906, Tonopah, NV (Courtesy of the Clara Logan Smith Family)

The day after the funeral, the *Sun* paid final homage to the man who had figured so prominently into the growth and development of their community:

A Tribute to Law and Order

It speaks well for the spirit of law and order in a new mining camp like this for such a tribute of respect to be paid to a dead peace officer as the out-pouring of the multitude do honor to the memory of the late Sheriff Logan. First in the thoughts of the people is respect to the office which is made vacant by the quick hand of death. Frontier fiction might tell the eastern mind that in a city situated as Tonopah is, there would be no veneration for the office of the man who preserves peace. The demonstration of yesterday was a contradiction of that false notion. It was proof that the people love peace and they love the man who, like Logan, preserves the peace by peaceable methods.

Tom Logan in his individual capacity commanded friendship. As sheriff he was more to the people than the individual. The official and the personality in this case were happily blended. To lose both, the loss of Tonopah and Nye County has been doubled.[15]

PERHAPS NOTHING BETTER symbolized the massive sea-change underway for Hannah Logan than did her signature on a court document accepting duties as Administratrix of the Thomas W. Logan estate on May 8, 1906. Writing first *Mrs. Thomas W. Logan*, that name was crossed out so she could rewrite *Hannah M. Logan*. At the age of 46 and mother of six minor children, the youngest being just three years old, she was on her own and confided in close friends that she wanted to stay at Smoky Valley. In that endeavor, the husband who could fill a doorway would soon struggle to occupy even the most remote corner of Hannah's aching heart.

Estimated by the *Sun* to be a man of considerable means, Tom owned several claims in various mining districts as well as interest in The American saloon.[16] Logan probate records indicate Hannah also had a residence in Tonopah on the northwest corner of St. Patrick and Tonopah Streets just below the courthouse. A onetime convenient residence for the sheriff, it was now equally well-situated for Hannah, considering the arduous legal task of unraveling her late husband's business affairs, outstanding debts, and any legal proceedings underway that involved Tom. The tedious and grueling course ahead would take several months, but Hannah's remarkable stamina once again confirmed her measure as a woman of principle and fortitude.[17]

Precisely what financial commitments and assets were known to her prior to his death, and what she was about to discover, cannot be fully distinguished.

Hannah first succeeded in gaining court approval to collect a monthly support allowance of $200 from the estate. George Swasey and George Logan posted bonds totaling $1,000 on behalf of Hannah, who initially estimated the Logan estate to be worth about $5,000. H. H. Bacon, Robert Govan, and County Treasurer Robert Gilbert were subsequently appointed to appraise all property and calculated that figure to actually be $13,200* That inventory included: two town lots in Tonopah ($2,200), mining claims primarily in the Manhattan and Golden Mining Districts ($7,200), mining stocks ($1,335), and cash and personal property totaling $1,300. A valuation of nearly $2,000 was given to fixtures, liquor, and cigar stock from The American.

The following summary provides an evocative glimpse inside the operation of that establishment.

Personal Property Situate at American Saloon: Bar and Back Bar-$500, Show Case-$100, Ice Box-$100, Safe-$150, Clock-$4, Register-$50, Cabinet-$100, Electric Fan-$10, Cart-$5, 2 Slot Machines-$10, 2 Fire Extinguishers-$20, Oil Painting-$50, 2 Lamps-$2, 9 Pictures-$50, Two Stoves-$20, Five Tables-$25, 18 Chairs [75¢ach]-$13.50, Contract for Piano Purchase-$50, 2 Couches-$30, 3 Rugs-$15, Carpet-$30, Linoleum-$50, 4 Pairs of Portaires [draperies]-$20, 10 Jars and Palms-$75, Punch Set-$5, Tom and Jerry Set-$5, and 5 dozen Glasses-$25. Alcohol on hand was valued at $588.25 and included more than 100 gallons of whiskey, some 35 gallons of sherry and a full array of standards such as wine, gin, rum, brandy, vermouth, sarsaparilla, and orange and wild cherry bitters. Nearly 2,500 cigars, worth $166.15, represented brands such as El Imperatrice, Espina, Alexander Humboldt, La Sinceridad, Camelo, Lajatroba and La Flor de Valaro.

Among Tom's personal property was a Remington typewriter and a ten-volume collection of *Messages and Papers of the Presidents*, a collection of proclamations, special messages, and speeches by U.S. presidents from 1887 to 1902. The appraisers summarized their accounting by adding this note: "Said Administratrix also believes that there is other property, real and personal not yet discovered, an inventory to which will be returned as soon as its whereabouts are ascertained."[19] A true and complete accounting was likely never compiled due to an inability to identify all verbal agreements made by Tom. The Smoky Valley ranch was not included in the Logan estate since Tom had not yet acquired legal ownership. Presumably, terms for purchasing the property had to have been well underway at the time of Tom's death for the deed holder to quitclaim the ranch to Hannah on August 28, 1906.[20]

Beginning on May 19, 1906, several public notices appeared in local newspapers notifying anyone who might have claims against the estate to file vouchers and affidavits with the county clerk. Nearly four months later, on September

---

* The equivalent of about $325,000 in 2014.[18]

8, 1906, Hannah submitted for Judge Peter Breen's approval an accounting, which included total receipts, expenses, and a statement of claims due payment:

ALLOWED CLAIMS[21] (with rounded figures):

Claimant	Claim (1906)	Approx. Value (2014)*
Frank Golden (co-investor, American saloon)	$637	$16,000
H. F. Nofsinger (sheriff's deputy)	440	10,775
George Swasey (Likely funeral expenses)	364	8,915
Tonopah Miner (perhaps sheriff office printing fees)	64	1,570
Jim Butler (Longtime friend, business associate)	200	4,900
M. Cronon Co. (nature of debt unknown)	1,033	25,300
Wetmore-Bowen Co. (California winery)	30	735
J. H. Nevin (Nevada State tax collector)	50	1,225
J. Bamberger & Co. (nature of debt unknown)	250	6,125
George Logan (Tom's brother)	569	$13,930
E. A. Fargo & Co. (whiskey wholesaler)	465	11,390
George Wingfield (Jointly owned mining claims)	1,000	25,000
TOTAL ALLOWED CLAIMS	**$5,102**	**$125,875**

Probate records provided no additional information stipulating the precise basis of each claim or which debts were applicable to Tom Logan as a private citizen, businessman, or sheriff; however, the total amount was substantial with one of the most notable claimants being George Wingfield. Hannah may have collected earnings from The American to offset claims against the estate, but before the end of summer, she had liquidated all the saloon's furnishings and inventory. She would eventually have to sell most of Tom's mining claims to satisfy the estate's outstanding liabilities.[22]

---

* Consumer Price Index Calculator, Bureau of Labor Statistics, US Dept. of Labor, Washington, DC.

Of the claims rejected by Judge Breen, one stood out—the Tonopah Lumber Company.* Assuming Tom owned the Jewel, they had filed a mechanics lien against the property for $912. Hannah Logan was named as the primary party and May Biggs identified as "junior to the rights of the plaintiff." [23] Hannah subsequently filed suit against May, claiming his estate owned Jewel.[24] May soon produced documents showing she held the title, which made her accountable to the lumber company.

Hannah inherited two other legal tangles in which Tom had been named a defendant. The first, filed on March 12, 1906, by G. M. Harris, charged Sheriff Logan and Sherman Crumley for having delayed the construction of his Manhattan saloon. His complaint alleged they had "wrongfully, tortuously, willfully and wantonly converted and appropriated to themselves and to their use" lumber and building materials Harris had purchased from the Nevada Coal and Lumber Company.[26]

Days before his death, Tom had filed two demurrers in the Harris case, one as sheriff and one as a private citizen, stating the damages valued at $3,600 lacked sufficient facts to constitute a cause of action. Hannah carried forward that defense and filed a response on October 30, 1906, asserting that since she had no proof of the allegations, she therefore had no responsibility to compensate Harris. By all indications, the complaint was dismissed.

The second matter involved former Nye County District Attorney Charley Richards and associate, W. J. Harris. At issue in the suit they filed on March 14, 1906, were possessory rights to the barber shop and bath house Tom had built next to The American in 1901. An apparent verbal agreement with Jim Butler had granted Tom use of a portion of the lot upon which The Butler saloon stood. When Butler conveyed title to the Tonopah Mining Company in 1904, he presumably did so with the full knowledge of the rights and equities in place for the barber shop. Indeed, county assessment records show Tom paid the annual property taxes.[27] However, when the Tonopah Mining Company quitclaimed Lot 14 to Richards and Harris, Butler's agreement with Logan, likely absent any written confirmation, became a point of contention. A settlement was reached between Hannah, Richards, and Harris by the end of 1906 in which she abandoned any claim to the property and they, in turn, compensated her $1,000 plus legal fees.[28]

Step by grueling step, with the assistance of the legal firm of Ford, Gibbons, Wheeler & Ford, Hannah pressed on. One of the most intractable quandaries to develop pertained to the discovery of a shortage in Sheriff Logan's accounts.

---

* The Tonopah Lumber Company and Manhattan Lumber Company had previously filed a lien against the Jewel property (Lot 12, Block N, Dexter Addition to South Manhattan). Naming Tom Logan as the "owner or reputed owner," they claimed an overdue account balance of $886.33. Coincidently, that document was officially filed by County Recorder Puddy Grimes on April 7, at 8:30 a.m.—almost the precise moment that Tom Logan died.[25]

Due in part to Tom's inclination to conduct business without a clear paper trail,
the matter would occupy the courts for more than five years as litigants sought
to determine who was liable for reimbursing the missing balance—the Logan
estate, his bondsmen, or both? From the *Gazette*, April 27, 1906:

Ex-Sheriff Thomas W. Logan was $9,000 short in his accounts, according to a report
of an expert examiner. Logan is dead, having been slain a few weeks ago by Walter A.
Barieau in a fight at Manhattan, but his bondsmen will have to make good the defi-
ciency. The friends of the dead official are greatly surprised, although about a year
ago an attack was made upon Logan for his failure to promptly report license collec-
tions.

Under the authority of the commissioners, Expert Louis Simonsen was employed and
has gone over all the accounts. He refuses to affirm or deny that the shortage exists,
but it has been admitted at all the county offices for some time the only question being
the amount....

There is some hope, though rather faint, that it will be yet discovered that Logan had
the amount on deposit in some bank. But to his private credit the local banks claim to
have no knowledge of such deposit. That makes the possibility of finding anything
rather meager.

Since the examination began it has developed that four years ago when Logan went
out of office as sheriff he was short $1,000. That occurred in the license collections
and before turning over the books he borrowed the amount and made his shortage
good. All who knew Logan agree that such was his probable intention this time, but
death overtook him and made restitution on his part impossible.

On May 8, 1906, the county commissioners ordered District Attorney William
Pittman to, "proceed without delay to notify the bondsmen on said Thomas
Logan's bond of said deficiency, and take all necessary and proper steps to collect the same and to protect the county from any loss on account of said deficiency." Those individuals included W. Trabert, H. Kind, W. J. Sinclair, Geo.
Watt, Al Revert, R. B. Davis, R. P. Stentson, Thos. Arden, Chas. Blumenthal,
and Tasker Oddie. Five months later, Pittman reported to the board that he had
billed both the Logan estate and his bondsmen, but neither had come forward
to pay the shortage.[29]

More than two years passed before legal action was brought against Hannah
and Tom's bondsmen. Their response, filed on January 9, 1909, cited insufficient evidence and breach of process as well as ambiguity regarding "how and
in what manner moneys collected is recoverable upon a bond conditioned for
the faithful performance of (Logan's) duties as sheriff and ex-officio assessor."
In general, doubt reigned as to whether the shortage was the result of under-
handedness by Tom or the unintended side effect of him being killed before he

had completed his collections and could personally rectify the discrepancies as had been his long-time habit.

After another two-and-one-half years passed, District Judge L. N. French ruled on May 11, 1911, to release Hannah from any further financial obligation. The outcome regarding the case against the bondsmen is unknown.[30]

BESIDES THE DIFFICULT chore of reconciling Sheriff Logan's books, the county commissioners' more immediate responsibility was to appoint a man to take his place. The situation "is agitating the street to a considerable extent," reported the *Sun* on April 13, 1906. Some predicted Tom's brother, George, was the most likely replacement, but the field of candidates rapidly filled with a range of prospects.[31]

Among the men who are mentioned capable of filling Tom Logan's place are Neil McLean of McLean & McSweeny, Alexander McKenzie, George A. Cole and Deputy Sheriff McDonald of Ryholite….

Today a new name has been added to the list of those being spoken of as good men for the position. A number of local men whose opinions count in Tonopah and who repre-sent the better element in this city have come strongly in favor of Daniel Robb, ex-sheriff of Esmeralda County. They claim that the county is so large that it will take an experienced man to give the county proper service, and that Robb possess all the nec-essary qualifications….

Strong influences are at work also in behalf of McKenzie, and the contest for the office promises to grow very warm before the question is settled." [32]

A few days later, the commissioners unanimously elected one of their more prominent citizens and a for-mer lawman, Tom McMahon, as the new Nye County Sheriff. Born in New Orleans, he was 38 years old and had lived in Texas, New Mex-ico, and Colorado, where he had served admirably as the sheriff of Teller and Denver Counties. He was also a civil engineer and had come to Tonopah to help build the water

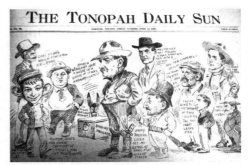

"Puzzle picture—find the Sheriff" (*Tonopah Daily Sun*, April 13, 1906, Arthur B. Buel, editorial artist, Tonopah, NV)

and sewer system. Regarding his new appointment, he told the *Sun*: "I appreciate the confidence which the county commissioners have placed in me and shall give my best efforts to fill the position acceptably, not only to them, but to the public at large as well." Outspoken against mob rule, he offered high praise for the law and order so well-enforced by the late sheriff and his deputies.[33]

McMahon's appointment heightened hopes in Manhattan that the local jail would soon be completed thereby better curtailing the criminal element. That relief quickly vaporized when an even greater threat to the camp's security and prosperity struck—the great San Francisco earthquake of 1906. Heavily financed by California investors, Manhattan residents with Bay Area ties would soon depart in droves to return to the stricken region. In less than two weeks, barely 100 people would be left in town.[34]

Dozens gathered outside the newspapers' offices throughout Nye County to read bulletins as fast as they were posted. The devastation from crumbling buildings and massive fires was unimaginable. The death toll reached into the thousands.[35] J. J. McSorely, a well-known mining man, told of how he had been asleep at the California Hotel when the shock occurred, quickly dressed, and went in search of other Tonopah people before making his way to Oakland to catch a train home. From the depot, he could see the burning city "as plain as if it was only a block away." Many high buildings were dynamited in an effort to check the flames.[36] George Wingfield had just recently traveled to San Francisco and was staying in the Palace Hotel at the time of the quake. The *Sun* reported, "Geo. Wingfield—cool, calm and collected under all circumstances, lost a few dress suits, but he didn't lose any time making his getaway."[37 & 38]

In Tonopah, where hard-driving people were accustomed to adversity and coveted "silver linings," the *Sun's* editor shared from on high the irrefutable value of that perspective by writing on April 19, 1906:

"The Silver Lining:" Great catastrophes like that which has befallen San Francisco naturally horrify and appall the world. The mind is staggered and stunned in the attempt to comprehend their magnitude and awful significance. Apart from the loss of life and property and the incalculable suffering entailed, there is in an earthquake disaster a special horror arising from the display of forces that are as mysterious as they are titanic....While it is true that nothing which may follow can give back the lives that have been lost, yet for the great city that today lies prostrate, mangled and bleeding, amid the wreck and ashes of her queenly habiliments there is a silver lining to the cloud that overhangs....Out of San Francisco's smoldering ruins will shortly arise a new city that will be both fairer and stronger than the old.

For Hannah, perhaps the one disguised blessing resulting from Tom's death was having summoned her daughters home from Oakland before the quake, thereby sparing them injury or even worse. However, like the day the earth trembled with such violence in California, she and her children had also been shaken to the core and were all but buried in the ruins of a former life. Forever lost in that rubble was Tom's promise to surprise Hannah with a trip to Oakland and the expected cash windfall to which he had alluded in his last letter to Annie. Whatever foothold he had managed to gain toward a more affluent, less laborious life had collapsed.

Salvaging what she could, Hannah Logan would rebuild the only way she knew how—one brick at a time.

There is No Death!

There is no death! The stars go down
To rise upon some fairer shore,
And bright in heaven's jeweled crown
They shine forevermore.

The granite rocks disorganize
To feed the hungry moss they bear;
The forest leaves drink daily life
From out of viewless air.

There is no death! An Angel form
Walks o'er the earth with silent tread;
He bears our best beloved things away,
And then we call them "dead."

He leaves our hearts all desolate;
He plucks our fairest, sweetest flowers;
Transplanted into bliss they now
Adorn immortal bowers.

The bird-like voice, whose joyous tones
Made glad this scene of sin and strife,
Sings now her everlasting songs
Amid the Tree of Life.

Born unto that undying life,
They leave us but to come again.
With joy we welcome them—the same,
Except in sin and pain.

And ever near us, though unseen,
The dear immortal spirits tread;
For all the boundless universe
Is life—there are no Dead.

—A fugitive poem that many authors claim,
Indianapolis Journal
Reprinted by *The Coconino Sun*, Flagstaff, AZ,
November 19, 1898 (condensed)

13

THE TRIAL: JULY 1906

Seldom if ever in the history of Nye County has there been such an interest dis-
played over the verdict of a jury as that displayed in the Barieau case. Practi-
cally the sole discussion on the streets and in the homes of Tonopah since the
jury retired yesterday was "What will the verdict be?"

Tonopah Daily Sun, July 14, 1906

WALTER A. BARIEAU was officially indicted by the Nye County Grand Jury
for the murder of Sheriff Thomas W. Logan on May 9, 1906. At his arraignment
the next day, the seemingly doomed gambler entered a plea "not guilty," was
summarily denied bail, and promptly escorted back to his cell by the jailer. His
new attorney was 49-year-old veteran litigator Stephen Flynn.[1]

The son of a sawmill worker, Flynn was born in Canada in 1857, and practiced law for more than two decades in Bay City, Michigan. After losing his
bid for a U.S. congressional seat and suffering a devastating financial loss in
the stock market, he, his wife, and daughter moved to Tonopah around 1904 to
start anew.[2 & 3]

Very few historical references today recognize Flynn as Barieau's lead attorney. Instead, Patrick McCarran is frequently credited with that distinction,
due in large part to his own personal account of what became known as "The
McCarran Miracle."[4] In a brief narrative he wrote several years later, McCarran
failed to even mention Flynn in his version of how he became involved in the
Barieau case:

The court looked over the vast array of eminent lawyers present and for some unknown
reason directed that I should defend Walter Bario [sic] the slayer of the sheriff of Nye
County. I had heard that there might be occasions in one's life when his knees would
go out from under him but I never believed it to be true until that moment, then for the
first time I realized what it was to be possessed of fear, embarrassment and consterna-
tion. But a wise old preceptor of the law had given me one admonition that came to
mind almost instantly. He said, "When you get in a tight place, ask for time." I asked
the court for time to inspect the indictment. It was granted. A few days afterwards Bario
[sic] pleaded "Not Guilty" to the indictment and I was in full charge of my first case,
to defend a man who had killed Tom Logan, the Sheriff of Nye County. I had nothing
else to do so I put my whole time into the case from then until the trial...."[5]

Although a captivating story, McCarran's recollection is not supported by Nye
County court records and minutes. Rather, when the Nye County Grand Jury
convened on May 9, 1906, they handed to the court several indictments along
with Barieau's. From the minutes:

The defendant Walter A. Barieau, being present in court, and represented by S. P. Flynn, as counsel—it is ordered that the name of S. P. Flynn be entered as counsel for said defendant. Upon request of counsel for said defendant, for time, the court sets the time for the arraignment of the said defendant at Thursday, May 10th, at 1 o'clock P.M., and the said defendant remanded to the custody of the sheriff.[6]

Immediately after Barieau appeared with Flynn, the next case called was that of the *"State of Nevada vs W. T. [Bilo] Boyd."* Charged with larceny, Boyd did not yet have anyone to represent him:

The defendant W. T. Bilo being present in court and not having counsel, at the request of said defendant, the court appoints P. A. McCarran as counsel for said defendant. With consent of counsel, the court sets the time for the arraignment of the said defendant for May 10th, to follow the case of the State of Nevada vs Walter A. Barieau, and the defendant remanded to the custody of the sheriff.[7]

McCarran further maintained that at the time of the Barieau trial, he "had nothing else to do." Multiple court minute entries during the spring of 1906 contradict that assertion. Not only was he one of four lawyers representing May Baric (Wingfield) in her divorce case, but McCarran's workload had so increased that he sought Flynn's assistance with several other clients.*

Not until the opening day of the Barieau trial was McCarran officially recognized by the court as an attorney for the accused. Flynn filed a motion requesting "P.A. McCarran be entered as of counsel for the said defendant."[9] Any number of reasons might explain why the silver-tongued sheepherder from Reno became one of Barieau's attorneys. Perhaps he recognized a plum opportunity to advance his professional ranking and either offered to assist or accepted an invitation to do so by Flynn. McCarran devoted every skill and tactic he could muster to help construct Barieau's defense and, years later, took considerable liberty recounting the magnitude of his contribution, once writing, "Never was there [a case] that meant more to a young man just commencing the practice of law."[10]

---

* When McCarran failed to compensate Flynn for his services, a lawsuit demanding payment was filed on September 14, 1906.[8] Flynn pulled no punches in his 11-page complaint against his co-counsel during the Barieau trial, stating: *"Because of the action of [McCarran] as herein set forth, disaffection and dissension has arisen between the parties hereto of such a nature as to render it impossible for [Flynn] to longer associate in business with defendant....Plaintiff further alleges on information and belief that said defendant is pecuniarily irresponsible, and that if he is not restrained by the injunction of this Honorable Court, that he will collect the moneys due and owing from said co-defendants as aforesaid and deprive the plaintiff of his right of participation therein, and his just and equitable share."* The ultimate resolution remains undetermined, but the irony hangs heavy that the relationship between the two men who pulled off one of the most sensational murder acquittals in Nevada's history would so rapidly disintegrate.

The prosecution team was composed of District Attorney William Pittman and Hugh Percy as co-counsel.[13] A former corporate attorney for the American Beet Sugar Company in the Los Angeles area, Percy had come to Tonopah about two years earlier. Considered a general practitioner, he specialized in mining law.[14] The presiding judge was Peter Breen, the first of three generations of well-regarded purveyors of justice from one of Nevada's most respected pioneer families. Born in Killarney, Ireland in 1847, he immigrated to the U.S. as a young man and worked as a painter and paperhanger before being admitted to the bar in Nevada. After 12 successful years as Eureka County district attorney, he was elected judge for the Third Judicial District in 1902.[15]

Scene of the Walter Barieau Murder Trial, Nye County Courthouse, c. 1980
(Courtesy of Bill Barieau)

The Walter Barieau murder trial began Tuesday morning, July 9, 1906. Barieau caused a considerable stir among those packed into the crowded courtroom when he arrived and took a seat near Flynn and McCarran:*

He plainly showed signs of long confinement and was decidedly nervous under the battery of glances that were directed toward him. His cheeks were sallow and sunken and his eyes rolled restlessly in their sockets. During the morning's proceedings the prisoner

---

* McCarran's daughter, Sister Margaret's belief that Barieau was a paid gun for Wingfield, loosely supports an opinion held by Nevada historian Bill Pettite.[11] As a young man in the early 1950s, Pettite routinely interacted with individuals from Wingfield's inner circle and from time to time, the Logan killing would come up in conversations. Although many disagree, Pettite still maintains, "Wingfield brought in McCarran because he didn't have faith in the other guy."[12]

rocked nervously back and forth in his chair and took only an ordinary interest in the questioning of the men of the venire.[16]

Convinced Barieau could not possibly receive a fair trial in Nye County, where Logan was held in such high regard, Flynn stepped forward to argue that point. From the *Sun*, July 9, 1906:

As the clerk was about to make the first drawing from the jury box, Attorney Flynn addressed the court on behalf of a challenge to the entire venire by the defendant. Flynn asked for an adjournment of two hours while he prepared his motion, but Judge Breen quickly decided that five minutes would be sufficient for the drawing of the document.

The challenge to the venire set forth four reasons of illegality, viz: (1) That the majority of the men of the venire were summoned by George Logan, brother of the man the defendant is accused of killing; (2) that the venire was not returned in the time prescribed by law; (3) that many names drawn from the box were not returned because the men were not known to those conducting the drawing; (4) that the men of the venire were not drawn from the county at large, but from the townships of Manhattan and Tonopah.

Judge Breen immediately overruled the challenge; Attorney Flynn noted an exception and the drawing continued.

A total of 55 names were called as potential jurors. Many were dismissed after confessing they held prejudiced opinions that would probably overtake any objectivity they might possess. Others were eliminated during several rounds of peremptory challenges by both sides, but by the end of the day, the following twelve men were selected to occupy the jury box and decide Barieau's fate: Thomas O'Neil, Dr. H.C. King, Elton Davis, George Coslett, J.E. Hart, John Erickson, George Strosnider, Roger Dougherty, W.A. Nagle, Charles L. Phillips, E.F. Prouty, and Dan Robb, former Sheriff of Esmeralda County, who would serve as foreman. All were placed in the custody of the sheriff to prevent interaction with anyone outside their ranks.[17 & 18]

While meticulous handwritten trial minutes on file with the Nye County Clerk provide dates, times, names, and court actions, not included with that record are witness testimony transcripts or attorney statements. Most likely, all handwritten notes taken by stenographer William Fuerste were destroyed rather than transcribed since Barieau was acquitted. Had he been found guilty of murder or manslaughter, a record of proceedings would be essential to a possible appeal of that conviction.[19] Consequently, newspaper accounts provide the best record and insights as to how the case unfolded.

On the morning of July 10, after opening remarks by Pittman, the state called its star witness, May Biggs, proprietress of the Jewel. From the *Sun*, July 10, 1906:

The direct examination of Miss Biggs brought out the statement that Barieau had agreed to leave the house when told to do so by Logan but that he [Barieau]) resisted at the front door and was shoved out on the porch in front of the sheriff. When asked to tell what followed, the woman graphically described the deadly struggle between Logan and Barieau. She turned to the jury and dramatically recited how Logan rushed from the house to overcome the armed Barieau; with many gestures she illustrated how Logan grappled with the man for possession of the gun; how the two fought like tigers in front of the house, and finally how Jimmy Bering, the piano player, rushed to Logan's assistance, with the sheriff's own gun, but did not fire as Logan commanded him not to. She told how Bering beat Barieau over the head with Logan's gun and rendered the man hors de combat.

When the witness was turned over to the defense for cross examination it was a signal for trouble between the attorneys of either side. Attorney Flynn attempted to show that Logan had showered costly gifts on the woman; that Logan had really bought the lumber to build her house, etc. This line of questioning was bitterly attacked by the prosecution, but Flynn persisted in the questioning and wrung many admissions from the woman.

At the noon adjournment, Miss Biggs was still on the stand and Attorneys Flynn and McCarran were propounding questions to her that brought the constant objection from the prosecution. From the line of questions asked and the statements of Flynn, it is plain to see that the hope of the defense is to discredit the testimony of the Biggs woman and in this way to try to show that her version of the tragedy is not to be relied upon.

Also taking the witness stand that day were Dr. George Von Wedelstaedt, Vivian Carlton, Jimmy Bering, Dan O'Brien, Deputy Scott Hickey, all of whom had testified at the coroner's inquest. Wedelstaedt again described the nature of Logan's wounds and cause of death. Carlton corroborated in detail Biggs' account. Bering did the same, describing how, when Barieau balked at leaving the house just as he reached the door, he tried to brace himself in the doorway and "Logan took him by the wrists and forced him out on the porch."[20]

On cross examination, Flynn questioned Bering in such a way as to suggest Biggs had not retrieved Logan's gun from its scabbard at the head of a bed, but had actually picked it up from the hallway where the sheriff had dropped it after using it to strike Barieau. Bering denied that was the case, restating that he and Biggs were in Logan's room when she gave him the weapon to take to the sheriff. Flynn further attempted to impeach Bering's testimony by reading to the jury what they believed to be conflicting statements from the preliminary hearing. To offset this ploy, the prosecution called Etta Hoffman to the witness stand. From the *Sun*, July 11, 1906:

Mrs. Hoffman testified that the transcript was not to be relied upon as, while she was taking down the testimony she was frequently interrupted by Judge Hoggatt, whom she charged with being badly intoxicated. Mrs. Hoffman was charged with going over the records of the preliminary hearing and picking out testimony that is unreliable.

Dan O'Brien and Deputy Sheriff Scott Hickey testified as to disarming Barieau and carrying Logan into the house. The state rested after Hickey testified.

Attorney Flynn made the opening statement for the defense. He stated that the prosecution hoped to prove by the defendant's testimony that the killing was justifiable; that the defendant was struck on the head with a gun by Logan twice before he was ejected from the house; that Logan dropped his gun and while he was groping in the hallway, Barieau, thinking himself in danger of being killed, fired. Also that the defense would show by books of a local lumber company that Logan bought the lumber for the house which the Biggs woman runs.

Trial proceedings continued well into the evening during which time the state rested their case and Flynn delivered his opening statement. The next day, the defense called several witnesses, including: Mabel Scott, Cecelia Fay, W. S Field, Lou Whitney, Dr. Jerry Garner, John Lynch, Fred Simonds, and Charles Morey. The intent behind each one's appearance is impossible to decipher within the abbreviated format of the trial minutes. However, based on the outcome of the trial, a general assumption could be drawn that the defense witnesses, none of whom were at the scene of the killing, were used to erode the reliability of the state's red light district witnesses; counter any attack against Barieau's supposed agreeable nature; reinforce declarations that the accused had never been in trouble before; and advance arguments condemning Tom's lack of moral integrity and abject disregard for his family.

Oddly, none of these witnesses were cross-examined by the prosecution. Trial minutes suggest that Pittman did little to refute those allegations and was perhaps over-reliant on May Biggs and Jimmie Bering. Once the defense was able to raise doubt as to the veracity of their accounts and could not disprove Tom's culpability in his own death, the case tipped irrevocably toward acquittal.[21]

As previously established, Volney Hoggatt,* Barieau's gambling companion at the Jewel and juiced-up legal counsel at the coroner's hearing, had temporarily disappeared from Nye County. That somewhat convenient void meant the jury had to rely exclusively on Barieau's version of why he brought a fully-loaded revolver to the Jewel. Hoggatt's absence also deprived the state of any substantive opportunity to discredit Barieau's version of events.

When court convened at 10 a.m. on July 11, Walter Barieau settled into the witness chair to speak on his own behalf. He explained that he had been induced by Hoggatt to join him and two others for a visit to the Jewel. Before they left, Hoggatt disclosed that he had considerable money and jewelry on his person

---

* After the boom years of Southern Nevada began to deflate, Hoggatt moved to Colorado where he was appointed to the post of Registrar for the State Land Board in 1912. Not long after, he championed a dry-land farming scheme promoting the colonization of more than a quarter-million acres. The project, which Hoggatt supported until his death in 1934, met with infrequent success and is considered by land management experts to be a "good historical example of unwise land use in the West." [22]

and asked if anyone had a gun. "Barieau said he seldom carried a gun," reported the *Sun*, "but always kept one in the drawer of the table at which he worked and when Hoggatt made this remark, he (Barieau) put his gun in his pocket."[23]

[Barieau] stated in effect that on the fatal morning he, in company with others, went into the Jewel saloon where he took one drink of wine, which made him sick and he went and lay down on the lounge. While there the woman, May Biggs, told him to go home. He protested that he was ill and begged that he be permitted to remain. She remained positive in her orders, however, so he proceeded to leave the place.

The woman thought he was not traveling fast enough and proceeded to push him along, when he struck back with his elbow, hitting her on the arm. She began to scream and he heard someone coming hurriedly and the next thing he knew he received a blow which knocked him down. He got up and was downed a second time by a blow. He was trying to back out of the house when he was struck on the head with some heavy instrument and then he noticed that his assailant had a gun, so he drew his pistol and fired a shot.

He finally succeeded in getting outdoors when he drew his pistol and fired four [five] more shots at the man with the gun who was still following him. In his backward retreat, he fell off the porch and Logan jumped upon him and a struggle for possession of the weapon followed. While they were thus engaged he was repeatedly struck upon the head by someone until Deputy Scott Hickey placed him under arrest. Barieau claimed he was not acquainted with Sheriff Logan, had never seen him before and did not know at the time who his assailant was.[24]

Margaret Chase, the manager of a restaurant where the Jewel residents ate their meals, answered questions from the defense about her past relationship with May Biggs. Stating they had met in Dawson, Alaska, when Biggs was working as a dancer, Chase told the court that she came to Tonopah after Biggs had arrived and went to work for her as a housekeeper. She went on to describe "frequent and costly gifts" Tom had supposedly given to May, including: "two vases that cost $250, a pair of diamond earrings worth $600, a beautiful work box with solid silver trimmings, a turquoise ring set with diamonds, two bedsteads, mattresses, pictures and many other things of lesser value." [25]

Pittman cross-examined with a series of inquiries related to Chase's blemished reputation, hoping to prove that she "was not of the best character." From the *Sun*:

Mrs. Chase caused some little amusement among the spectators by the manner in which she vehemently denied that she ever drank or associated with men. It turned out that Mrs. Chase was known in Dawson as Mother Woods. While in the north it is said that she made many friends by caring for sick miners. She denied that she was ever known in Dawson as "Stampede" Woods.[26]

Even though the prosecution objected to the relevance of testimony about how Tom had charged the Jewel lumber to his account, Judge Breen was persuaded that this information helped illustrate a certain intimate connection between Tom and May. George Andrews, the manager of the Manhattan branch of the Tonopah Lumber Company, confirmed that Tom had ordered the lumber used to build the Jewel:

Mr. Andrews further stated that May Biggs had nothing to do with the transaction until about a month ago when she came to the office of the company and asked to be allowed to pay the account which stood in Logan's name. She was told that nothing could be done as proceedings had commenced on the lien. Later Attorney McClellan for the Biggs woman effected an arrangement with the company, payment was made and McClellan was given a receipt for May Biggs. On the cross examination Mr. Andrews said that May Biggs stated to him that she had given Mr. Logan $400 to pay toward the account.[27]

Continuing to solidify Barieau's self-defense claim, Flynn and McCarran contended Sheriff Logan's size and strength compared to Barieau was a significant factor and sought confirmation from Tom's longtime friend, business associate, and fellow law enforcement official, Alex McKenzie:

Constable Alex McKenzie told of the appearance of Barieau the day after he was brought to jail and during the time while McKenzie was keeper at the jail. In answer to questions by Attorney Flynn the witness stated that Logan weighed, in his judgment, over fifty pounds more than the defendant. He also stated that Logan was a very powerful man. Attorney Pittman caused a laugh in the courtroom when he asked McKenzie if he was not present in a saloon in Tonopah when Sheriff Logan tried to put him [Pittman] out and he threw the sheriff down and held him on the floor. McKenzie denied being present….

Among those who have followed the trial from the start there was considerable comment as to the alleged discrepancies between the statements of May Biggs, while under oath and giving testimony, and the statements made by Margaret Chase….[28]

Shortly after court reconvened on the afternoon of July 12, Flynn called a most unexpected witness to the stand for questioning—his own co-counsel, Patrick McCarran.[29] A rare and historically unconventional maneuver in any courtroom, this tactic allowed him the opportunity to influence the jury both as the defendant's attorney and as a supporting witness. The precise advantage achieved by McCarran taking the stand shortly before he began closing arguments is impossible to ascertain, other than to conclude there had to have been one. As the ensuing years would prove, McCarran's courtroom prowess was akin to that of a theatrical wizard directing a cast of actors.* He spoke slowly in a high-pitched

---

* McCarran's daughter, Sister Margaret, told the author in 1985, "I used to tell him 'don't you use your eloquence on me. I'm not a jury!'"[31]

tone, and, as described by a future colleague, his speeches were "glacial rather than volcanic, moving slowly but unceasingly and irresistibly."[30]

During the final few hours of the trial, several witnesses were recalled including Hickey, Carlton, Biggs, and Barieau. Before court adjourned Thursday afternoon all were excused for McCarran and Percy to commence closing statements.[32] From the *Sun*, July 13, 1906:

Attorney P.A. McCarran for the defense opened and the unanimous opinion of those present in the courtroom was that no finer argument, from the standpoint of eloquence and logic, has ever been delivered in the courthouse. During the course of the argument, Attorney McCarran demonstrated that as a dealer in sarcasm and invective he is without a peer at the local bar. His arraignment of the characters and testimony of many of the witnesses of the prosecution will long be remembered.

In his opening argument Attorney McCarran did not go into the details of the testimony adduced at the trial but confined himself to a general talk on the merits of the case as presented by the defense and prosecution.

During the course of his remarks Mr. McCarran took the opportunity to comment on the reliability of the chief witnesses of the state—May Biggs he characterized as an "enchantress who had wound herself into the life of a man inclined to do right and making him a slave to her every will and wish."

There were few dry eyes in the courtroom when Mr. McCarran touchingly referred to the family of Thomas Logan. He stated that while the sheriff, under the influence of the Biggs woman, was showering presents upon her, the family of the man in Smoky Valley had but few of the necessities of life.

Wilson J. Bering, the piano player of the Jewel and a former employee of Dunham, Carrigan and Hayden of San Francisco, was bitterly denounced by Attorney McCarran. The speaker commented on the mentality of the man who would give up an honorable position with a big firm to enter a house like the Jewel as a piano player. The general demeanor of Bering while on the stand and previous to the trial also brought forth striking rebuke from the speaker.

In conclusion Attorney McCarran explained that his arraignment of the state's witnesses and his review of their various characters was done for the purpose of showing the jury and the world at large that the prosecution's witnesses was not to be relied on and that the general sense of the law was to discredit people of their reputations.

Assistant District Attorney Percy followed McCarran, also speaking along broad lines. He acknowledged that Tom Logan was wrong to have visited the Jewel and said the same about Barieau. As a point of ridicule and weak effort by the accused, Percy singled out Barieau's statement that he "carried a revolver mostly for protection against wild horses while prospecting." Hoping to rehabilitate the credence of the state's witnesses, in particular Biggs and Bering, Percy argued that nothing had been brought out to show the actual testimony to in any way be faulty. He concluded by asking the jury for "justice and nothing more."[33]

Flynn and Pittman delivered the final closing arguments. Flynn spoke for slightly more than two hours reviewing witness testimonies for both the prosecution and defense, comparing varying statements, and portraying his client as the true victim. He dwelt upon Barieau's "previous good reputation" and praised the unflinching faithfulness of his devoted wife. Flynn portrayed Barieau as a law-abiding man who had never been in trouble before.[34] The *Sun* reported:

A point particularly dwelt upon was the whereabouts of the Logan revolver which was not produced at the trial. Mr. Flynn suggested that Bering used his own revolver to beat Barieau with and that Logan's revolver was laying [sic] in the hallway where the Sheriff had dropped it. The production of the revolver, he argued, would have allowed the prosecution's testimony to coincide.

Attorney Flynn waxed eloquent as he characterized May Biggs as a perjurer and charged that the woman had no regard for the truth. "All she thought about was to sustain the theory of the state and not to tell the truth. This woman perjured herself, not once, but a dozen times," he said.[35]

Many of those who heard District Attorney Pittman's comments to the jury believed his presentation on behalf of the state was a masterful effort:

His tribute to the memory of Thomas Logan was a most beautiful one and reached a climax when the speaker, a close friend of the dead man, burst into tears and sobbed out the remaining words of his sentence. The breakdown of Attorney Pittman was not without its effect on the jury and several of those in the jury box who knew Tom Logan could not keep back tears.

In defense of the bitter attacks of the attorneys for the defendant, Mr. Pittman spoke eloquently on the charity which all men should display toward unfortunate women and begged the jury not to be influenced by the continual arraignment of the state's witnesses by the defense.

The theory of the defense that Bering could not have inflicted the wounds on Barieau's head because of the position of Logan over the defendant during the fight was dwelt on to some length by Mr. Pittman. Crouching over an imaginary body before the jury box the district attorney demonstrated how Bering could have inflicted the wounds and refuted the claims of the defense.

As if to offset his many vituperations that had been cast as the prosecution's case, Mr. Pittman devoted no little time to an expression of opinion as to the malice of the defendant in his killing of Logan and ended with the plea to the jury not to turn Walter Barieau lose on the public to give him the opportunity to commit further criminal acts.[36]

Both the prosecution and defense teams provided Judge Breen with separate sets of recommended instructions for him to present to the jury. The state delineated various grounds upon which Barieau could be found guilty, and the defense summarized rationales upon which he should be acquitted.*

On behalf of the prosecution, Breen provided the jury with a specific definition of "murder," observing that deliberation and premeditation need not be long. He also stipulated criteria differentiating between manslaughter, and first and second degree murder:

...defendant must be presumed to know that the effect is likely to be deadly, and knowing this must be presumed to intend death, which is the probable and ordinary consequence of such an act, and if such deadly weapon is used without just cause or provocation, he must be presumed to do it wickedly or from a bad heart, and if the jury believe that defendant took the life of deceased by shooting him in a vital part with a pistol, as set forth in the indictment, with manifest design to use such weapon upon him, and with sufficient time to deliberate and fully form the conscious purpose to kill and without sufficient reason or cause or extenuation, then such killing is murder in the first degree, and whilst it devolves on the State to prove the willfulness, deliberation and malice aforethought, all of which is necessary to constitute murder in the first degree, yet these need not be proved by direct evidence, but may be deduced from all the facts and circumstances attending the killing, and if the jury are satisfied, they will be warranted in finding the defendant guilty of murder in the first degree.

You are instructed that if you believe that the defendant did, with malice aforethought, but without willful, deliberate premeditation shoot the deceased, with the intent then and there to kill him, and while so engaged did kill the deceased, you will find the defendant guilty of murder in the second degree.

The court instructs that manslaughter is the unlawful killing of another without malice and may be either voluntary, as where the act is committed with a real design and purpose to kill, but through the violence of sudden passion occasioned by some great provocation, which in tenderness for the frailty of human nature, the law considers sufficient to palliate the criminality of the offense, or involuntary, as where the death of another is caused by some unlawful act not accompanied with any intention to take a life.[37]

In regard to determining whether or not Barieau had indeed acted in self-defense, Breen informed the jury that the evidence must prove the threat of danger was so urgent that killing the other person was absolutely necessary to prevent death or great bodily harm, and that "the slayer had really, and in good faith, endeavored to decline any further struggle before the mortal shot was given." Furthermore:

Gentlemen, you are instructed that a bare fear of personal violence or danger to the life of the defendant at the hands of deceased, to prevent which the homicide is alleged to

---

* A complete copy of instructions, both those that Breen accepted and those he rejected appear in the Appendix section of this book.

have been committed, shall not be sufficient to justify the killing. It must appear that the circumstances were sufficient to excite the fears of a reasonable man and that the party killing really acted under the influence of those fears, and not in a spirit of revenge.

Breen explained, as a standard of proof, "reasonable doubt" is one based on reason and must be actual and substantial, not mere possibility or speculation. And finally, in regard to the credence of witness testimony, the judge asked the jury to consider the demeanor of witnesses while on the stand, and:

...if you believe from all the evidence, that any witness has willfully sworn falsely on this trial as to any matter or thing material to the issue in this case, then you are at liberty to disregard his entire testimony, except in so far as it has been corroborated by other evidence, or by facts and circumstances proved on the trial.

Proposed instructions from the defense team were far lengthier in verbiage and scope of intent. Understandably, ample attention was dedicated to the cardinal principle of presumed innocence until proven guilty beyond reasonable doubt, and criterion for justifiable homicide. Breen also reinforced the importance of weighing testimony from the standpoint of probability or improbability, and asked the jury to fully consider the character of the witness, when material and put in evidence, their motives, interests, or bias. However, the following examples of defense directives *disallowed* by the judge as inappropriate for the jury provide additional insight into the thrust of Flynn and McCarran's case for acquittal:

Refused by Judge Breen and not given to the jury: *The character of the several witnesses should be considered, the good character of the witness should weigh in the witness' favor; while on the other hand, the bad character of a witness should weigh against the witness; and I charge you that if you find from the evidence that one of the witnesses for the State is the keeper of a disorderly house, or a house of ill fame and that other witnesses for the State are prostitutes, I charge you as to the testimony of those witnesses that it should be disregarded unless corroborated in every essential particular by the testimony of credible witnesses.*

Refused by Judge Breen and not given to the jury: *It is understood that the deceased was not acting in his official capacity as Sheriff of Nye County or in any other official capacity when he met his death at the hands of the Defendant. He wore no insignia nor badge of office, nor is it claimed that he informed the Defendant or that the Defendant knew that he was Sheriff of Nye County before the shooting took place, I charge you therefore that the fact that he was Sheriff of this County should not weigh against the Defendant in this case.*

Refused by Judge Breen and not given to the jury noting "not law:" *If you find from the evidence that deceased was a powerful man and that Defendant was in a weakened physical condition, and deceased assaulted Defendant with the fist alone, if there was apparent purpose and ability to inflict death or serious bodily injury upon Defendant,* *and Defendant believed in good faith that such was the purpose of deceased, such an assault was sufficient to justify killing in self-defense....And further Defendant was assaulted with a deadly weapon and he did not provoke the assault or bring on the difficulty, he was not bound to retreat, but had a right to stand and defend himself; and if the necessity arose for taking the life of the deceased in order to save himself from death or serious bodily injury, such killing is justifiable on the ground of self-defense.*[38]

Judge Breen appears to have most fairly exercised proper judicial authority in the process of conveying to the jury their scope of responsibilities and the fundamental parameters of applicable law. As the trial neared conclusion, it was evident that Pittman and Percy, without "respectable" witnesses, could not convincingly demonstrate how Barieau was unjustified in the degree of lethal force inflicted on Sheriff Logan. On the other hand, Flynn and McCarran's barrage of counter arguments steeped in invective and blame unleashed tremendous doubt as to who was telling the truth.

Apparently undetected by the prosecution, and perhaps even unknown to the defense, was Barieau's history of lawlessness. Had his past offenses and true core character been exposed, he may have been much less credible. Instead, Flynn and McCarran were able to deflate key testimony from Biggs, Bering, and Carlton—despite the corroborative substance of their independent accounts—on the basis of their sordid lifestyles. Then, by placing Tom in such company, the defense gained more latitude toward portraying him as the aggressor and Barieau as the innocent victim of his uncontrollable rage. In short order, the sheriff known throughout the land for his quiet ways and devotion to law and order was, in many ways, put on trial without the benefit of due process or the opportunity to lend his voice to the proceedings.

After the jury was dismissed to deliberate, some twenty hours before they would reach a verdict, McCarran wrote the following request addressed to District Attorney Pittman for Barieau to sign:

Mr. W. B. Pitman, Dist. Attorney:
Dear Sir:

Please deliver my gun now in the custody of the County Clerk of Nye Co. to bearer, P.A. McCarran.

Respectfully,
W.A. Barieau

(Nye County Clerk's Office, Tonopah, NV)

Nye County Courthouse, from a period postcard, c. 1910, Tonopah, NV
(Logan Family Collection)

McCarran's note could be interpreted as an audacious display of confidence in the jury about to acquit his client, but might also suggest an anticipated need for Barieau to arm himself in such an event. Deliberations began at 12:30 p.m. on Friday and would conclude at 5:30 a.m. the next morning, July 14.

DURING THE ENTIRE Walter Barieau murder trial, the jurymen were lodged at the courthouse under constant surveillance by a deputy sheriff:

They were permitted to converse with no one, nor were they allowed to discuss the merits of the case among themselves until the proper time. Cots were provided for them in the courthouse and they appeared on the streets only at meal time, and then always in charge of the deputy.[39]

The first ballot taken by the jury resulted in a vote of six for acquittal and six for conviction with varying viewpoints as to what degree of murder applied. It then became the task of those united in favor of a "not guilty" verdict to sway the inclinations of those so opposed. Ballot after ballot, argument after argument, one by one the reluctant abandoned their quest for conviction. Two unidentified members apparently held out for manslaughter through the night but, after a strenuous review of the testimony, were eventually persuaded otherwise.[40] From the *Sun*, July 14, 1906:

The scene in the court room at 9 o'clock this morning when the defendant, his wife and child and a few spectators gathered to hear the verdict was very impressive and the fact that the life of a man was at stake gave additional solemnity to the occasion. The jury was already in the box when the court was called to order and Barieau brought in by the sheriff a moment afterward....

The jury announced that a verdict had been arrived at and the court ordered the clerk to read it. The defendant, his wife and child listened breathlessly to each word and when the clerk pronounced "not guilty," Mrs. Barieau threw her arms around her husband's neck and kissed him again and again, and weeping, not from fear this time, but from sheer joy. Barieau's little daughter climbed into his lap and embraced him fondly. The man whom the law had declared not guilty of murder, who slipped from the shadow of the gallows with the reading of the verdict, who unflinchingly looked District Attorney Pittman in the eye during the terrible arraignment yesterday, now gave way and bending over with his head in his hands, Walter A. Barieau wept and his lips moved in audible thanksgiving to his lawyers who rushed over to congratulate him....The immense popularity of Thomas W. Logan has manifested time and again since he was killed on April 7, and the general opinion about town seemed that Barieau would be held at least for manslaughter.

Varying perspectives will surely continue to ride the winds of time as to whether or not Walter Barieau got away with murdering Nye County Sheriff Tom Logan. Although an intriguing prospect, no evidence beyond innuendo implicates Barieau as a hired gun for perhaps George Wingfield, a labor union, or some other "contractor." Certainly, Tom had his share of enemies, some of whom may have even wished him harm. However, in those pre-dawn hours at the Jewel on April 7, 1906, it is quite possible that the events leading to his death were profoundly uncomplicated. No conspiracy, no woman to avenge, no abuse of power. Instead, the local sheriff attempted to do what he had done on countless occasions, at all times of the day or night, in all manner of attire—firmly escort a nuisance into the street so he could be on his way.

Barieau, not averse to threatening a lawman with a gun as he had done in Sacramento, had taken extreme offense to being forced out of the Jewel and, in protest, upped the ante and drew his gun. Perhaps that first shot was not intended for the tall man standing in the doorway, but when Tom bolted toward the indignant gambler to disarm him, Barieau panicked and pumped five bullets into his body. The most riveting irony of that bloody skirmish outside the Jewel dwells in the haunting voice of the very man Barieau thought was about to kill him, and instead saved his life.

"Don't shoot him," Sheriff Logan told the piano player, and in that instant probably exercised his last breath of authority as a man sworn to uphold the sacred tenants of law and order.

Southwest from Bullfrog

Out there in the land o' sagebrush, in the brown horn-toad's domain,
Where the clouds float 'round moth-eaten—in the land of stingy rain;
   Where the birds are only sage hens, where the grey coyote slinks:
      Where each little drop o' water is a shinin' pearl that stinks:
   Where the trailless, silent desert like a windin' sheet has grown—
      Alkali made even whiter; redhot sunshine crumbles bone!
   Where you swing a pick in anguish, probe the bowels of a hill,
P'raps you'll hear the nuggets callin'—Then it's time to scrawl your will.

Out there in the land of gamble, where the chance is swift and steep,
   Where each man gives in his little so that some may take a heap:
   Where the life rips off the covers, stamps his breed upon each lad—
      Where a man is clean and quiet, or is rotten, shoutin' bad:
   Where the fightin' ground is ready for the man who cannot wait,
      Where he sheds his extra linen, has his battle out with Fate:
   Where a man may win a fortune, where he'll lose all but his name,
I have cut the deck for the dealer, tried to play a white man's game.

      I recall when I first saw it, saw this hidin' ground of gold;
   It's not hard to recollect it—these grey hairs don't mean I'm old.
      Stood above a new rag village on a bit of risin' ground—
You could hear the click of glasses, roulette wheels a clickin' round.
   But my thoughts were on the desert, shimmerin' in devil's breath,
   On the bare hills that meandered to the valley they call Death.
         Any man can be a hero, gladly go to eat his dirt,
   When he's got a proper purpose buttoned in his flannel shirt.

Learned a mite of human nature from the men who came and went,
      Men of fifty occupations on one occupation bent.
   Learned that overalls and whiskers do not make a sameness when
      They are part of ev'ry fellar; dogs are dogs, and men are men.
   Had my share of sour moments: it will sometimes turn your head,
This hard life among the raw things, too much flesh, too little bread.
   But I carried with me somthin' that could banish ache and pain—
      Just a mem'ry of a someone wavin' good-bye to a train.

—Rufus Milas Steele, c. 1906 (excerpt)

14

THE ENSUING YEARS

The world is inclined to smile at many things laid at "human nature's" door, but sooner or later a man's misdeeds are liable to come back to him in ways that are not pleasant. But what's the use of preaching? We all keep doing those things that we ought not to do, and leave undone those things that we ought to have done.

Beatty Bullfrog Miner, July 20, 1906

AFTER MORE THAN three months in the county jail, Walter Barieau was set free on July 14, 1906. The following day he attended mass with Patrick Mc-Carran and, on the next day, District Attorney William Pittman returned his gun.[1] Soon thereafter, likely funded by an unidentified benefactor, the Barieau family made their way to San Francisco and boarded a steamer bound for Panama.[2] Presumably, discontent with the verdict was still prevalent enough to warrant he leave not just the state, but the country as well.

Nevada newspapers, in a rare departure from their typical propensity to lash out against any perceived injustice to have transpired in a court of law, were uncharacteristically silent regarding any opinions related to Barieau's acquittal, with the exception of the *Beatty Bullfrog Miner*:

There is no doubt a wide difference of opinion regarding the jury's verdict in the Logan murder case, yet this fact seems plain, that here in the West a man must act on the square if he receives the sympathy of his fellows. In many ways Sheriff Logan was honored and admired by his friends and associates, and evidently with good cause, yet when he neglected his wife and children for a public character who cared only for his money and was shot down as a direct result of such illicit relations, a jury of representative citizens says his slayer was justified in causing his death.[3]

Walter Barieau, his wife, and daughter returned to San Francisco in early October 1906, and would eventually make their way to Las Vegas where the 1910 U.S. Census indicates he was employed as a "miner." However, scant evidence exists that he ever truly traded in his gaming tackle for a pick and shovel. Five years later, while living in Bakersfield, California, it was apparent Bareiau had well-resumed his preferred line of work. From the *Morning Echo*, December 14, 1915:

Officer Joe Deuel arrested W. A. Barieau and confiscated a punch board from the stand in front of the Old Crow saloon. The punch board contained an automatic revolver as a prize. Deuel will file a complaint against Barieau for having a lottery game. He will be arraigned today before Judge Flournoy.

As had been his habit since leaving home at the age of 14 and typical of most itinerant gamblers, Barieau didn't stay in any one place very long. The 1920 U.S. Census placed him in Los Angeles and unemployed. His wife Margaret was listed as the "head of household" since she had a job as a sales lady. In 1927, property he had acquired in the Bakersfield area, and then later apparently abandoned, was on the Maricopa Delinquent Tax List.[4] Moving south to San Diego, Barieau worked as real estate salesman.[5] By 1930, he had gained ownership of an apartment house where he was the manager.[6]

Margaret Barieau filed for divorce in Reno during the summer of 1936.[7] Her complaint alleged that Barieau had left her on March 24, 1931, and never returned. Margaret told the presiding judge during a brief trial, "We didn't get along and many things were disagreeable." Her husband of 43 hardscrabbled years was again living in Las Vegas. According to Barieau's nephew Bill, also during this time period, his uncle had gone to Ensenada, Mexico, to "run a plush gambling casino for Jack Dempsey" at a popular destination for movie stars, high society types, and rich businessmen. [8 & 9]

From the *Pittsburg Press*, "Mexico Casino is Next Venture for Mr. Dempsey," by Theon Wright, August 8, 1935:

Los Angeles—Jack Dempsey, the beetle-browed maestro of maulies, today prepared to launch the latest venture of his checkered career—a gambling resort at Ensenada, Mex., with the government of Mexico as a "partner." The fact the Mexican government's current head-man, President Lazaro Cardena, has forbid gambling specifically at the luxurious Agua Caliente Casino operated by American promoters did not discourage Dempsey."

In his book *Roots of Reno*, author Al Moe expanded on Dempsey's involvement in the gaming industry in Mexico and how he had fronted for Wingfield and many of his operatives:

Walter Barieau, an old friend of Wingfield's from Tonopah and Manhattan, Nevada, ran the casino [in Mexico]. Barieau had once been tried for murder after killing Sheriff Tom Logan....The jury found his actions to be self-defense. His friendship with Wingfield at the time was instrumental in his acquittal.

Moe's source for these insights was Nevada historian Bill Pettite. A longtime friend of Dempsey's, Pettite once described Wingfield as the only man in Nevada history to have been both the "ruler of the state and the underworld at the same time." He also recalled how much Dempsey liked Barieau and occasionally referred to him as, "Frenchie, the guy who got away with killing that sheriff."[10]

Before his death at the age of 84, Barieau connected briefly with a nephew stationed with the Marines in San Diego and confessed that once, when he was in San Francisco, he went to visit family (likely a sibling), but after walking by the house a couple of times he left.[11] His daughter became a nurse and married but had no children.[12] With little to his name but a checkered past, Walter Amphiloque Barieau died alone in a San Diego hospital on July 4, 1953. His last known occupation had been that of "bartender." The next of kin notified of his passing was his former wife who had remarried several years earlier.[13]

AS BARIEAU'S DEFENSE team, Stephen Flynn and Patrick McCarran proved themselves a potent combination of legal expertise and ravenous ingenuity. Yet, in the aftermath of the verdict, the veteran Flynn would inexplicably spiral into obscurity while the gifted upstart from Reno soared to extraordinary heights—many of his future accomplishments spilling into realms populated by magicians and miracle workers.

Perhaps no headline is more indicative of McCarran's prominence as a litigator than one published by the *Gazette* on November 17, 1906: "Leo Buncell Acquitted at Elko: Lawyer McCarren [sic] Makes a Strong Plea for Prisoner and *Jury Returns Verdict without Leaving the Box.*" The accused had been charged with arson for setting fire to a local livery stable. Previously arrested for the same offense at the same place, the man would have more than likely been convicted but for a dose of McCarran "eloquence." Biographer Jerome Edwards observed that McCarran was a much better defense attorney than a prosecutor because, "his heart was with the sinner."[14]

However, the fall of 1906, McCarran was elected Nye County's new district attorney in a landslide vote of 1,799 to 435 against J. H. Roche.[15] The seemingly star-struck county commissioners subsequently approved a staggering annual salary increase for the D.A.'s office from $1,500 to $7,500 (the equivalent of nearly $200,000 in 2014), plus expenses, along with a steady stream of monthly invoices for vagrancy convictions.[16 & 17] Nevada law at the time also permitted McCarran to maintain his private practice.[18]

Midway through 1907, Nye County found it was unable to meet basic expenses. The commissioners assigned McCarran the task of going to Carson City to negotiate with the State Board of Revenue for an emergency loan for $10,000. Less than five months later, they would seek an additional $40,000.[19]

McCarran served just one term as district attorney before moving back to Reno's greener pastures in 1910 and soon became the most widely known orator in Nevada.[20] He became chairman of the Nevada State Board of Parole Commissioners (1913-18), a Nevada Supreme Court Justice (1917-18), and chairman of the Nevada State Board of Bar Examiners (1919-32).[21] After two unsuccessful runs for the U.S. Senate, he was elected in 1933 and served 22 years. Throughout his prestigious and often controversial political career, McCarran frequently cited the Barieau case as one of the most pivotal moments of his life.

In stark contrast to McCarran, Stephen Flynn, who had practiced law for nearly 25 years, would not be catapulted into fame by the Barieau verdict. Instead, not long after that trial, he moved to the San Francisco area where his final days would be as tragic as McCarran's were triumphant. Nearly three years to the day after the two had won their "miracle verdict," Flynn was found hanging from a pair of clothes hooks in a rooming house, his mouth badly burned by the carbolic acid he had ingested.[22]

The *San Francisco Call* compassionately memorialized Flynn on July 27, 1909, beneath the headline: "Lawyer Ends His Life by Hanging: S.P. Flynn, Once of Most Brilliant Attainments, Commits Suicide at San Jose." A published excerpt from a letter written to his wife and daughters offered some insight into the tortured state and poignant acquiescence that drove him to take his own life:

My Wife and Daughters: I have deemed it best not to express regret for the reason that I am not conscious that I entertained any. My frame of mind may be described as that of complete resignation to what I at this moment believe to be my fate, inevitable fate. Were I upon the scaffold with the black hood drawn over my head I could not be better convinced of the fact, and I believe that I am immeasurably more resigned than I would be if I occupied the latter position....One can be insane and be conscious of every act and the probable result thereof. It is just 5 o'clock, and I am prompted to make my exit with a feeling of charity, if, not indeed, love in my heart for every human being.

Flynn was 20 years older than McCarran and apparently a man of palpable, if not overwrought, sensibilities. Had he, like his one-time co-counsel, celebrated the Barieau verdict as a monumental triumph of justice, or could Flynn's demise be due in part to a conscience left to reconcile improprieties taken to win at any cost? Perhaps the demise of their short-lived partnership was caused by more than differences over legal fees. Whether ethics or personal philosophies were contributors, only they knew why each went such divergent and separate ways.

A bit more than four decades later, during the fall of 1954, U.S. Senator Patrick McCarran made a round of campaign appearances to support Democratic Party candidates. At the time, one of Tom Logan's grandsons, 24-year-old Loran Logan, was working as a part-time director for a CBS affiliate in Reno. The instant he learned McCarran was scheduled for a studio interview, he asked to borrow the badge he knew his father, Roy, had kept stored among his most prized possessions for nearly 50 years.[23]

For as long as he could remember, Loran had heard infrequent snippets from Roy about "a famous sheriff" killed by some lowlife gambler, and the fancy-talking attorney who helped him beat a murder conviction. The entire case, sorely complicated by Tom's patronage of a house of ill-fame, had settled into the Logan family history as a persistent source of disgrace. A half century later,

Patrick and Martha McCarran, c 1910
(Nevada Historical Society, Reno, NV)

most descendants had resigned themselves to there being no hope of ever finding a way to restore some portion of Tom Logan's otherwise respectable reputation.

At the television station, Loran refused to be intimated by McCarran's formidable stature and, reaching into his pocket, asked, "Senator McCarran, have you ever seen this?" Now 78 and rotund, the senator briefly glanced up at Loran, who had inherited Tom's tall, slender build, and then looked into the open hand holding the small five-point silver star, "No, I don't think I have," he answered. Loran responded, "This is Tom Logan's badge." McCarran froze on the spot, said not a word, and then gathering his poise, turned and walked away.

Roy Logan (likely wearing his father Tom's chaps) and sister Kate Logan, Smoky Valley, c. 1915 (University of Nevada, Las Vegas Libraries, Special Photo Collections, Las Vegas, NV)

A cameraman hurried over to Loran to find out what he had said to have caused such a blanched look on McCarran's face. "I showed him this," Loran said, revealing the badge. "It was my grandfather's and (McCarran) was the instigator who got the killer off."

"Oh, no wonder," said the cameraman. "I can see how that would make him go white."

Loran long-relished a personal swell of satisfaction, believing that in the span of those few seconds he had wordlessly conveyed to McCarran that his so-called "miracle" had not been forgotten by the Logan family. Slipping the precious, tarnished badge back into his pocket, he was once and forever convinced that Nevada's most prestigious politician, by way of his sudden silence and ashen expression, had acknowledged the obvious—he had helped a guilty man go free.[24]

Not long after his encounter with Loran Logan, McCarran suffered a fatal heart attack on September 28, 1954, following a campaign speech in Hawthorne, Nevada. He died immersed in his one true passion—wrangling extravagant hyperbole to persuade those most reluctant to his way of thinking.

Some 20 years later, still yearning for morsels of redemption on behalf of their father, Tom's 79-year-old daughter, Amy, then living in Minden, Nevada, received new information related to McCarran's role in the Barieau acquittal. She revealed that discovery in a letter to her older sister, Hazel, then 82:

Dear Hazel,

Jim is gone deer hunting so I am here alone. The wind is blowing a gale. Leaves blowing everywhere and nice big red apples falling all over the ground. Hate to see them go to waste but I can't save all of them.

Thought I could explain about Papa's murder. Pat McCarran was a young lawyer at that time. It was his first big murder case so he decided if he won, he could make a big name for himself, which he did. He became U. S. Senator. Has airports named after him and has been in the lime light for years. A few years ago—his own daughter (who is a Catholic nun) told Loran's wife that her father was so determined to win that he framed our father and she could even name the witnesses who were paid to testify falsely at the trial. So—because of that dirty stinker, we have lived under a cloud for these 70 years. But—it is a good thing to know that it isn't so and I'm sure McCarran will pay for his sins. We all do sooner or later....

Love, Amy" [25]

Although tempting to contemplate whether or not any witness was paid or otherwise influenced by the defense, such an exercise would likely prove futile—with one exception: Margaret Chase, May Biggs' former housekeeper and one-time sister "doxy" in Dawson. Her revelations of a veritable treasure trove of gifts given to May by Tom, and her first-hand observations regarding May's disreputable "line of work" seriously undermined the state's case. Flynn and McCarran capitalized on Chase's statements to erode the jury's confidence in May, Jimmie, and Vivian, even though all were eyewitnesses and provided seemingly near identical, unyielding accounts. Given Chase's apparently questionable background, she may very well have been open to compromise. She appears to have crossed paths with several of the heavy-hitters acquainted with Walter Barieau, such as Tonopah Club owners, Tom Kendall and George Wingfield:

*The Tonopah Block was erected a few months ago by Thomas Kendall, James McQuillan and George Wingfield, and cost over $45,000. It is one of the most substantial structures in the West and was constructed entirely of stone and steel. It has a frontage on Brougher Avenue extending from St. Patrick Street to Summit. The Kendall-Mason Drug Co., McNamara Shoe Co., Wells Fargo and B. Rutholtz occupy the stores on the ground floor, while the handsome office rooms are occupied by Senator Oddie, Southwestern Nevada Mines Co., R. P. Dunlap, Lookout Mining Co., Empire Lumber Co., C.H. McIntosh, Prescott Ely, **Miss Chase** and Western Ore Purchasing Co.[26]*

At the time of the Barieau trial, the Tonopah Block was located across the street from McCarran's office. Untold opportunities existed for individuals affiliated with the trial or keenly interested in the outcome to conspire on any number of matters—from witness management to pooling funds to pay for Barieau's voyage to Panama. George Wingfield was unquestionably the most powerful capitalist in Sheriff Logan's jurisdiction, which required there be a connection of some kind. Logan could have just as easily functioned as a stick caught in the wheels of Wingfield's operation as he could have been a well-greased cog assuring certain favors, or a little of both.

Wingfield's relationship with McCarran, not unlike that of many others, was tangled and complicated. Sally Zanjani wrote in the biography of her father George Springmeyer, a Goldfield attorney and a one-time leader in the Progressive Party:

Pat McCarran was widely regarded as [a crank], not only by my father and Wingfield, but by most of the political elite of the period. There had always been something strange and repellant about McCarran...and no one liked him much.[27]

Obviously, Sister Margaret McCarran had a different opinion. Certain her father abhorred Wingfield, she remembered a dog he gave their family. The children loved the black Labrador they named Wingfield, but McCarran lacked the same affection, occasionally grumbling, "I hate that dog." Sister Margaret would remind him it wasn't fair to be mad at an innocent animal. "After all, the dog didn't do anything wrong."[28]

At constant issue was the proverbial and frequently indecipherable line between right and wrong. Wingfield thrived on blurring the boundaries, as happened during his ultimate conquest over the volatile labor union unrest* between 1906 and 1908.

Intent on breaking the strike against his and other area mining companies, Wingfield and a committee of other supporters went to Carson City under the pretext of selecting a site for a new smelter. At the meeting, he and five others actually convinced Governor Sparks of the need for U.S. Army troops to maintain peace in the highly charged atmosphere of Goldfield. President Roosevelt was telegraphed about the need and, after a formal request was issued, troops from the Presidio in San Francisco were sent by train to Goldfield. Many individuals had previously contacted Governor Sparks about the perceived inability of local law enforcement to handle the volatile situation, but Wingfield was, in reality, exercising his increasing power and influence. Individuals with a more pro-labor viewpoint disagreed with both the Governor and the man who would later be known as "King George."[29]

Perhaps Nevada underworld scholar Bill Pettite best nutshells the association between the two power brokers by simply stating, "McCarran was part of the Wingfield machine." Whether hailed as a genius or a snake in the grass, Wingfield continues to conjure an array of sentiments, generally displaying a mixture of both. According to Sister Margaret:

I learned that [in 1922] on another occasion [McCarran] was an attorney for a bootlegger in Tonopah and they got a "not guilty" verdict, which surprised him. It was something he did not show, so he was surprised. It was a federal case and the jury had been bringing in guilty verdicts one right after the other....[McCarran] was driving out of Tonopah afterwards with a judge, another attorney, and George Wingfield in an auto because the trains were no longer running to Tonopah. They turned to Wingfield and said, "George, how come that jury brings in guilty verdicts all through the session and suddenly one 'not guilty?'" George replied, "Oh, I owed that guy something." That's all I know about that, but there was a man with the power to sway a jury by means we know nothing about.[30]

Judge Peter Breen II, son of the judge who had presided over the Barieau trial, May Baric Wingfield's divorce case, and Hannah Logan's probate hearings, was particularly familiar with how Wingfield operated. Nicknamed "Judge Pete," he served ten years on the Fifth District Court bench for Nye County, beginning in 1957. Prior to that, he had been the Esmeralda County district attorney for 20

---

* Labor unrest was rumored to have contributed to Tom Logan's death. In the September 22, 1906, *New York Evening Post* writer Barton W. Currie reported: "The boycott of the two newspapers came about in this way: Several months ago, two men were clubbed to death in Tonopah. They had some time before refused to join the I.W.W. The *Tonopah Sun* ventured the editorial opinion that members of the union had been guilty of both crimes. The killing of the sheriff of Tonopah two months ago was said to have been inspired by the Industrial Workers of the World. Bradley C. Branson, the editor of the *Tonopah Sun*, a young man who has edited dailies in Nome, Dawson, and other camps…frankly charged the I.W.W. with the crimes."

years. While hospitalized in Reno at St. Mary's Hospital for the heart ailment that would take his life in the fall of 1967, Sister Margaret came to visit:

I said something about my father having defended Sage, a man who had killed another person in Silver City, Nevada. My father had forced us, in a gentle way, to give up a party and reception for guests, this was in the early 1920s, and to go to Yerington for the plea to the jury which he was about to make in the Sage case. And Judge Breen interrupted me and said, "Sage was a paid gun for Wingfield."[31]

Clarence Sage had been one of the "detectives" hired by Wingfield the winter of 1906 to help quell labor union interference in the operation of his many mines.[32] In regard to Wingfield's connection to Sage, biographer Elizabeth Raymond, wrote:

Perpetually wary of the dangers of radical "infiltration," George Wingfield for years employed detectives at his mining properties to report on any union activities. Clarence Sage, who was appointed as one of the deputies of the new State Nevada Police, and who was arrested later in life for rape (in Arizona) and manslaughter [in Nevada], was one of the most notorious of the operatives....[33]

The prosecuting attorney in the Sage case was Lyon County District Attorney Clark J. Guild, who would later preside over the grueling Wingfield bank receivership hearings that resulted in the catastrophic collapse of his financial kingdom (1931-33). In a 1967 interview archived with the University of Nevada "Oral History Program Collection," Guild recalled prosecuting Sage:

[Sage] got into an argument with these three boys and one of them hit him pretty bad. And he went up to the Winn Hotel, where he was staying, and come back with a gun, and come in the door, and he dropped his gun on the boy and killed him....

Well, at the time of the trial, Pat McCarran defended this man. I was right up against it. And he testified, in defense, after all of these other boys had testified to the scrap and about how he left there and come back with a gun and so on, that he had the gun in his pocket when he had the struggle with the boy in the saloon. I had him nailed to the wall. The gun was in evidence. In my address to the jury, I got up and took the gun and stuck it in my back pocket, and I said, "Gentlemen, when you get to the jury room, you do the same thing. Jump up and down a little bit and see if it'll fall out of your pocket." I turned around and that fellow was as pale as a sheet. And old Pat McCarran just stared at me. They found him guilty of manslaughter, which was very, very light because it was cold-blooded murder.

Sister Margaret, intermittently defensive and critical of her father's manipulation skills, described how during McCarran's closing arguments, as if on cue and likely prearranged, Sage's little girl broke away from her mother and "trotted up to sit in her Daddy's lap. My father said to the jury, 'Those of his flesh and blood cry to you for mercy.'"[34]

As he had done in the Barieau trial, McCarran was able to heap doubt into the jury's lap as to whether Wingfield's detective had indeed left the scene to retrieve a gun or had it with him at the time of the initial altercation. That uncertainty and discrediting prosecution witnesses was enough to have the verdict reduced from murder to manslaughter, even though "what really happened," conceded Sister Margaret, "was that [Sage] came into the saloon, spotted the man, went out and got the gun, came back and killed him."[35]

With any major event or development in Nye or Esmeralda County from 1902 to 1908, the question was not *if* Wingfield was involved, but *how*? His ability to neutralize obstacles and engineer outcomes to his advantage, be they of the regulatory variety or of flesh and bone, was astounding. Sometimes he made things happen and, other times, he would shrewdly exploit an unforeseen opportunity, as occurred on March 10, 1907, when gunfire broke out on a picket line in Goldfield. When the dust settled, restaurant owner John Silva was dead.

Witnesses described how IWW* leader Morrie Preston had shot Silva in self-defense. Preston was arrested and charged with murder and Joseph Smith, even though nowhere near the crime scene, was charged with conspiracy to commit murder. Preston was found guilty of second-degree murder and sentenced to 25 years. Smith was convicted of manslaughter and received a ten-year sentence. How the two were railroaded by Goldfield's anti-union barons like Wingfield was the subject of a 1986 book by Sally Zanjani and Guy Rocha titled, *The Ignoble Conspiracy: Radicalism on Trial in Nevada*.

Driven much like Logan descendants have been to set straight a perceived faulty record, Smith's granddaughter, Diane Varni, summarized the "atrocious errors in jurisprudence" in an article she wrote for the Watsonville, California *Register-Pajaronian*, November 14, 1986. Stopping short of a wholesale condemnation of Wingfield, Varni addressed distorted reports by Goldfield newspapers in 1907, paid witnesses for the prosecution, false defense claims, and death threats against Judge Frank Langan. While both men would eventually be paroled, Smith after five years and Preston after seven, additional efforts to be pardoned failed:

Throughout the remainder of his life, the effects of the trial and five years in Nevada State Prison would echo in everything Joseph Smith attempted to do. His health and spirit were permanently affected by the poor treatment he received and he really never

---

* Industrial Workers of the World, also known as "Wobblies," formed in Chicago in 1905 by often combative unionists at odds with the conservatism and philosophies of the American Federation of Labor. A major point of contention was the AFL's practice of separating out crafts and trades into different unions. The IWW considered itself "One Big Union," placing all workers into a single organization.

prospered during his lifetime....Eventually his wife left him. My grandfather, Joseph William Smith, died a pauper in 1935.[36]

Working in concert with Zanjani and Rocha, Smith descendants eventually persuaded the Nevada Pardons Board to grant their request to exonerate Smith and Preston on May 12, 1987. Among the evidence was a letter Wingfield's one-time bodyguard, Diamondfield Jack Davis, wrote to Governor Tasker Oddie in 1913 hoping to gain his help in forcing Wingfield to pay an overdue debt. Davis claimed Wingfield owed him $9,500 for money he fronted as requested to hold "witnesses together and other things" at the trial:

I stayed with Wingfield through thick and thin. Did he stay with me? He sold me out... I would not trust George Wingfield as far as I could throw a bull by the tail. His motto is to use anyone that he can and then throw them aside like a broken branch...."[37]

Jewel inmate Vivian Carlton, as did most tarnished women, vanished into the magenta ethers of her trade. Young Jimmie Bering returned to California where multiple city directories between San Francisco, Denver, and Los Angeles chronicle a long life as a musician interspersed with supplemental day jobs as a salesman or accountant. Before he died in Napa, California, at the age of 82, he surely must have entranced many through the years with vivid tales of tinkling the ivories in the rough and tumble, sometimes bloody, commotion of a frontier mining camp.[38 & 39]

Traces of May Biggs fade quickly. Nye County property records indicate she operated the Jewel for about two more years after the killing. In 1909 and 1910, tax bills were sent to Denver in care of M. L. Jacob, the identity of whom has yet to be determined. The next year, she sold the property to Charles. E. Blaker, who lived on the site with his wife Anna, while operating a blacksmith shop and ore wagon service.[40] Today, nothing remains of the Jewel except the sky above and the ground below where it once stood, although even local old-timers can't agree on the precise location.

District Attorney William Pittman's co-counsel, Hugh Percy, would also relocate to Reno where he practiced estate law until his death in 1927.[41] Pittman, in partnership with his brothers Key and Vail, provided private legal services to the citizenry of Nye and Esmeralda Counties until about 1911, when William moved to the Territory of Hawaii. There he married and, in 1934, was elected Attorney General. Just two years later, suffering from a kidney ailment, he died at the age of 60.[42]

THE UNRESOLVED MATTER of where Tom Logan had deposited or stored public monies missing at the time of his death created enormous confusion as to how to distinguish between what belonged to his estate, what was due county coffers, and what had yet to be collected. In the absence of a logical explanation that his friends and colleagues were confident he could have provided, Tom was vulnerable to outright attack for the shortages. Ironically, the same turmoil would erupt when his elected successor, Jack Owens, vanished in early May of 1910 on his way back to Tonopah from San Francisco.

Newly married at the age of 40 and in the final year of his second term, Sheriff Owens' mysterious disappearance produced many eerily similar circumstances as those related to Tom's death. Both situations would lay bare how swiftly a man of notable stature and esteem, who dies or goes missing, can have their good name stripped away as others commence to theorize. Accusations roll like giant tumbleweeds in a windstorm of public condemnation and suspicion.

To this day, it has not been fully proven one way or the other what caused the shortage in Logan's account. The same is true for Sheriff Owens as far as determining if he chose to disappear or met with foul play. Slated to run and predicted to win the coveted office of Secretary of State in 1910, Owens was well-respected throughout the state. The *Gazette* reported on November 10, 1909, that in conducting the affairs of the Nye County Sheriff's office, Owens' honesty was "his resounding virtue." From that same article:

When the State Bank and Trust Company closed their doors, the institution had on deposit a sum of money belonging to the sheriff's office that totaled somewhere around $10,000. This amount has been greatly reduced owing to the fact that Sheriff Owens has been paying large sums monthly into the county treasury, thus reducing the amount he is liable for. When the Nye and Ormsby County bank failed, Mr. Owens immediately released his bondsmen and secured a surety bond. The above facts are not of general knowledge and they go to show the caliber of Sheriff Owens. The indebtedness caused by the closing of the banks will have been paid within a short time and when J.J. Owens completes his term of office the affairs will be turned over to his successor without a shortage of one cent.

In April 1910, Owens honeymooned in Southern California before returning to Nye County to resume his duties. A few weeks later, he sold a small portion of his mining stock, took $2,000 in gold, notified colleagues of his travel plans, and boarded a northbound train. Such travel was not uncommon. Undersheriff Vail Pittman received a telegraph on May 11 from Owens informing him that he was in San Francisco and planning to leave for Tonopah the next day with a stopover in Ely. He never arrived.[43] Some friends speculated that while in San Francisco, Owens had "gazed into the deep little hand mirror once too often, and been taken in by some of the smooth gentry who are now said to be plentiful in the city by the bay."[44]

Rumors swirled about Sheriff Owens' whereabouts, including an alleged sighting in Portland, Oregon, another in Seattle, Washington, and the unconfirmed belief that he was on his way to Alaska. In June, the Nye County Grand Jury advised the District Attorney that Owens' accounts were short and likely why "the idol of the desert" had abandoned his new wife, his public duties, and substantial assets. Assuming the financial deficiency was the result of a deliberate act, the D.A. filed suit against the Owens' estate in an attempt to somehow recuperate missing county money. His property was also attached.[45]

As in the months following Tom Logan's sudden death, supporters and detractors of Sheriff Owens had colliding perspectives. The *Tonopah Miner* criticized both men for negligent bookkeeping methods in a June 1910 editorial, "Another Nye County sheriff has gone wrong!" and offered the following:

Notwithstanding the full knowledge of the dire results, the Miner nearly two years ago exposed the methods pursued by Sheriff Owens, "king of the politicians," showing conclusively and beyond the shadow of doubt that the door was left wide open for fraud…

The Miner showed, and submitted unquestionable proof, that Mr. Owens was collecting thousands of dollars in taxes and not turning them in, in direct violation to every conceivable construction of the law which is most explicit on the subject. This proof was so strong that the grand jury was forced to admit that Mr. Owens had disobeyed the law, but that learned body found that his predecessor [Tom Logan] had done the same thing, and therefore, there was no blame to attach to Mr. Owens….

At the time of making the complaint, the Miner did not accuse Mr. Owens of dishonesty, but it pointed out the fact that the door for fraud was left wide open…and that sooner or later the county would come to grief. That time has come….

Owen's wife waited eight lengthy years before filing for divorce in 1918.[46] Dan Robb, former sheriff of Esmeralda County and foreman of the Barieau jury, was appointed to complete Owens' term. Undersheriff Vail Pittman assumed the daunting task of identifying the substantial, if not catastrophic, pitfalls wrought by mixing personal and public monies.

A resident of Tonopah for six years and in the early stages of developing a newspaper publishing career, Vail was William and Key Pittman's younger brother. Vail would be elected governor of Nevada in 1945. However, in 1910 as Nye County's undersheriff, he found himself thrust into the position of making sense out of the chaos that had once again erupted regarding county funds kept in personal bank accounts. There still being no designated depository accounts for the sheriff and assessor's office, the practice was not only legal but purely routine.

William, Key, and Vail Pittman, early 1900s
(Central Nevada Historical Society, Tonopah, NV)

Vail Pittman wrote a detailed letter to Nye County authorities concerning the current disposition of Owens' private assets and what measures might be taken to gain access. That report was published in the *Tonopah Daily Bonanza* on May 31, 1910, and in part, reads:

[Frank Mannix, Nye County Treasurer] urged me to draw a check on Mr. Owens' account in the Nevada First National Bank for the full amount there in favor of the treasurer of Nye County. While I was then and am now desirous as any of you that this money should be immediately available o the county, I considered the matter too complex and my duty and authority too uncertain to permit me to comply with your request without a fuller investigation and the assistance of legal advice....

The statutes of the state do not require that the sheriff shall keep moneys collected for the county on deposit in the name of the county or in any trust fund for the benefit of the county or at any particular safe or place. The statutes apparently permit the sheriff to use the money so collected as he sees fit and to mix them with his own funds or to do what he pleases with them so that he pays the amount due the county at certain periods of time. In other words, the sheriff, instead of holding the money collected for the county, simply owes the county and his obligation is settled by making the payments at the time required.... Money belonging to the state and county, I not only have no authority to disperse it but can conceive of no scheme by which I could equitably divide it.

Pittman further assured colleagues that Sheriff Owens' $55,000 surety bond would amply protect the county from any anticipated shortages and, as he had been advised, a creditor had more latitude than he toward making any withdrawals from Owens' personal accounts estimated to be in excess of $20,000. This being the second time in less than four years that Nye County had suddenly lost a sheriff, igniting a fretful buzz about "missing funds," Pittman meticulously outlined the policies he wanted to inaugurate while in command—all of which seemed to be dreadfully late in coming to Nye County.

First clarifying it was the duty of the sheriff and assessor to collect licenses, poll tax, personal property tax, office fees, and bullion tax, Pittman next suggested there be five separate corresponding deposit accounts and all checks drawn be payable only to the county treasurer. Acknowledging this required more effort on the part of the depository, it would allow the county auditor to more quickly detect errors, plus reduce the potential for incriminations associated with intentional or unintentional withdrawals for personal use however legitimate a final tally might reveal.[47]

Pittman's recommendations to upgrade Nye County's imperiled bookkeeping system surely set into motion efforts to minimize the hazards of relying on the good faith of elected officials. Logan descendants have long wrestled with the prospect that Tom was pocketing money for personal use or selectively conducting that duty by not collecting from all those who owed payment. Given the increasing transient nature of the population, the often undocumented transfer of business and property, the sheer geographical size of Nye County, and Tom's heretofore trustworthiness, he may very well have had to rely on personal contributions to balance the sheriff and assessor's books from time to time. By the same token, he could have just as likely used county dollars for personal use until required to square up. Obviously, it becomes apparent why co-mingling funds soon not only became unacceptable but subject to criminal action.

THE AMERICAN SALOON would remain standing until the night of May 11, 1908, when the entire block burned to the ground. The origin of the fire was traced to a rooming establishment over the Merriman-Fasset billiard parlors. Flames could be seen from Goldfield, 25 miles away, and were so intense that all the plate glass windows in buildings on the other side of Main Street were broken.[48] From the *Bonanza*, May 13, 1908:

Chief McKenzie had two fingers of his right hand cut by glass and was taken to the hospital, where Dr. Mapes dressed the wounds. Dick Rainville, of the fire department, was burned when he fell through the roof of the American saloon building.

During the progress of the fire, a dispute arose on three or four occasions between Chief McKenzie and members of the volunteer fire department. It is alleged that the chief lost his temper and deliberately struck three men, Paul McGuire, Will Grimes and Ambrose Murphy, and threatened to disembowel Don Gillies….

That the women of Tonopah were not one whit behind the men as fire fighters was demonstrated Monday night when Mrs. Barker and Mrs. Malin discovered a residence on South street on fire, which had caught from falling cinders. They immediately secured buckets and in a very short time quenched the fire, thus saving the city further loss, for had the fire gained headway in the residence portion of town, untold damage would have ensued.

Smoldering ruins of The American saloon, southeast corner of Main and Brougher, Tonopah, NV Central Nevada (Historical Society, Tonopah, NV)

Along with The American saloon, some 30 other businesses and homes were destroyed by the fire—all of which were among Tonopah's earliest original structures. Gone, for instance, were the National Safe Deposit and Trust Company, Dr. Davis' dental parlors, Warren's Grocery Store, Collins' Electrical Works, the Grotto ice cream store, Mrs. Richardson's millinery, and the popular Palace Hotel. Even though most of The American and The Butler were burned, their storefronts remained standing and were refurbished for the new businesses that took their place.[49] Tonopah's "most disastrous conflagration," as described by the *Bonanza*, proved particularly emblematic of all that was disappearing from the Old West.

The New West

Oh, have you seen, my traveled friend
The expurgated west,
Where men longer tote their guns
Attention to arrest,
Where little Willie Tenderfoot
No longer gets a shock,
But where they gather round the boy
And sell him mining stock?

Gone are the glories of the land
Where once the cowboy ranged.
That chap is now a hired man,
For, lo, the times have changed!
No longer hardship stalks abroad,
For if the grub is shy
They call the store by telephone
And get a new supply.

The wild and wooly mining camp
Most of its wool has shed;
The bold, bad men who used to roam
The streets have gone to bed.
They do not now shoot up the town—
That wouldn't be polite.
Besides, it doesn't seem the way
To treat the electric light.

A new and milder race of men
Now monkey with the game.
And when they get their dress suits on
The scene is trite and tame.
You note them in the swallowtail,
Tall hat and fancy vest,
And looking all around you see
The passing of the west.

—Duncan M. Smith, December 21, 1907,
Bisbee Daily Review, Bisbee, Arizona

15

AN INCONSOLABLE WIND: 1907-2013

FOR HANNAH LOGAN, in the years to come, life was a constant search for balance between deciding what to give up and devising ways to keep what was left, especially the Smoky Valley ranch. Nye County property records from 1907-1920 along with several faded letters* written by Hannah to her eldest daughter Annie, then living and working in Tonopah as a single woman, help to map the family's whereabouts as well as the nature of their struggles. The new reality required that the ranch generate income plus the older girls had to find employment anywhere they could. Hazel, likely referred by one of Tom's cousins in the Sacramento area, journeyed to Sutter, California, to work for a brief period of time as a servant for a widowed farmwoman named Vita Gray.[1]

Concerned about the four younger children's education, Hannah boldly chose in 1909 to sell her cattle, lease the ranch, and move to Pasadena where she purchased two small houses—one in which to live and the other to rent. Annie remained her mother's touchstone in Nye County. On October 29, 1910, Hannah wrote:

So much to attend to that I couldn't think to write. Kids have all been under the weather. Kate is not a bit well yet, but she keeps right on at school. They are all doing well at school…only they send Roy home afternoons as he is ahead of some five year olds and keep them afternoons so they can catch up with him. Quite a scheme don't you think to keep an eight-year-old out to accommodate kids under school age….If you know of anyone to loan a thousand dollars for two years on [the ranch], let me know and find out what interest one would have to pay. The place is good for that in that country, but people down here can't loan money on a place so far away…so don't fail to send me some money and we will all come out all right as this place will be worth something when I get it cleared.

Hannah also mentioned that Jessie, Joie, and Hazel, who had left her job in Northern California to rejoin her mother, were all working, but "we cannot rely on Hazel, no matter how good a chance she has as she is fit to fly the track any minute." Exhaustion was as much a central theme to Hannah's narratives as were comments related to her financial woes. November 6, 1910:

Hazel is almost done up and she will never be any better unless she can get where she can rest her nerves. Anything she works at seems to wear her out in less than a week. She always tries to do what would take anyone else a week all in one day and when she can't, her nerves get the best of her. She has been home again since Thursday. She

---

* Logan family letter excerpts are from The Logan Family Archives in the author's possession.

can't stay with anything long enough to pay for what it cost to get there. I had to make her come home this time as she was so determined to stay with it...but she was fainting away all the time and could not work. The folks left her alone so much I made up my mind that we would have to get her home as much for their good as for her own. The children all wrote cards to you about the things you sent and I forgot to write thanks. Lovingly, Mama (Annie, burn all my letters as long as you have to be in other people's houses.)

From Kate Logan, about to turn age 12:

Dear Ann, I received card but am busy at school. I want to ask you to not send Roy and I any birthday present, because you sent Mama that money and we get just as much good out of it as any of the rest. Got the card and that was enough.

Everyone contributed to "a never-ending drain" of household expenses. At age 16, Amy clerked in a grocery store for $5 a week, Jessie earned board and room as live-in help in the Los Angeles area, and Joie was briefly employed as a private servant near Bishop, California, before she was able to get a stenographer job in Bakersfield. For Thanksgiving that year, Hannah wanted to do something special since they hadn't had meat for five months unless one counted the 10-cent soup bone she picked up twice a week. The extravagance came in the form of a 50-cent pot roast, homemade cranberry sauce, mashed potatoes, and hot rolls. To begin the New Year, the family went to the 1911 Rose Bowl Parade, but the glow of that festive affair soon faded. Hannah wrote Annie on January 18, 1911:

Hazel Logan (left) and friends,
c. 1911, Venice Beach, CA
(Logan Family Collection)

You ask what I am going to do about the ranch. I don't know what I am going to do as it seems that everything I calculate on falls through. Sometimes I am sorry that I did not sell it and again I think it was best that I did not, but it is scratching sure now that I am not getting anything out of it and have to pay to keep it up besides keep up interest and expenses here, but if I can only manage to hang on, it may be worth it later on.

Hannah reported the children were doing fine in school although it had been difficult being in classrooms with 50 to 60 children they didn't know, and continued writing:

Ted was in a room where larger boys even told things on him that they did themselves and he took the punishment until he got disgusted and left school. He was never afraid of them and would not tell the teacher, of course he did not get his promotion card and is in the same room, but they have all gone in the next grade and he has not had one bit of trouble so far this term. Roy and Kate got the same deal. Roy did not get promoted so he is with kids more his size. They are all three favorites with their teachers now, so you see one has to catch on here to get on.

Desiring to keep the ranch operational so they had a home to come back to and another source of income, Hannah went into partnership with Mr. "Red" Redmond, explaining to Annie:

Mr. Redmond expects me to be (at the ranch) to start spring work and get things running and I am very anxious to go long enough to get the papers made out properly I am almost afraid to have left that too long now, but it is going to take quite a bit of means to get started. I will have to have enough to pay my fare up there, and pay for the provisions and seed grain and for some help besides the cost of harvest besides keep up here and the worst of it is I will have to cut Jess out of her wages and have her stay with the children and then either go up there alone or cut off Amy's wages. They are not very much but a steady thing and a chance of a raise if she stays with it and then another thing—we can't count on Hazel. She has the best thing of any of them but you can't tell when she will jump, tho she has been pretty steady lately. She don't take any more care of her health tho. Of course I would be obliged to borrow money but don't want to borrow too much….

I might rent the ranch but it is a loss in the end as the party renting will never take care of anything that they are not making money out of…those people sure use up every wagon tool, harness and horse and everything they handled…. Mr. Redmond has done good work up there already getting things together shoeing horses but of course he has had to buy a good many things. They either lost or stole most of my tools used up the wagons and harnesses and it will cost considerable to get things back so that one can get along…. The agreement was that they would keep everything in repair, so I think it best to go in pardners [sic] with someone and they will be more apt to take an interest unless they are the kind that are careless with everything and then it makes it just as bad as one partner is responsible for the other's debts.

On January 25, 1911, Hannah further solidified plans to move back to Smoky Valley and wrote Annie to do what she could to help her the borrow money to do so:

I will have to buy quite a lot of things before I go as I haven't much bedding now or anything left up there…there are lovely winter suits on sale here. If I only knew the size and color you would want I might do pretty well…. Amy says there is going to be a big sale on underwear of all kinds beginning Monday and if you answer the card I wrote and give the size, Amy will do the rest. Tho Annie the things on sale now are higher than they were a couple of years ago for the regular price. Cotton goods is getting higher every day…. Must close as Roy has been having an earache for four or five nights and I have not had much rest and have an awful cold myself tonight. Lovingly, Mama

Certainly, Pasadena offered Hannah and her children many enticements compared to life in the remote Smoky Valley of Nye County, the least of which were better schools, medical services, and employment opportunities. However, after two years of testing her chances in modern southern California while also trying to preserve her interests in the ranch, it became apparent that Hannah had to decide between one or the other, or risk losing what she termed, "the whole cheese." Once so close to achieving a fair measure of "the good life," Tom Logan's widow recalibrated by instead embracing "the familiar life."

The Logan Ranch: Three ranch hands (far left) with Ted, Roy, and Amy Logan
(standing), Kate and Jessie (seated), and Hannah Logan (chair), c. 1910,
Smoky Valley, NV (Logan Family Collection)

Back in Smoky Valley, dealing with people she knew and those who trusted her, Hannah embarked on the arduous course of overseeing the ranch's revival. At least three times between 1912 and 1916, she borrowed against the property, but always paid her debts back in full, on time, and with interest. Annual Nye County Assessment Rolls chronicled the success of her efforts, delineating a steady increase in livestock and expanding crops. For instance, in 1913, the ranch was described as having 240 acres of hay and pasture land with improvements consisting of a frame house, sheds, barn, cellar, stable, corral, and fencing. Livestock was limited to two work horses, one saddle horse, one harness, and ten stock cattle.

By 1916, total acreage had grown to 360 upon which grew: 3 acres of alfalfa, 22 acres of meadow, 4 acres of vegetables,135 acres of pasture, and 196 acres of grazing. In addition to property improvements previously noted, also listed were three horses, 20 stock cattle, and 10 poultry. All but Annie and Joie returned to Smoky Valley with Hannah to help operate the ranch. Amy was the first to leave after she married one of the Darrough brothers in 1913 but remained for a time in the area, where they ran their own spread.

In May 1914, Hazel wed George Barton, a miner from Maine, in Bishop, California, and promptly boarded a train to Oregon, where, besides mining, he would operate a produce transportation service. They would have 11 children.

George and Hazel Barton Family, (l. to r.) Coral with baby Anna Mae, Ruth, Bethany, George, Dorothy, Eldon, Fern, Hazel, Bethel, Quinton, and Harold with Richard, Eugene, OR, c. 1936 (Logan Family Collection)

Stories related to Jessie revolve around what many in the family consider to have been a chronic and debilitating mental condition that developed while the Logan's were living in Pasadena. A letter Hannah received in October 1912 from a man apparently helping her to determine whether to sell or rent out her Pasadena house included this note: "I trust Jessie is much improved with you and that all the balance of the family are well." Based on a related response written by Amy to her mother, Hannah was then visiting her ailing daughter in a Salt Lake City hospital. Jessie would never marry, remain always in her mother's care, and die at the age of just 47.

Hannah's decision to sell the Smoky Valley ranch in 1919 can be summed up in three words: *It was time*. She was about to turn 60 and her youngest child, Roy, was now 17. Before the end of the year, Kate would also marry a Darrough boy. They would remain in Smoky Valley where she worked as the Round Mountain postmistress for many years.

Ted Logan married Ruth Averill in 1922. She was the daughter of Tonopah attorney and former Esmeralda County assemblyman, Mark Averill, who succeeded Judge Peter Breen in 1908 as presiding judge for the Fifth District and served until 1923. A Republican, Ruth blazed a political trail of her own when she was elected to the State Assembly in 1920 for Nye County, and distinguished herself as the first woman to chair a legislative committee for the state of Nevada.[2]

"One woman among so many men naturally has a problem on her hands," Ruth wrote about herself in *The Woman Citizen* magazine, July 30, 1921. "Luckily, I am a true Nevadan and not a radical reformer....One of my first moves was to suspend the rule against smoking in the legislature. Although I would never smoke myself and hate to see a woman doing it, I feel that men are very much easier to get along with when they have something sticking in the mouths to talk around and look wise over."

Roy and Ted Logan, c. 1914, Logan Ranch, Smoky Valley, NV
(Logan Family Collection)

Ruth completed one term in the assembly and then, in 1923, moved with Ted Logan and her father to Turlock, California. There, Ted worked as a power company lineman and was nearly electrocuted to death the spring of 1925, when he came in contact with a high-tension line.[3] Although Ted found work as a laborer, he reportedly never fully regained his former robust health, and their marriage faltered from that point on. Ted eventually moved to Reno to live with Hannah. Sadly and inexplicably, his one-time shining-star wife spent most of her final years in a mental institution in Stockton, California.[4]

William Henry Berg, one of four brothers from Ohio who had come west around 1906 and owned a general merchandise store in Round Mountain, officially purchased the Logan ranch on June 18, 1919, for $7,000.[5 & 6] Hannah was well-settled in her new home in Reno by 1920. There, in "The Biggest Little City in the World," on East 4th Street, she would live for more than two decades caring for Jessie and Ted before they preceded her in death. Ever the consummate mother hen, Hannah did once travel to Eugene, Oregon, to look after the brood of Barton children during one of Hazel's "attack of nerves." She is remembered as being stricter than most, intolerant of picky eaters, and tirelessly dedicated to her family.[7]

Left to right, Ted Logan, Grandma Rogers (grandmother to Irene "Rene" Rogers Berg Zaval) and Hannah Logan; in foreground is Aunt Emma Rogers and Rene as a child, taken at the R. O. Ranch during one of Hannah's return visits to Smoky Valley after she had moved to Reno, c. 1925. (University of Nevada, Las Vegas Libraries, Special Photo Collections, Las Vegas, NV)

Arguably one of Nevada's most resilient pioneer women, Hannah Mariah Hamblin Logan passed away at daughter Annie's home in Verdi, just west of Reno, Nevada on July 12, 1942. At the time, she had 21 grandchildren and nine great-grandchildren. She is buried in Reno's Mountain View Cemetery between Jessie and Ted, the two children who, in the end, needed her most by their sides.

ONE HUNDRED AND five years after Tom Logan's death, on Memorial Day 2011, and the occasion of his 150th birthday, nearly three dozen descendants and guests gathered in Tonopah to honor his life during the 41st Annual Jim Butler Days. A welcoming breeze accompanied those who gathered together in the old Tonopah cemetery. Ranging in age from 15 to 79, several had brought handfuls of soil from their hometowns to sprinkle over Tom's grave—their way of connecting the present to the past. Heartfelt personal thoughts of appreciation were shared, Cousin Joan Armstead sang an original song, and Nye County Sheriff DeMeo enlightened all with a history lesson on sheriffing, spanning from medieval times in England to the Wild West days of the late 1800s. DeMeo presented the family with a framed rubbing of Sheriff Logan's name from an engraving on the National Law Enforcement Officer Memorial Wall in Washington, D.C.

Finally, beneath a cheerful sun and to everyone's surpirse, Sheriff DeMeo posthumously awarded Sheriff Tom Logan the Nye County Sheriff's Office Medal of Valor and Purple Heart. Suggesting it mattered not if Tom had been killed on the steps of a bordello or a church, DeMeo acknowledged Tom Logan had acted in the interest of public safety and deserved recognition for having made the ultimate sacrifice. In part, the resolution read, *whereas*:

...Sheriff Logan attempted to settle the disturbance by escorting the suspect Barieau from the establishment.

Suspect Barieau brandished a weapon and shot six times at point-blank range striking Sheriff Thomas Logan with five rounds.

Although mortally wounded, Sheriff Logan was able to subdue the suspect until a deputy was able to arrive on scene and took the suspect into custody.

Before the suspect was removed from the scene of the shooting, it was reported that Sheriff Logan protected the suspect from bystanders who were about to assault the suspect in Sheriff Logan's custody.

It is hereby ordered Sheriff Logan will be awarded posthumously The Purple Heart for injuries suffered...and The Medal of Valor for his resolve to his Oath of Office, after being mortally wounded, he not only subdued an armed suspect, through his actions he safe-guarded the suspect from possible serious harm or death...."

An upwelling of pride in the man none had met, but all were finally getting to know, moved many to unexpected tears. Family—forever bound by blood and history, most of which cannot be changed nor should be. But every once in a while, when the moon is blue and the wind inconsolable, the past, however tragic or glorious, comes calling...and then anything is possible.

EPILOGUE

WHEN LIFE GOT hectic, which happened a lot in my grandmother's Oregon home during the 1950s and '60s, she often wished aloud that she was in Nevada and could just jump on a horse and ride off into the desert. I long imagined she merely wanted to escape the turmoil of a bad day or her over-crowded house. Now, after gathering so many buried fragments of our family history, much like the dogged prospectors who fanned out over the craggy terrain of Nye County so long ago, I think differently. Instead of running away, maybe there was some place in Hazel's past that she yearned to revisit, or perhaps something she was longing to find but never got that chance. Should that be the case, then maybe this book is that ride and, if nothing else, has brought some semblance of clarity to the burdensome throes of the unknown.

Hazel Logan (left) and friend, c. 1913, Nye County, NV (Logan Family Collection)

As a child, I was riveted to television programs like *Death Valley Days; Rawhide; Gunsmoke; Have Gun, Will Travel;* and *Bonanza*. My first crude attempt to write a book at the age of 14 was a western. The protagonist was a rebellious young woman, who could ride, rope, and shoot as well as any man, and wanted to make her own way in life. I still have the worn, spiral-spine notebook in which I created the Old West world I wished I had lived in—close to the earth, governed by the golden rule and common horse sense, replete with magnificent adventures, simple furnishings, and a hat for every occasion.

Ironically, my fictional western was randomly set in 1861, the year Tom Logan was born. Also, before knowing anything about his life, I would have three children, all three of whom would by chance be given names that had belonged to three of Tom and Hannah's eight children. Our oldest daughters share the name Elizabeth, our first-born sons the name Jay, and my youngest son was given "Logan" as his middle name. Adding to the intrigue, he was born on November 18, the same date as Tom's youngest son Roy, one week after Roy's death in 1982.

Had these connections occurred by coincidence, or were they attributable to the stealthy, inexplicable influence of bloodline? More than a few paranormal devotees have suggested influence from "the other side." For certain, I was driven by the same curiosity most have to know more about our roots and the historical context of those branches from which we grew. My search for answers related to the life and death of Tom Logan revealed to me a purposeful, imperfect life of value. With that awareness has come understanding and healing for me and other descendants of Tom and Hannah Logan. Like many others who lived and died during those early days of Nevada history, they are not unique, but that does not mean their time spent was not meaningful.

Finally, I appreciate discovering how profoundly truth can surprise and inform, disappoint and inspire, and be denied or accepted—*all at the same time*. Truth is not the same as fact. Still, in any form and forever wildly subject to interpretation, it certainly does have a way of finding voice if given the chance… even when it's buried six feet deep.

TODAY, THE JIM Butler Inn occupies the southeast corner of Main Street and Brougher Avenue in Tonopah where The American saloon once stood. This is the location where I intentionally "bunk" while doing research in Nye County. One guest unit in particular is positioned within a few feet of where the front door of my great-grandfather's saloon once swung open for patrons to come and go.

From inside my room, seated at a small table with a laptop and reams of notes, I can visualize through the lace-curtained window some of what I imagine Sheriff Tom Logan saw from this very spot more than a century ago. Surely, he too had watched the pale light of dawn brush the top of Mt. Brougher with a copper glow and transform a gray sky to blue as sunlight seeped into the awakening town below.

Where I now watch pedestrians hurry across the street between coasting tractor trailers, four-wheel-drive trucks, packs of motorcycles, and sleek, air-conditioned sedans heading to Las Vegas, the ancient winds still whistle in to sweep away modern-day trappings, and sepia-toned images flicker into view....

Once these unpaved thoroughfares swarmed with industry, and from lands, near and far, came prospectors with over-loaded burros, 20-mule-team freight wagons laden with sacks of ore, buckboards jammed with crates and furniture, horse-drawn buggies conveying officials to and fro, and thirsty cowboys, miners, and weary stage passengers in search of refreshment, refuge, and reward.

When I visit Tom Logan's grave, the wrenching stillness reminds me that here lies his body but not his life. Only at Main and Brougher do I best sense the initiative he brought to his work, his community, and his family. In this space, in front of the saloon bearing an eagle emblem, he had emerged countless times, signature cigar clenched in his teeth and hat firmly anchored, to mount his horse and take on the day.

Tom Logan's grave on the morning of his 150th birthday (Author Photo)

I hear the tin rattle of spurs, the groan of a saddle, and the enveloping clamor of a mining camp. In the air swirls the smell of burning wood, sizzling bacon, and simmering beans amid whiffs of whiskey and sagebrush. The tall, lanky man wearing a silver star on his chest nods hello to friend and newcomer alike. Lawman that he is, his keen gaze lingers slightly longer on the strangers and, with the squint of an eye or a tap of the pistol holstered on his hip, he quietly signals anyone plotting mayhem to step carefully under his watch…until that watch came to an end.

Here, in the heart of Tonopah, the intersection of Main and Brougher hosted drilling and mucking competitions, boxing matches, and countless processions—from jubilant holiday celebrations with marching bands and elaborate floats to columns of tearful mourners, dressed in black, accompanying the newly departed down the hill to the desert-encrusted cemetery.

There, rounding the corner near the stone-block Golden Building, inside a long, flower-draped coffin on a hand-drawn fire truck, once passed the earthly remains of Sheriff Thomas Walter Logan on his way through this intrepid little town for the last time....

Now, more than a century later, when I visit Nye County and the timeless, foraging winds circle around to greet me, I celebrate all that was *not* lost so long ago: letters, photos, news clippings, property deeds, court records, and family memories. With each discovery came fresh insight and more understanding about my great-grandfather's virtues and faults, how he lived and died, and his personal contribution to "Battle Born" Nevada.

Most of all, I am grateful for having at last found his voice. This is, after all, *his* story—one that he never had a chance to tell, and one I pray will finally allow "our Tom" to truly rest in peace.

ACKNOWLEDGMENTS

THIS BOOK OWES its existence to countless family, friends, and scholars known to me as the "Logan Posse." While many members have now "crossed the great divide," others continue to search for yet one more undiscovered facet that might enlighten, answer a lingering question, or fill a void in the life and times of Sheriff Tom Logan. To all of you, I am eternally grateful for your patience, diligence, and commitment to reconstructing his impact on the waning days of the Wild West.

To my soul mate and benevolent sounding board, Dean Hupp, I express my deepest appreciation for your stalwart company on this sometimes magical, often bumpy, always dusty journey. Also ever-present with an encouraging word, editorial comment, and red cowboy boots was my dear friend, Marsha Lang.

Cheerleading credits are owed Jeanette Sartain and Carol Wright; my brothers Randy, Ron, and Fred Otremba; my sister, Paula Lang; sons Jay and Eric Boor; daughter Stacey (Boor) Morgan and her husband Dave. Grandchildren Elizabeth and Joseph Morgan were exuberant, living reminders of the oft overlooked importance of preserving family history and building a legacy.

Four generations of Logan descendants have contributed memories, photos, letters, and other material vital to authenticating family history and events. Those individuals are: Clara (Logan) Smith, Hazel (Logan) Barton, Roy Logan, Amy (Logan) Darrough, Wesley and Dorothy Logan, Adele Eicher, Glen and Eleanor-Ann Logan, Loran Logan, Fern (Barton) Armstead, Harold Barton, Coral (Barton) Blake, Quintin Barton, Ruth (Barton) Davis, Dorothy (Barton) George, Bethany (Barton) Otremba, Bethel (Barton) Wormington, Richard Barton, Anna Mae (Barton) Caldwell, Ellen and Melvin Smith, Norm Rose, and cousins galore including Dale Rodrigues, Charles Clausen, Barbara Clausen, James Darrough III, Sue Hagner, and Helen (Charley) Hosburgh.

Invaluable research assistance was furnished by Heidi Englund, Michael Maher, Lee Brumbaugh, and Arline LaFerry from the Nevada Historical Society in Reno, NV. Equally willing to "go digging" with me was Eva LaRue, Allen Metscher, and Angela Haag from the Central Nevada Historical Society in Tonopah, NV. Their cumulative expertise was exceptional and their passion for early Nevada history wonderfully contagious.

Additional archival support was provided by: Jeff Kintop and Elizabeth Moore, Nevada State Archives, Carson City; Kelli Luchs and Delores Brownlee, University of Nevada Las Vegas Special Collections Division; Aina Trodden, Nevada Division of State Lands, Reno; Crystal Van Dee, Nevada State Museum, Las Vegas, NV; Wally Trapnell, Austin Historical Society, Austin, NV; Kay Ellerman, Mojave Museum of History and Arts, Kingman, AZ; Barbara Moss, Bishop Museum and Historical Society, Bishop, CA; Jim Ducker, Alaska Historical Society, Anchorage, AK: Sandra Johnston, Alaska State Library

Historical Collections, Juneau, AK; Cheryl Thompson, Carrie Mclain Memorial Museum, Nome, AK; Elizabeth Bouvier, Head of Archives for the Massachusetts Supreme Judicial Court; and Martha Reagan, Library Director at the *Boston Herald*.

Each widely published and recognized for their historical expertise, the following authors greatly helped guide me to set the political, economic, and social context of turn-of-the-century Nevada: Phillip Earl, Anne Seagraves, Michael Green, PhD, Sally Zanjani, Guy Rocha, Bill Pettite, Dana Bennett, Al Moe, Bob Nylen, David Beltran, Elizabeth Raymond, PhD. and Michael Fischer.

The Nye County clerk's office was a tremendous ongoing source of support in the process of researching civil and criminal court records. A huge thank you goes to County Clerk Sandra (Sam) Merlino and staffers Debra Melott, Amy Dowers, and Lisa Westerland. Special guidance for navigating antiquated public records was also provided by the Nye County assessor and recorder offices including: County Recorder Deborah Beatty, Theresa Pate, Vicky Walker, Dawn Gudmunson, and Jolyne Zimmerman. County Commissioner Joni Eastley and Sheriff Tony DeMeo could not have been more generous with their time and resources. They each exhibited extraordinary enthusiasm for honoring the history of the community they serve.

In neighboring Esmeralda County, Clerk-Treasurer Lacinda (Cindy) Elgan graciously facilitated research efforts in Goldfield. Special appreciation is extended to the one and only Virginia Ridgeway and the host of tenant spirits who provided a personal tour of the famed Goldfield Hotel built by George Wingfield in 1907.

Other long-time Nevada residents, from Reno to Las Vegas, who munificently shared the benefit of their knowledge include: Anne Berg, Henry and Bertie Berg, Claire Blackburn, Bob Bottom, Peter Breen, James Eason, Doug Gist, Tony Grimes, Shirley Ann Berg Henle, Jeanne Sharp Howerton, Ron James, Ron Matheny, Joe Mizzi, Sharon Pauley, Bob Perchetti, Bill Roberts, Terry Terras, "Banjo Bob" Beville, Rene Berg Zaval, and Tonopah's own Nancy Drew, Katherine Mizzi.

Frequent lodging accommodations at the Jim Butler Inn in Tonopah were made especially accommodating by owner Shirley Van Houten with the able assistance of Wanda Crisp and Andrea Williams Moss. Bunk facilities in Reno were routinely provided by Joan and Patrick Cringle—she being a dear childhood friend, who long ago became accustomed to my penchant for story-telling.

A heartfelt debt of gratitude is owed Sister Margaret McCarran and William (Bill) Barieau, both now deceased. Nearly 30 years ago, they each politely indulged my curiosity, and we soon found ourselves an unlikely trio united in a common quest to better comprehend the events surrounding Tom Logan's death.

Finally, I heap praise on my editor and publisher, Nan Wisherd. She is an author's dream—accessible, seasoned, thoughtful, tolerant, and thorough. In an industry where relationships are often trampled in the production process, I do not take for granted the personal touch she brings to her work. To Nan and her exceptionally talented Cable Publishing crew of Larry Verkeyn, Debbie Zime, and super intern Amanda Brown, thank you for believing in Sheriff Tom Logan's story.

APPENDIX

Judge Peter Breen's instructions to the jury in the Walter Barieau murder trial, Tonopah, NV, July 13, 1906.

Instructions submitted by the prosecution, District Attorney William Pittman and Hugh Percy:

1. Murder is the unlawful killing of a human being, with malice aforethought, either expressed or implied. The lawful killing may be affected by any of the various means by which death may be occasioned.

2. Express malice is that deliberate intention unlawfully to take away the life of a fellow creature, which is manifested by external circumstances capable of proof.

3. The court instructs that the time for deliberation and premeditation need not be long. If it furnishes room and opportunity for reflection, and the facts show that such reflection existed, and that the mind was busy with its designs, and made the choice with full time to choose otherwise, and for sufficient deliberation.

4. The court instructs that the law knows no specific time within which an intent to kill must be formed, so as to make it murder. If the will accompanies the act a moment antecedent to the act itself which causes death, it is as sufficient to make the offense murder s if it were a day or any other time.

5. The court instructs the jury that if they believe from the evidence that the defendant willfully, that is intentionally used upon deceased at some vital part, a pistol, in the absence of qualifying facts, defendant must be presumed to know that the effect is likely to be deadly, and knowing this must be presumed to intend death, which is the probable and ordinary consequence of such an act, and if such deadly weapon is used without just cause or provocation, he must be presumed to do it wickedly or from a bad heart, and if the jury believe that defendant took the life of deceased by shooting him in a vital part with a pistol, as set forth in the indictment, with manifest design to use such weapon upon him, and with sufficient time to deliberate and fully form the conscious purpose to kill and without sufficient reason or cause or extenuation, then such killing is murder in the first degree, and whilst it devolves on the State to prove the willfulness, deliberation and malice aforethought, all of which is necessary to constitute murder in the first degree, yet these need not be proved by direct evidence, but may be deduced from all the facts and circumstances attending the killing, and if the jury are satisfied, they will be warranted in finding the defendant guilty of murder in the first degree.

6. You are instructed that if you believe that the defendant did, with malice afore-thought, but without willful, deliberate premeditation shoot the deceased, with the intent then and there to kill him, and while so engaged did kill the deceased, you will find the defendant guilty of murder in the second degree.

7. The Court instructs that manslaughter is the unlawful killing of another without malice and may be either voluntary, as where the act is committed with a real design and purpose to kill, but through the violence of sudden passion occasioned by some great provocation, which in tenderness for the frailty of human nature, the law considers sufficient to palliate the criminality of the offense, or involuntary, as where the death of another is caused by some unlawful act not accompanied with any intention to take a life.

8. Gentlemen, you are also instructed that, if a person kill another in self-defense, it must appear that the danger was so urgent and pressing that, in order to save his life, or to prevent his receiving great bodily harm, the killing of the other was absolutely necessary; and it must appear that the person killed was the assailant, or that the slayer had really, and in good faith, endeavored to decline any further struggle before the mortal shot was given.

9. Gentlemen, you are instructed that a bare fear of personal violence or danger to the life of the defendant at the hands of deceased, to prevent which the homicide is alleged to have been committed, shall not be sufficient to justify the killing. It must appear that the circumstances were sufficient to excite the fears of a reasonable man and that the party killing really acted under the influence of those fears, and not in a spirit of revenge.

10. You are instructed that in the commission of every crime or public offense, there must be a union of joint operation of act and intent. The intention is manifested by the circumstances connected with the perpetration of the offense and the sound mind and discretion of the accused.

11. The Court instructs that a person must be presumed to intend to do that which he voluntarily and willfully does in fact do, and he must be presumed to intend all the natural, probable and usual course even if of his own acts.

12. Gentlemen, you are instructed that a "reasonable doubt" is one based on reason. It is not mere possible doubt, but is such a doubt as would govern or control a person in the more weighty affairs of life. If your minds, after the entire comparison and consideration of all the evidence, are in such a condition that you can say you feel an abiding conviction of the truth of the charge, there is not a reasonable doubt. Doubt to be reasonable must be actual and substantial, not mere possibility or speculation.

13. You are instructed that you are the sole judges of the facts and of the credibility of the witnesses, and in weighing their testimony, you can take into consideration their demeanor on the stand, and it is your duty to consider anything adduced by the evidence touching the credibility of a witness.

14. The Court instructs you, gentlemen, that if you believe from all the evidence, that any witness has willfully sworn falsely on this trial as to any matter or thing material to the issue in this case, then you are at liberty to disregard his entire testimony, except in so far as it has been corroborated by other evidence, or by facts and circumstances proved on the trial.

Instructions submitted by the defense, Lead Counsel Stephen Flynn and Patrick McCarran:

I

(a) It is a cardinal principle of the law that the Defendant in a criminal trial must be presumed innocent of the crime for which he is indicted until guilt is proven beyond a reasonable doubt, and in this case I charge you it is your duty to give the Defendant the benefit of that presumption of innocence.

(b) That presumption of innocence does not cease when you as a Jury retire to deliberate upon you verdict. It accompanies this Defendant through the Trial, down to and through you deliberations after you have retired, and it is your duty if possible to reconcile the evidence with this presumption of the Defendant's innocence.

(c) AND FURTHER I charge you that the facts established by the evidence should not only satisfy you that they are consistent with the Defendant's guilt, but inconsistent with any other reasonable hypothesis, if they do not so convince you, the Defendant should be acquitted.

II

(a) In determining the weight or effect you should give to the testimony of the several witnesses you should consider their respective testimony from the standpoint of its probability or improbability, you should also take into consideration the character of the witnesses (added by Breen: when material and put in evidence) —their motives, their interests, their prejudices or their bias.

(b) After having done so the effect to be given to the testimony of any witness solely rests with you. If you should believe the testimony of any one or more witnesses because of its inherent probability, or because of its agreement with the material circumstances surrounding the main or principal event, which in this case would be the shooting of the deceased, you have the right to accept the testimony of that witness or witnesses, though you find it to be in conflict of all other testimony in the case; and this applies to the testimony of each and every witness, including the defendant.

(c) If you find that a witness, or witnesses, have willfully sworn as to any material fact you may disregard her or his or their testimony, or such parts thereof as is uncorroborated by the testimony of credible witnesses.

(d) *Refused by Judge Breen and not given to the jury*: The character of the several witnesses should be considered, the good character of the witness should weigh in the witness's favor; while on the other hand, the bad character of a witness should weigh against the witness; and I charge you that if you find from the evidence that one of the witnesses for the State is the keeper of a disorderly house, or a house of ill fame and that other witnesses for the State are prostitutes, I charge you as to the testimony of those witnesses that it should be disregarded unless corroborated in every essential particular by the testimony of credible witnesses.

(e) *Refused by Judge Breen and not given to the jury*: It is understood that the deceased was not acting in his official capacity as Sheriff of Nye County or in any other official capacity when he met his death at the hands of the defendant. He wore no insignia nor badge of office, nor is it claimed that he informed the defendant or that the defendant knew that he was Sheriff of Nye County before the shooting took place, I charge you therefore that the fact that he was Sheriff of this County should not weigh against the defendant in this case.

III

If you find on all the evidence that deceased assaulted Defendant, and that it reasonably appeared to Defendant that deceased was about to take his life, or inflict serious bodily injury upon him, and to prevent this result Defendant shot at deceased, he should be acquitted; and further, that Defendant would have the right to continue to shoot as long as there was an appearance of danger to his life or serious bodily injury; and that it was not essential to the right of self defense that imminent danger should actually exist,—if it were reasonably apparent from the circumstances, the Defendant would have the same right to defend himself against it as he would have had were the danger real, —the appearance should be viewed from the Defendant's standpoint.

IV

If the Defendant, in the position in which he was placed, and with the light and knowledge which he then had, had reasonable ground to believe that the deceased intended to kill him or do him some great bodily injury, and the circumstances as they came to his knowledge were sufficient to excite the fears of a reasonable person, that the deceased was about to murder him or do him great bodily injury, and that the danger thereof was imminent, and, if, acting on his fears he killed deceased to protect himself, then such killing was justifiable and the Defendant should be acquitted.

V

Refused by Judge Breen and not given to the jury on the basis of being contra-dictory and redundant: Although the necessity for taking deceased's life was not actual, present and urgent, the right of self defense was properly exercised by Defendant if he was assaulted by deceased and had reasonable ground to believe, and in good faith did believe, from the conditions present, that death or the infliction of great bodily harm was imminent.

VI

Refused by Judge Breen and not given to the jury noting "not law:" If you find from the evidence that deceased was a powerful man and that defendant was in a weakened physical condition, and deceased assaulted Defendant with the fist alone, if there was apparent purpose and ability to inflict death or serious bodily injury upon Defendant, and Defendant believed in good faith that such was the purpose of deceased, such an assault was sufficient to justify killing in self defense.

VII

(a) *Refused by Judge Breen and not given to the jury:* If before defendant fired the first shot, deceased attacked him with a weapon calculated to produce death or serious bodily injury, the law presumes deceased intended to murder or aimed to inflict serious bodily injury on the Defendant, and if on a consideration of all the evidence you find such to be the fact, or if you entertain a reasonable doubt as to whether or not such was the fact you must resolve that doubt in Defendant's favor and bring in a verdict of not guilty.

(b) *Refused by Judge Breen and not given to the jury:* And further Defendant was assaulted with a deadly weapon and he did not provoke the assault or bring on the difficulty, he was not bound to retreat, but had a right to stand and defend himself; and if the necessity arose for taking the life of the deceased in order to save himself from death or serious bodily injury, such killing is justifiable on the ground of self defense.

VIII

(a) That in deciding on Defendant's guilt, you should determine what an ordinary and reasonable man might have fairly inferred from all the facts and circumstances surrounding Defendant, and in so going must not try him in the light of subsequent developments, nor must you require of him the same cool judgment that you can now bring to bear upon the occurrence. You must put yourself in the Defendant's place and then judge whether the danger was apparent or should have been considered apparent by a man of ordinary caution and prudence in like condition, and you must consider that the danger need not have been real, present or urgent at the very moment of killing, but only apparently so.

(b) *Refused by Judge Breen and not given to the jury on the basis of redundancy:*
A reasonable doubt is one based on reason. It is not mere possible doubt, but
is such doubt as would govern or control a person in the more weighty affairs
of life. If in the mind of the jurors, after the entire comparison and consideration
of all the evidence, are in such a condition that they can say they feel an abiding
conviction of the truth of the charge, there is not a responsible doubt. Doubt
to be reasonable must not be actual and substantial, not mere possibility or
speculation.

CHAPTER NOTES

Chapter One

1. *Logan Family Reunion: Overton, NV*, transcript of recollections, November 28, 1953, Logan Family Archives.

2. Clara Logan Smith, *My Mother's Trip Across the Plains in the Year 1856*, a personal essay, 1935, Logan Family Archives.

3. Conrad P. Cline, b. 1756, Warwick, PA; d. 1837, Marlborough, OH; Genealogical Records, Logan Family Archives.

4. "Marriages," *Daily Bee*, Sacramento, CA, July 9, 1860.

5. *Reunion*, transcript.

6. Laura Haffey, personal letter to Clara Logan Smith, 1935, Logan Family Archives.

7. Susannah Perkins lived out her days toiling against the elements with meager means until her death in 1906. Robert Perkins, also with little to show for his lifelong ventures, died five years earlier in Los Angeles at the age of 83.
Genealogical Records, Logan Family Archives.

8. Ellen Smith Papers, photocopied packet of family research, 1990, Logan Family Archives.

9. Edward B. Scott, *Saga of Lake Tahoe*, (Crystal Bay, Lake Tahoe, NV: Sierra-Tahoe Publishing Co., 1957, Volume I), pp. 257-59; (1973, Volume II), pp. 70-71.

10. "DIED," *Virginia Daily Union*, Virginia City, NV, August 7, 1864.

11. Oscar Lewis, *The Town That Died Laughing* (Boston, MA: Little Brown, 1955), p. 3.

12. *Daily Reese River Reveille*, Austin, NV, October 11, 1865.

13. Lewis, p. 99.

14. *Reveille*, October 11, 1865.

15. Nevada State Parks, Dept. of Conservation & Natural Resources, 10. www.park.nv.gov/parks/belmont-courthouse, 2012.

16. "Our Hidden Wealth: The White Pine Silver Mines," *New York Tribune*, New York, NY, August 10, 1869.

17. Lincoln County Nevada, *The Town of Pioche*, www. lincolncountynevada.com.

18. Sam Davis, *History of the State of Nevada* (Reno, NV: The Elms Publishing Company, Inc., 1913), p. 487.

19. Ibid., pp. 653-54.

20. *Reunion*, transcript.

21. Arabell Lee Hafner, *100 Years on The Muddy* (Springfield, UT: Art City Publishing, 1967), p. 131.

22. Ellen Smith Papers.

23. *Reunion*, transcript.

24. Dorothy Logan, personal letter to Norm Rose, September 26, 1986.

25. Dorothy Logan, letter to Norm Rose.

26. "Death of Mrs. Logan," *Pioche Daily Record*, Pioche, NV, March 11, 1882.

27. Paul Bailey, *Jacob Hamblin: Buckskin Apostle* (Los Angeles, CA: Westernlore Press, 1948), pp.7-8.

28. Robert D. Arner, *The Story of Hannah Duston: Cotton Mather to Thoreau*, American Transcendental Quarterly, 18, 1973, pp. 19-23.

29. "Local Intelligence," *Daily Record*, Pioche, NV, June 2, 1883.

30. Dorothy Logan, letter to Norm Rose.

31. Ibid.

32. *Mojave County Miner*, Mineral Park, AZ, September 9, 1884.

33. *Mojave Miner*, January 25, 1885.

34. *Reunion*, transcript of recollections.

35. *Mojave Miner*, December 26, 1884.

36. *Pioche Weekly Record*, Pioche, NV, January 11, 1907.

37. "Local Intelligence," *Pioche Weekly Record*, Pioche, NV, May 1, 1886.

38. *Arizona Weekly Journal*, April 28, 1886.

39. *Mojave Miner*, Mineral Park, AZ, August 8, 1886.

40. Dan Messersmith, *Mohave Memories: Kingman a Short History*, Mojave Museum of History & Arts, 2000.

41. *Mojave Miner*, February 25, 1888.

42. Anna Mae (Barton) Caldwell, personal letter to author, September 17, 1977.

43. Robert Logan Note to Surveyor General, February 24, 1892, Logan Family Archives.

44. "Commissioner's Proceedings," *Weekly Record*, June 8, 1893.

45. *Pioche Daily*, April 18, 1895.

46. Ibid., May 7, 1896.

47. *Reunion*, transcript.

Chapter Two

1. Sheriff Tony DeMeo, Nye County, NV, grave-side presentation on the occasion of Sheriff Tom's Logan's 150th birthday, May 28, 2011.
2. *Belmont Courier*, Belmont, NV, January 7, 1899.
3. *Population of Counties by Decennial Census: 1900 to 1990*, compiled and edited by Richard L. Forstall, Population Divisions, US Bureau of the Census, Washington, DC, March 27, 1995.
4. Jim Butler essay photocopy, unknown author, c. 1920s, Logan Family Archives.
5. Sally Zanjani, *Jack Longstreet: The Last of the Desert Frontiersmen* (Athens, OH: Swallow Press/Ohio University Press, 1988), p. 81.
6. James Warren Nye, *Biographical Directory of the U.S. Congress*.
7. P.E. Keeler, "Chapter LV: Nye County," *The History of Nevada*, Vol. II, Sam P. Davis, ed. (Reno, NV: The Elms Publishing, 1912), p. 962.
8. Zanjani, p. 84.
9. *Courier*, December 2, 1899.
10. *Courier*, April 29, 1899.
11. *Mojave Miner*, November 27, 1897.
12. *Mojave Miner*, September 16, 1899.
13. Zanjani, pp. 94-95.
14. *Reunion*, transcript.

Chapter Three

1. William Douglas and Robert Nylen, ed., *Letters from the Nevada Frontier: Correspondence of Tasker L. Oddie, 1899-1902* (Reno, NV: University of Nevada Press, 2004) p. 191.
2. Ibid., p. xii.
3. Ibid., p. xii, 184.
4. Ibid., pp. 191-194.
5. Ibid., p. 209.
6. *Courier,* July 7, 1900.
7. Douglas and Nylen, *Letters*, p. 178.
8. *Reunion*, transcript.
9. Douglas and Nylen, *Letters*, p. 358.
10. Robert "Bob" McCracken, "Questions linger in Nye legend," *Pahrump Valley Times*, Pahrump, NV, March 12, 2012.
11. Butler essay.
12. Ibid.
13. *Courier,* September 8, 1900.
14. *Courier*, September 15, 1900.
15. Douglas and Nylen, *Letters*, p. 240.
16. *Courier,* November 6, 1900.
17. Butler essay.
18. James W. Travers, *Tonopah, Past, Present, Future: History of the World's Greatest Mining Camp* (publisher unknown, 1902), Nevada Historical Society, Reno, NV.
19. Richard G. Lillard, *Desert Challenge: An Interpretation of Nevada* (New York, NY: Alfred A. Knopf, 1949), p. 241.
20. "Tonopah's Looking Back on Half Century of History," *Nevada State Journal,* Reno, NV, May 14, 1950.
21. Robert "Bob" McCracken, *History of Tonopah, Nevada* (Tonopah, NV: Nye County Press, 1990).

Chapter Four

1. Minutes of Meeting, State Board of Assessors with the State Revenue Board, Carson City, April 1 to 4, 1901 (Carson City, NV: State Printing Office), p. 4.
2. Ibid., pp. 22-23.
3. Ibid., pp. 10-11, 25.
4. *Tonopah Bonanza*, Tonopah, NV, June 29, 1901.
5. *Bonanza*, August 10, 1901.
6. *Bonanza*, July 6, 1901.
7. *Bonanza*, July 27, 1901.
8. *Bonanza*, August 17, 1901.
9. *Bonanza*, July 13, 1901.
10. *Bonanza*, August 10, 1901.
11. "A Man Sits on 25 Pounds of Giant Powder and Applies Match," *Bonanza*, July 13, 1901.
12. *Bonanza*, July 20, 1901.
13. *Bonanza*, August 3, 1901.
14. *Bonanza*, October 5, 1901.
15. *Bonanza*, November 9, 1901.
16. *Bonanza*, December 21, 1901.
17. JoVon Sotak, Oldhouseweb.com, August 29, 2011.
18. "Tonopah's First Funeral," *Reno Evening Gazette*, September 13, 1950.
19. *Bonanza*, November 23, 1901.
20. *Bonanza*, January 4, 1902.
21. Casey Tefertiller, *Wyatt Earp: The Life Behind the Legend* (Hoboken, NJ: John Wiley & Sons, Inc., 1997), pp. 1-2.
22. Ibid., pp. 306-310.
23. Mrs. Hugh (Marjorie Moore) Brown, *Lady in Boomtown: Miners and Manners on the Nevada Frontier* (Reno-Las Vegas, NV: University of Nevada Press, 1968), pp. 35-36.
24. Josephine Sarah Marcus Earp, *I Married Wyatt Earp* (Tucson, AZ: The University of Arizona Press, 1979), p. 212.
25. "Sheriff Thomas Logan is Shot and Killed by Walter Berieau [sic]: He Cowed Earp," *Tonopah Daily Sun*, Tonopah, NV, April 7, 1906.
26. *Minutes of Assessors' Meeting*, State Board of Assessors with the State Revenue Board, Carson City, January 13-15, 1902 (State Printing Office, Carson City, NV), pp. 2-16.

27. Butler essay.

28. *Report of the State Board of Health, 1901-02,* Appendix to Journals of the Senate and Assembly, 1905, pp. 5-7.

29. *Bonanza,* February 8, 1902.

30. Ibid.

31. "Samuel Findley Fails in his Endeavor to Kill Wm Lavelle and in Return is Shot Through the Head," *Bonanza,* March 1, 1902.

32. Ibid.

33. Ibid.

34. *Bonanza,* June 21, 1902.

35. *Bonanza,* July 12, 1902.

36. "Tonopah Happenings," *Nevada State Journal,* Reno, NV, August 21, 1902.

37. *Bonanza,* August 23, 1902.

38. *Bonanza,* September 14, 1902.

39. *Bonanza,* April 5 & 26, 1902; June 7, 1902.

Chapter Five

1. "The Conventions," *Gazette,* August 26, 1902.

2. "A Political Directory of Nevada—A project of the Nevada Historical Society," Retired Seniors Volunteer Program (RSVP), Waller H. Reed, volunteer, Nevada Historical Society, Reno, NV.

3. "Unfair Tactics," *Bonanza,* November 1, 1902.

4. *Bonanza,* October 18, 1902.

5. *Bonanza,* November 1, 1902.

6. *Bonanza,* November 22, 1902.

7. *Bonanza,* November 15, 1902.

8. "News of the State," *Journal,* September 24, 1902.

9. Bill Pettite interviews, Spring 2013, Sacramento, CA.

10. *Bonanza,* January 10, 1903.

11. *Bonanza,* January 3, 1903.

12. *Bonanza,* February 14, 1903.

13. "Butler Saloon Held Up," *Bonanza,* January 24, 1903.

14. Ibid.

15. *Bonanza,* February 21, 1903.

16. *Bonanza,* January 17, 1903.

17. *Bonanza,* February 7, 1903.

18. *Bonanza,* February 21, 1903; March 14, 1906.

19. *Bonanza,* March 21, 1903.

20. *Bonanza,* April 4, 1903.

21. *Bonanza,* April 11, 1903.

22. *Bonanza,* May 9, 1903.

23. Edwin Hamblin, personal letter to granddaughter, Annie Logan, Letter, January 25, 1903.

24. Hazel Logan Barton, family recollections known to author.

25. *Bonanza,* May 9, 1903.

26. *Bonanza,* May 23, 1903.

27. "An Official Outrage: Nightwatchman Booth Arrested on Flimsy Pretext," *Bonanza,* May 23, 1903.

28. "Festivities of the Fourth End With Cruel Murder: Walter Dunn the Victim of a Fiend," *Bonanza,* July 11, 1903.

29. *Bonanza,* July 11, 1903; August 1, 1903.

30. "Woeful Miscarriage of Justice in Belmont Court," *Bonanza,* August 8, 1903.

31. "Gang of Thugs Attach Chinese Quarter: Kill One, Murderously Assault Others and Then Attempt to Drive Them Out of Town," *Bonanza,* September 19, 1903.

32. Sue Fawn Chung with Elmer Rusco, *Chinese America: History and Perspectives 2003,* "The Anti-Chinese Riot in Tonopah, Nevada, 1903," pp. 35-44, Chinese Historical Society of America, 2003.

33. Ibid.

34. "Must Comply with Law," *Bonanza,* September 26, 1903.

35. "As to Sheriff Cushing," *Bonanza,* October 10, 1903.

36. *Bonanza,* October 24, 1903.

37. *Bonanza,* December 12, 1903.

38. *Gazette,* December 15, 1903.

39. "Dunn's Slayer Set Free," *Bonanza,* December 19, 1903.

40. "Prisoners Escape from County Jail," *Bonanza,* October 10, 1903.

41. *Bonanza,* October 3, 1903.

Chapter Six

1. C. Elizabeth Raymond, *George Wingfield: Owner and Operator of Nevada* (Reno, NV: The University of Nevada Press, 1992), pp. 8-10.

2. Ibid., pp. 23-26.

3. Mining Locations, Book J, pp. 59-66, Nye County Recorder's Office, Tonopah, NV.

4. David H. Grover, *Diamondfield Jack: A Study in Frontier Justice,* (Reno, NV, University of Nevada Press, 1968), pp. 142-145.

5. Ibid., pp. 159-60.

6. Loran Logan interviews with author, 2011-12, Reno, NV.

7. *Journal,* November 24, 1901.

8. Douglas and Nylen, *Letters,* p. 355.

9. Deeds, Book R, pp. 241-43, Nye County Recorder's Office, Tonopah, NV.

10. Dale Rae Rodrigues (great-granddaughter of James Darrough and Tom Logan) interviews with author, 2012-13, Smoky Valley, NV.

11. Ibid.

12. Nye County Tax Assessment Rolls, 1903, 1904, and 1905, Nye County Recorder's Office, Tonopah, NV.

13. Raymond, *Wingfield,* p. 23.

14. "R.F. Gilbert Died at Noon," *Bonanza,* April 15, 1920.

15. "Indian Dan Goes a Gunning, but Meets His Waterloo," *Bonanza,* July 2, 1904.

16. "Shooting Affray: W.S. Elliott Kills Madigan and Wounds Hamilton," *Bonanza,* August 20, 1904.

17. Chas. L Richards, District Attorney of Nye County, personal letter to the State Board of Prisons, July 20, 1904, Nevada State Library and Archives, Carson City, NV.

18. "Communicated," *Bonanza,* August 6, 1904.

19. "Program of Railroad Day Celebration," *Bonanza,* July 23, 1904.

20. "The Democratic Split in Nye: Farmers and Miners were Ignored," *Gazette,* September 25, 1904.

21. "Democratic Ticket," *Bonanza,* October 1, 1904.

22. "A Political Club," *Bonanza,* October 8, 1904.

23. "Candidates for Sheriff: Two Sterling Good Men are in the Field for this Office," *Bonanza,* November 5, 1904.

24. "Horrible Murder in Tonopah: Dead Body of a Man Found in North Star Tunnel." *Bonanza,* November 19, 1904.

Chapter Seven

1. *Bonanza,* November 12, 1904.

2. "Nevada Interests in 1904: Nye County," *Salt Lake Tribune,* January 1, 1905.

3. Minutes of Meeting, State Board of Assessors with the State Revenue Board, Carson City, January 9-10, 1905 (Carson City, NV: State Printing Office), pp. 4-20.

4. Ibid., pp. 14-15.

5. Ibid. p. 16.

6. "The News from Carson," *Sun,* January 22, 1905.

7. "The County Seat," *Bonanza,* January 28, 1905.

8. James Cushing, resignation letter to Governor John Sparks, May, 4, 1906, Sparks Papers, Nevada State Library and Archives, Carson City, NV.

9. Governor John Sparks response letter, May 8, 1906, Sparks Papers, Nevada State Library and Archives, Carson City, NV.

10. "Tonopah is Now Actually the County Seat," *Sun,* May 2, 1905.

11. Arrest Warrant, Justice Court of Tonopah Township, Criminal Records, January 27, 1905, Nye County Clerk's Office, Tonopah, NV.

12. "Simpson Shot by William Shipe: Wounded Man Still Alive and May Recover—Cause of Trouble Unknown—Assailant Surrenders," *Sun,* January 28, 1905.

13. Sister Margaret, *McCarran 1876-1954.*

14. Patrick A. McCarran, Unpublished Autobiography (undated), McCarran Papers, Nevada Historical Society, Reno, NV.

15. Sister Margaret, *McCarran 1876-1954.*

16. McCarran, Autobiography.

17. Sister Margaret, *McCarran 1876-1954.*

18. "The State Senatorship," *Gazette,* October 25, 1904.

19. "The Eve of the Election," *Gazette,* November 7, 1904.

20. "Charged with Destroying U.S. Telephone Poles Placed on his Ranch," *Gazette,* July 13, 1905.

21. Sister Margaret, *McCarran 1876-1954.*

22. Jerome E. Edwards, *Pat McCarran: Political Boss of Nevada* (Reno, NV: University of Nevada Press, 1982), p. 8.

23. "New Legal Firm," *Sun,* September 24, 1905.

24. "Will Enforce Sanitation Laws in Tonopah: District Attorney Pittman Emphatically Declares Himself—Sheriff Logan to Stand by Him," *Sun,* January 12, 1905.

25. "Will Abate the Nuisances: Owners Agree to Clean their Back Yards," *Sun,* February 26, 1905.

26. "Should Help Desert Mariners," *Sun,* February 3, 1905.

27. Phillip Earl, "This Was Nevada: Desert Frontiersman Featured in New Exhibit," *Henderson Home News, Boulder City News,* and *Grass Valley News,* March 14-15, 1991.

28. "Highwayman Lynched by Mob of Angry Citizens," *Sun,* March 1, 1905.

29. "George Logan Appointed Night Watchman," *Sun,* February 4, 1905.

30. "Wyatt Erb [sic] Coming to Goldfield: His Brother Already in the Camp," *Sun,* February 11, 1905.

31. "Nye County Salary Measure," *Sun,* March 14, 1905.

32. "Disease Breeders Must Go:
Commissioners Take Most Emphatic Stand,"
Sun, March 23, 1905.

Chapter Eight

1. "Does His Duty in Face of Death," *Sun*,
March 24, 1905.
2. "Pitched Battle with Outlaws," *Bonanza*,
March 25, 1905.
3. Ibid.
4. *Oakland Tribune*, Oakland, CA, April 7, 1905.
5. "$400 is Offered for Arrest of Crouch,"
Gazette, April 19, 1905.
6. Phillip I. Earl, "Killer of Nye County lawman
never captured," *Gazette*, Reno, NV, June 14,
1987.
7. "Don't Ask Too Much," *Bonanza*,
March 25, 1905.
8. "This Stampede is No Fake: Grafters Find Poor
Picking Here," *Sun*, April 9, 1905.
9. *Bonanza*, April 8, 1905.
10. "Let Fears Be Calmed and Liars
Be Silent," *Sun*, April 11, 1905.
11. "Alarming Tales From Tonopah: Stories of
Death Harvest Denial Comes from the Camp—
Governor Sparks will Act at Once," *Gazette*,
April 14, 1905.
12. Ibid.
13. "He Died About One Hour Ago,"
Journal, April 15, 1905.
14. "Reno Journal Condemned by Citizen's
Committee," *Sun*, April 16, 1905
15. "Disease Raging in Reno: Overrun by
Smallpox and Pneumonia," *Sun*, May 4, 1905.
16. "Body of Thomas Logan Laid at Rest,"
Manhattan News, April 14, 1906.
17. "Disease is Under Control: L. De. Sallier Says
Tonopah is Cleaning House and Caring for the
Sick," *Gazette*, April 24, 1905.
18. "Expectoration on Tonopah Sidewalks," *Sun*,
March 10, 1905.
19. "Court House Should be on Brougher
Avenue," *Sun*, March 17, 1905.
20. "About the Court House Site,
Gentlemen," *Sun*, March 19, 1905.
21. "Contract Let for Building Nye County Court
House," *Sun*, April 14, 1905.
22. "Divide the County," *Beatty Bullfrog Miner*,
Bullfrog, NV, May 20, 1905.
23. "Vigilantes May be Organized," *Sun*, April 7,
1905.
24. "New Township and Jail," *Bullfrog Miner*,
May 13, 1905.
25. "A Gala Day in Tonopah," *Bonanza*,
June 10, 1905.
26. *Lovelock Review Miner*, July 22, 1932.
27. "Law and Justice are Now Holding Sway in
Tonopah," *Sun*, June 8, 1905.
28. "Grand Jury makes Report," *Bonanza*, June 17,
1905.
29. Ibid.
30. "Just Plain Folks garbed in Cotton Garments,"
Sun, May 11, 1905.
31. "The Night that Pomeroy was Introduced in
Tonopah City," *Sun*, July 18, 1905.

Chapter Nine

1. "Shocking Murder and Suicide in the Tonopah
Tenderloin," *Sun*, September 3, 1905.
2. Nye County Commissioners' Minutes, Book D,
September 14, 1905, Nye County Clerk's
Office, Tonopah, NV.
3. *Tonopah Directory, Southern Nevada –
Consolidated Telephones and Telegraph
Company*, January 1906, Central Nevada
Historical Society, Tonopah, NV.
4. "Biggs v. Biggs," (#3170), divorce action filed
April 15, 1903, 2nd Judicial District, Cochise
County Clerk's Office, Bisbee, AZ.
5. "Wanted in Phoenix," *Weekly Orb*, Bisbee, AZ,
July 2, 1899.
6. "Biggs v. Biggs."
7. Chattel Mortgages, Cochise County, June 9,
1903, p. 171, Cochise County Clerk's Office,
Bisbee, AZ.
8. Deeds, Cochise County, August 6, 1903,
Cochise County Clerk's Office, Bisbee, AZ.
9. "Advertised Letter List," *Journal*,
October 18, 1904, May 3, 1905, and
December 19, 1905.
10. Coroner Jury's Inquest, transcribed by Etta
Hoffman, April 7, 1906, p. 14, **"State of
Nevada v. W. A. Barieau,"** Nye County Clerk's
Office, Tonopah, NV.
11. "They Who Dally with Justice," *Sun*,
October 9, 1905.
12. Ibid.,
13. "Grand Opening," *Bonanza*, July 29, 1905.
14. "Board of Trade Gets Support of all Labor
unions," *Sun*, August 2, 1905.
15. "Incompetent and Unwilling," *Sun*, August 6,
1905.

16. "Tonopah Business Houses Must Pay Licenses," *Sun*, August 9, 1905.

17. "An Ordinance," *Bonanza*, August 12, 1905.

18. "Prisoners Will do the Work," *Sun*, August 10, 1905.

19. Commissioners' Minutes, September 6, 1905.

20. "Handsome badge for McKenzie: Presentation Made at Tonopah Club," *Sun*, November 11, 1905.

21. "Tonopah's Young Poundmaster," *Bonanza*, October 14, 1905.

22. "Heavy Taxpayers: Names of Those who Help Pay the County Expenses," *Bonanza*, October 28, 1905.

23. Commissioners' Minutes, November 9, 1905.

24. "Water Pipes Frozen," *Bonanza*, December 30, 1905.

25. "Indian's Absence Still Clogs Wheels of Justice," *Sun*, November 13, 1905.

26. "Big Law Suit Draws to a Close," *Sun*, November 16, 1905.

27. Ibid.

28. Tom Logan, personal letter to Annie, Josephine, and Jesse, December 13, 1905, Logan Family Archives.

29. "Death of W. H. Cowan: A Popular Public Official Passes Away," *Bonanza*, November 18, 1905.

30. *Bonanza*, December 23, 1905 and January 6, 1906.

31. "County Officials on the Rack: Grand Jury Recommends that Commissioners No Longer Violate the Statutes and Reprimands Sheriff," *Sun*, November 24, 1905.

32. "Grand Juror Makes Sharp Reply to Sheriff Logan," *Sun*, March 10, 1906.

33. "Letter Writer Called a Liar," *Sun*, March 11, 1906.

34. "Thomas W. Logan, Sheriff v. F. W. Schmalling," public auction, Third Judicial District Court of the State of Nevada, Nye County, March 2, 1906, Book Q, pp. 430-435, Nye County Clerk's Office, Tonopah , NV.

Chapter Ten

1. Deeds, Book Z, p. 638, Nye County Recorder's Office, Tonopah, NV.

2. Bob Bottom interview with author, 2013, Manhattan, NV.

3. 1900 U.S Federal Census, San Francisco City, San Francisco County, CA.

4. "Nevada's Gold Camp is Growing Rapidly," *San Francisco Call*, San Francisco, CA, January 29, 1906.

5. E. Marks, subpoena, July 9, 1906, Nye County Court Records, Nye County Clerk's Office, Tonopah, NV.

6. "How it All Started," *Bonanza*, June 20, 1906; Robert "Bob" McCracken, *Manhattan: The Land of Heart's Desire* (Tonopah, NV: Nye County Press, 2008) p. 14.

7. Mine location documents, July 24, 1905 to March 8, 1906, Nye County Recorder's Office, Tonopah, NV, Logan Family Archives.

8. Edwin W. R. Lawrence, "Manhattan, Nevada," *The Pacific Monthly*, Vol. 16, Portland, OR, pp. 539-42.

9. Cada Castolas Boak, personal letter to his wife, MSNC 60, Nevada Historical Society, Reno, NV.

10. *Crocker-Langley Directory*, 1901-05, San Francisco, CA.

11. Barton W. Currie, "Wild West in Nevada," *New York Saturday Evening Post*, September 22, 1906.

12. "Attempt to Rob a Saloon," *Sun*, January 6, 1906.

13. Ibid.

14. *Sun*: "Jury Decides Accused Guilty," February 3, 1906; "Arthur Morgan Shot Four Times this Morning at Manhattan by Jack Evans," February 17, 1906; "Man Hurt in Shooting Fray at Manhattan," March 20, 1906; and "Self-Defense is the Jury's Verdict," March 22, 1906.

15. "Handcuffed in Tall Cedars," *Gazette*, March 8, 1906.

16. "Clampers and no Mistake," *Carson City News*, January 9, 1906.

17. "Assessors have a Feast," *Gazette*, January 8, 1906.

18. "Railroad Man Dines Assessors," *Journal*, January 10, 1906.

19. "A Beautiful Site," *Bonanza*, February, 24, 1906.

20. "Union Miners Shot Down: During Quarrel in Southern Country," *Gazette*, January 29, 1906,

21. "J.C. Hennessy Held for the Grand Jury," *Sun*, February 3, 1906.

22. Nye County Court Records, June 18, 1906, Nye County Clerk's Office, Tonopah, NV.

23. *Appendix to Journals of Senate and Assembly of the Twenty-third Session of the Legislature of the State of Nevada, 1907, Carson City, Nevada*; Biennial Report of the Nevada State Prisons for the years 1905-06, Nevada Historical Society, Reno NV.

24. Commissioners' Minutes, February 5, 1906.

25. "Race War in Berlin is Averted," *Sun*, March 7, 1906.

26. "Bravery of Deputies Prevents Riot in Berlin," *Sun*, March 8, 1906.

27. "Race War in Berlin is Averted," *Sun*, March 7, 1906.

28. "May Wingfield v. George Wingfield," Answer to Plaintiff, Third Judicial District Court of the State of Nevada, Nye County, March 2, 1906, pp. 19-22, Nye County Clerk's Office, Tonopah, NV.

29. Raymond, *Wingfield*, pp. 49-50.

30. Olephia "Leafy" King, *"Dust and Desire, Laughter and Tears: Recollections of a Nevada Cowgirl and Poet,"* interviewed by Carol E. Colip, p. 12, University of Nevada Oral History Program, 1980, Reno, NV.

Chapter Eleven

1. "Sheriff Thomas Logan is Shot and Killed by Walter Berieau (sic): In an Accident," *Sun*, April 7, 1906.

2. Inquest, p. 13.

3. William G. Barieau Family History Papers, 1971, given to author at the 1985 Logan Family Reunion, Belmont, NV, Logan Family Archives.

4. "The Merrimac Street Wife Murder," *Boston Journal*, Boston, MA, July 18, 1872.

5. Ibid.

6. Barieau Papers, 1971.

7. Ibid.

8. "Games Pulled: Seven Festive Sports Arrested by the Police Last Night," *Sacramento Daily Union*, May 3, 1893.

9. "Barieau Once made Home in Sacramento," *Sacramento Evening Bee*, April 9, 1906.

10. "Standing Fat: The Chinese Lottery Men Still Refuse to Pay their Losses," *Union*, March 2, 1895.

11. Ibid.

12. "Two Lottery Joints Broken Up: Successful Raids Made by Determined Policemen," *Union*, March 4, 1895.

13. "Barieau Discharged," *Union*, March 20, 1895.

14. "Seized the Furniture: Constable Faris Had a Very Lively Time of it Monday, *Union*, March 13, 1895.

15. "Last Sad Rites for the Dead Sheriff: Berieau [sic] is Calm," *Sun*, April 10, 1906; Barieau Papers, 1971.

16. *Rhyolite: Metropolis of Southern Nevada* (Rhyolite: Richard E. Sinclair, 1907), Central Nevada Historical Society, Tonopah, NV.

17. "Maxwell, Sunday, Hoggatt All Boyhood Chums; L.Q. Hoggatt was Noted Story Co. Character," *Ames Daily Tribune*, Ames, IA, July 18, 1934.

18. Ibid.

19. "Milestones," *TIME Magazine*, July 23, 1934.

20. "Schwab Gets Into Manhattan: Buys Interest in the Bronco Mine," *Gazette*, March 6, 1906.

21. Mining Records, Books T, U, V, W and Y, Esmeralda County Recorder's Office, Goldfield, NV.

22. "Stampede to New Camp Growing Larger," *Bonanza*, January 20, 1906.

23. Lucille Glasgow, "The Death of Tex Rickard," Clay County Museum, Henrietta, TX.

24. Barieau Papers, 1971.

25. Inquest, p. 16.

26. Ibid. pp. 13-14.

27. "Tom Logan is at Rest: Concealed Weapons," *Bonanza*, April 14, 1906.

28. Inquest, pp. 1-2.

29. "Defense Attempts to Show that Barieau was Justified in Shooting," *Sun*, July 11, 1906.

30. "Popular Sheriff Killed: Thomas Logan is Murdered in Cold Blood this Morning," *Bonanza*, April 7, 1906.

31. *Journal*, July 9, 1905.

32. Inquest, pp. 4-5.

33. Inquest, pp. 6-10.

34. Inquest, pp. 11-12.

35. Inquest, pp. 23-24.

36. Inquest, pp. 24-26.

37. Inquest, pp. 17-19.

38. "Berieau [sic] Falls Into Fit," *Sun*, April 9, 1906.

39. Inquest, cover material.

40. Inquest, pp. 20-22.

Chapter Twelve

1. Ruth Barton Davis, personal letter to author, November 23, 1985.

2. Fern Barton Armstead, personal letter to author, 1985.

3. "Sheriff Tom Logan Slain at Manhattan," *Gazette*, April 7, 1906.

4. "Sheriff Logan Shot, Makes Heroic Fight: Beats Assailant then Dies of Wounds," *Journal*, April 8, 1906.

5. "Jury Hears Story: We Greatly Deplore the Killing of Sheriff Logan," *Sun*, April 9, 1906.

6. Ibid.

7. Georgiana Logan, personal letter from her Cousin Florence, April 10, 1906, Logan Family Archives.

8. "Last Sad Rites for the Dead Sheriff: Barieau is Calm," *Sun*, April 10, 1906.

9. "Guilty of Murder: So Said the Coroner's Jury in the Case of the late Tom Logan," *Goldfield Daily Sun*, April 9, 1906.

10. "Thousands of People Mourn for Late Tom Logan," *Goldfield Daily Sun*, April 10, 1906

11. E. Marks, subpoena.

12. "Body of Thomas Logan Laid at Rest," *Manhattan News*, April 14, 1906.

13. "Tom Logan Killed by Goldfield Man," *Goldfield Review*, April 12, 1906.

14. "Tom Logan at Rest," *Bonanza*, April 14, 1906.

15. "A Tribute to Law and Order," *Sun*, April 13, 1906.

16. "Last Sad Rites for the Dead Sheriff: Logan Man of Means," *Sun*, April 10, 1906.

17. The Thomas W. Logan Estate, Probate Records, April—December, 1906, Nye County 13. Clerk's Office, Tonopah, NV.

18. Consumer Price Index Calculator, Bureau of Labor Statistics, US Dept. of Labor, Washington, DC

19. Logan Estate, Probate.

20. Land Patent Contract No. 2765, Application No. 6913, Thomas Tate, applicant, August 3, 1886, Nevada Division of State Lands, Carson City, NV.

21. Logan Estate, Probate.

22. Ibid.

23. "Tonopah Lumber Company v. Hannah Logan & May Biggs," Civil Case #1307, May 31, 1906, District Court of the Third Judicial District (now Fifth), Nye County, State of Nevada, Nye County Clerk's Office, Tonopah, NV.

24. "Hannah Logan v. May Biggs," (Civil Case #1315), June 6, 1906, District Court of the Third Judicial District (now Fifth), Nye County, State of Nevada, Nye County Clerk's Office, Tonopah, NV.

25. "Manhattan Lumber Co. and Tonopah Lumber Co. of Manhattan Nevada v. T.W. Logan," (File 10948), April 7, 1906, Nye County, State of Nevada, Nye County Clerk's Office, Tonopah, NV.

26. "G.M. Harris v. Thomas Logan and Sherman Cromley," (Civil Case #1251), March 12, 1906, District Court of the Third Judicial District (now Fifth), Nye County, State of Nevada, Nye County Clerk's Office, Tonopah, NV.

27. Nye County Assessment Roll, 1904, Nye County Recorder's Office, Tonopah, NV.

28. C. L. Richards and W. J. Harris v. Thomas W. Logan, et. al.," (Civil Case #1257), March 14, 1906, District Court of the Third Judicial District (now Fifth), Nye County, State of Nevada, Nye County Clerk's Office, Tonopah, NV.

29. Commissioner's Minutes, May 8, 1906, Book D, p. 475; October 1, 1906, Book E, p. 30.

30. "State of Nevada v. Hannah M. Logan as Executrix of the Estate of Thomas Logan, Deceased. T. L. Oddie. et.al.," (Civil Case #2095), January 9, 1909, District Court of the Third Judicial District (now Fifth), Nye County, State of Nevada, Nye County Clerk's Office, Tonopah, NV.

31. *Bonanza*, April 7, 1906.

32. *Sun*, April 13, 1906.

33. "T.J. McMahon Will be the Sheriff of Nye County," *Sun*, April 18, 1906.

34. McCracken, *Manhattan*.

35. "San Francisco Destroyed," *Bullfrog Miner*, April 21, 1906.

36. "The terrible Disaster in City of San Francisco," *Bonanza*, April 21, 1906.

37. "George Wingfield over from Goldfield Monday," *Sun*, April 12, 1906.

38. "Rebuilding Starts Before the Ashes are Cool," *Sun*, April 25, 1906.

Chapter Thirteen

1. Minutes of Criminal and Civil Actions, Book D, pp. 539-41, 1May 10, 1906, District Court of the Third Judicial District (now Fifth), Nye County, State of Nevada, Nye County Clerk's Office, Tonopah, NV.

2. Michigan Official Directory and Legislative Manual for the Years 1905-1906, compiled by George A. Prescott, Michigan Secretary of State, 1905.

3. "Lawyer Ends His Life by Hanging," SF Call, July 27, 1909.

4. Sister Margaret interview.

5. McCarran, Autobiography.

6. Minutes of Criminal and Civil Actions, Book D, pp. 534-538, 9 May 1906, District Court of the Third Judicial District (now Fifth), Nye County, State of Nevada, Nye County Clerk's Office, Tonopah, NV.

7. Ibid.

8. "S. P. Flynn v. P.A. McCarran," (Civil Case #1419), Complaint, September 14, 1906, District Court of the Third Judicial District (now Fifth), Nye County, State of Nevada, Nye County Clerk's Office, Tonopah, NV.

9. Minutes of Criminal and Civil Actions, p. 586, July 9, 1906.

10. Sister Margaret interview.

11. Bill Pettite interviews.

12. McCarran, Autobiography.

13. Minutes of Criminal and Civil Actions, p. 586, July 9, 1906.

14. "Deputy Appointed," Bonanza, July 7, 1906.

15. Lovelock Review Miner, July 22, 1932.

16. "Walter Barieau is Placed on Trial for his Life," Sun, July 9, 1906.

17. Minutes of Criminal and Civil Actions, pp. 587-594, July 9, 1906.

18. "Testimony in Barieau Trial Begins in District Court," Sun, July 10, 1906.

19. Judge Peter Breen, personal letter to author, May 27, 1986.

20. "Defense Attempts to Show that Barieau was Justified in Shooting," Sun, July 11, 1906.

21. Minutes of Criminal and Civil Actions, pp. 598-600, July 11, 1906.

22. "Defense Attempts to Show that Barieau was Justified in Shooting," Sun, July 11, 1906.

23. "Logan Slayer is Found 'Not Guilty,'" Bonanza, July 14, 1906.

24. "Defense Attacks Credence of State's Witnesses," Sun, July 12, 1906.

25. Ibid.

26. Ibid.

27. Ibid.

28. Minutes of Criminal and Civil Actions, p. 601, July 12, 1906.

29. Fred E. Whited, Jr., Senator Patrick A. McCarran: Orator From Nevada, Nevada Historical Society Quarterly, Vol. XVII Number 4, Winter, 1974, p. 193 (Reno, NV)

30. Sister Margaret interview.

31. Minutes of Criminal and Civil Actions, p. 602, July 12, 1906.

32. "Fate of Logan's Slayer is with Jury: Attorney P. McCarran Delivers Eloquent Address in Behalf of Defendant—Mr. Percy Makes Strong Reply," Sun, July 13, 1906.

33. Ibid.

34. Ibid.

35. Ibid.

36. "State of Nevada v. Walter Amphibius [sic] Barieau," Jury Instructions, District Court of the Third Judicial District (now Fifth), Nye County, State of Nevada, July 13, 1906, Nye County Clerk's Office, Tonopah, NV.

37. Ibid.

38. "Logan Slayer is Found 'Not Guilty,'" Bonanza, July 14, 1906.

39. "Jury Finds Barieau Not Guilty of Murder: Logan's Slayer Given freedom After Seventeen Hours' Deliberation—Affecting Scene in Court," Sun, July 14, 1906.

Chapter Fourteen

1. Bill Pettite interviews, Spring 2013.

2. Inward Passenger List, 5 Oct 1906, SS Newport, Pacific Mail Steamship Company, San Francisco, CA.

3. Editorial, Bullfrog Miner, July 20, 1906.

4. Maricopa County Delinquent Tax List, Bakersfield Californian, Bakersfield, CA, June 13, 1927.

5. San Diego City Directories, 1925-1931.

6. United States Federal Census: San Diego Township, San Diego, CA, 1930.

7. "Margaret Barieau v. Walter A. Barieau," Civil Case #53656, August 5, 1939, District Court of Second Judicial District, Washoe County, State of Nevada, Reno, NV.

8. Barieau Papers, 1971; Paul J. Vanderwood, *Satan's Playground: Mobsters and Movie Stars at America's Greatest Gaming Resort* (Durham, NC and London, England: Duke University Press, 2010).

9. Al W. Moe, *The Roots of Reno*, (Charleston, SC: BookSurge Publishing, 2008), p. 139.

10. Bill Pettite interviews, Spring 2013.

11. Barieau Papers, 1971.

12. Barieau Papers, 1971.

13. Edwards, *Political Boss of Nevada*, p. 8.

14. "A Political Directory of Nevada, Reed.

15. Whited, *Orator From Nevada*, p. 187.

16. Commissioner's Minutes, April 1, 1907, Book E, p. 97.

17. Guy Rocha, former Nevada State Archivist, "Myth #130 – Changing Murder Trial Venues," Nevada State Library and Archives, Nevada Department of Administration, www.nsla.nevadaculture.org.

18. Commissioner's Minutes, April 7, 1907, Book E, p. 128; September 25, 1907, Book E, p. 157.

19. Whited, *Orator From Nevada*, p. 185.

20. Whited, *Orator From Nevada*, p. 192.

21. *SF Call*, July 27, 1909.

22. Loran Logan interviews.

23. Ibid.

24. Amy Logan Darrough, personal letter to Hazel Logan Barton, October 22, 1973, Logan Family Archives.

25. *Bonanza*, March 10, 1906.

26. Zanjani, p. 240.

27. Zanjani, p. 241.

28. Sister Margaret interview.

29. Michael E. Fischer, Former Director, Nevada Dept. of Cultural Affairs and Nevada History Scholar.

30. Sister Margaret interview.

31. Ibid.

32. Raymond, *Wingfield*, p. 71.

33. Raymond, *Wingfield*, p. 9.

34. Sister Margaret interview.

35. Diane Varni, "A Story Out of the Past," *Register-Pajaronian*, Watsonville, CA, November 14, 1986.

36. Sally Zanjani and Guy Louis Rocha, *The Ignoble Conspiracy: Radicalism on Trial in Nevada*, (Reno, NV: The University of Nevada Press, 1986), p. 147.

37. *An Isolated Empire: A History of Northwestern Colorado,* Chapter X: Development of Northwestern Colorado,1890-1940, BLM Cultural Resource Series (Colorado: 12), October 31, 2008.

38. California Death Index, Napa, CA.

39. United States Federal Census: Reno, NV, 1910; City Directories, Reno, NV (1913-27); Funeral Notices, *Gazette*, July 16, 1927.

40. Nye County Tax Assessment Rolls, Manhattan, 1912, p. 6, Nye County Recorder's Office, Tonopah, NV

41. United States Federal Census: Reno, NV, 1910; City Directories, Reno, NV (1913-27); Funeral Notices, *Gazette*, July 27, 1927.

43. "W. B. Pittman Seriously Ill," *Journal*, November 25, 1936; "W. Pittman Dies in Honolulu," *Journal*, December 21, 1936.

43. "Sheriff of Nye was Seen at Portland," *Gazette*, June 2, 1910.

44. "Sheriff Owens of Nye County is Missing," *Gazette*, May 30, 1910.

45. "Sheriff of Nye was Seen at Portland," *Gazette*, June 2, 1910.

46. "Wife of Jack Owens Divorced: Case Recalls Mysterious Disappearance of Former Sheriff of Nye County," *Journal*, April 10, 1918.

47. "Vail Pittman Outlines his Policies as Acting Sheriff," *Bonanza*, June 3, 1910.

48. *Bonanza*, May 13, 1908.

49. *Bonanza*, May 12, 1908.

Chapter Fifteen

1. United States Federal Census: Sutter Township, Sacramento, CA, 1910.

2. Nevada State Legislature Fact Sheet, "Women in the Nevada Legislature," prepared and updated by the Research Division, Legislative Counsel Bureau, November, 2013.

3. "Former Tonapahn is Electrocutes," *Gazette*, March 20, 1925.

4. United States Census, 1930 and 1940

5. Shirley Ann Berg Henle interview, 2011

6. Nye County Recorder, Deed Book 34, p. 285, Tonopah, NV.

7. Loran Logan interviews.

BIBLIOGRAPHY
Interviews and Oral Histories

Cited sources:
- Bottom, Bob, 2013, Manhattan, NV.
- Henle, Shirley Ann Berg, 2011, Round Mountain, NV.
- King, Olephia "Leafy," interviewed by Carol E. Colip, University of Nevada Oral History Program, 1980, Reno, NV.
- Logan, Loran, 2011-13, Reno, NV.
- McCarran, Sister Margaret, McCarran Ranch, 1985, Sparks, NV.
- Pettite, William "Bill," 2012-13, Sacramento, CA.
- Rodrigues, Dale Darrough, 2011-13, Smoky Valley, NV.

Contextual input:
- Barton, Richard, 2012, Springfield, OR.
- Beltran, David Jimenez, 2013, Chula Vista, CA.
- Berg, Anne, 2012-13, Smoky Valley, NV.
- Berg, Irene "Rene," 2012, Smoky Valley, NV.
- Blackburn,Claire, 2011, Tonopah, NV.
- Breen, III, Peter, 1986, Reno, NV.
- Clausen, Barbara, 2011-13, Eugene, OR.
- Clausen, Charles, 2011-12, Grants Pass, OR.
- Darrough, III, James, 2012, Minden, NV.
- DeMeo, Sheriff Tony, 2011-12, Tonopah, NV.
- Earl, Phillip, 1987-2013, Reno, NV.
- Eastley, Joni, 2011-13, Tonopah, NV.
- Englund, Heidi, 2011-14, Reno, NV.
- Hosburgh, Helen (Charlie), 2011-13, Reno, NV.
- Howerton, Jeanne Sharp, 2014, Las Vegas, NV.
- La Rue, Eva, 2011-13, Tonopah, NV.
- LaFerry, Arline, 2012-13, Virginia City, NV.
- Metscher, Alan, 2011-13, Tonopah, NV.
- Perchetti, Bob, 2011, Tonopah, NV.
- Seagraves, Anne, 2012, Hayden, ID.
- Zanjani, Sally, 2012, Reno, NV.

Manuscripts and Letters
- *Appointments of U.S. Postmasters*. 1900-30.
- Arner, Robert D. *The Story of Hannah Duston: Cotton Mather to Thoreau*, American Transcendental Quarterly, 1973.
- Austin Historical Society, Austin, NV.
- Barton, Fern. Personal letter. Logan Family Archives.
- Barieau, William G. Papers. Logan Family Archives.

- Barton, Anna Mae. Personal letter. Logan Family Archives.
- Bureau of Land Management Cultural Resource Series, *An Isolated Empire: A History of Northwestern Colorado*, 2008.
- Jim Butler Essay. Unpublished manuscript. c. 1922. Logan Family Archives.
- Central Nevada Historical Society, Tonopah, NV.
- Clay County Museum, Henrietta, TX.
- Cochise County Records. Cochise County Courthouse, Bisbee, AZ.
- Crosby, Jr., George H. "History of Edwin Hamblin." Unpublished and undated essay. Logan Family Archives.
- Cushing, James. Letter. Nevada State Library and Archives, Carson City, NV. 1905.
- DeMeo, Sheriff Tony. Untitled and unpublished manuscript. Logan Family Archives. 2011.
- Esmeralda County Records. Esmeralda County Courthouse, Goldfield, NV.
- Haffey, Laura. Letter. Logan Family Archives. 1935.
- Hamblin, Cyril, Unpublished and undated essay. Logan Family Archives.
- Hamblin, Edwin. Letter. Logan Family Archives. 1903.
- *History of Edwin Hamblin*: http//www.geocities/hamblinancestors/edwinhamblin
- Logan Family Reunion. Unpublished transcript. Logan Family Archives. 1958.
- Logan, Georgiana. Letter. Logan Family Archives. 1906.
- Logan, Robert. Letter. Logan Family Archives. 1892.
- Logan, Tom. Letters. Logan Family Archives. 1905-06.
- McCarran, Patrick A. Papers. Unpublished and undated autobiography. Nevada Historical Society, Reno, NV. c. 1935.
- Miner, Mark. "Miner Descent," Ancestral blog, www.miner descent.com. 2012.
- Mojave Museum of History and Arts, Kingman, AZ.
- Nevada Division of State Lands Records, Carson City, NV. 1886.
- Nevada Historical Society, Reno, NV.
- Nevada State Records. Nevada State Archives, Carson City, NV.
- Nye County Records. Nye County Courthouse, Tonopah, NV

• Prescott, George A. Michigan Official Directory and Legislative Manual for the Years 1905-1906.
• Smith, Clara Logan. "My Mother's Trip Across the Plains in the Year 1856." Unpublished manuscript. Logan Family Archives. 1935.
• Smith, Ellen. "Thirty-Six Years with the Logan's." Unpublished manuscript. Logan Family Archives. 1990.
• Suffolk County Records. Suffolk County Courthouse. Boston, MA.
• U.S. Federal Census Records, 1850 to 1950.
• Washoe County Records. Washoe County Courthouse, Reno, NV.

Newspapers and Periodicals

• *Ames Daily Tribune*, Ames, IA.
• *Arizona Weekly Journal*, Prescott, AZ.
• *Bakersfield Californian*, Bakersfield, CA.
• *Beatty Bullfrog Miner*, Beatty, NV.
• *Belmont Courier*, Belmont, NV.
• *Boston Journal*, Boston, MA.
• *Boulder City News*, Las Vegas, NV.
• *Bulletin*, Casa Grande, AZ.
• *Carson City News*, Carson City, NV.
• *Daily News*, Huntington, PA.
• *Daily Reese River Reveille,* Austin, NV.
• *Goldfield Daily Sun,* Goldfield, NV.
• *Goldfield Review*, Goldfield, NV.
• *Grass Valley News*, Grass valley, CA.
• *Henderson Home News,* Henderson, NV.
• *Manhattan News*, Manhattan, NV.
• *Mojave County Miner*, Mineral Park, AZ.
• *New York Saturday Evening Post,* New York, NY.
• *Nevada Historical Society Quarterly,* Reno NV.
• *Nevada State Journal*, Reno, NV.
• *Oakland Tribune*, Oakland, CA.
• *Pacific Monthly*, Portland, OR.
• *Pahrump Valley Times*, Pahrump, NV.
• *Pioche Daily Record*, Pioche, NV.
• *Pioche Weekly Record*, Pioche, NV.
• *Reno Evening Gazette,* Reno, NV.
• *Sacramento Bee*, Sacramento, CA.
• *Sacramento Daily Union*, Sacramento, CA.
• *Salt Lake Daily Tribune*, Salt Lake, UT.
• *San Francisco Call*, San Francisco, CA.
• *TIME Magazine,* New York, NY.
• *Tonopah Bonanza*, Tonopah, NV.
• *Tonopah Daily Sun*, Tonopah, NV.
• *Virginia Daily Union*, Virginia City, NV.
• *Weekly Orb*, Bisbee, AZ.

Secondary Sources

• www.Ancestry.com
• Bailey, Paul, *Jacob Hamblin: Buckskin Apostle*. Los Angeles, CA: Westernlore Press, 1948.
• Beatty, Bessie, *Who's who in Nevada*. Los Angeles, CA: Home Printing Company, 1907.
• Brown, Marjorie. *Lady in Boomtown: Miners and Manners on the Nevada Frontier*. Reno, NV: University of Nevada Press, 1968.
• Chung, Sue Fawn with Elmer Rusco. *Chinese America: History and Perspectives 2003*. Chinese Historical Society of America, 2003.
• *Crocker-Langley Directory,* San Francisco, CA 1901-05.
• Davis, Sam. *History of the State of Nevada*. Reno, NV: The Elms Publishing Company, Inc., 1912-13.
• Douglas, William and Robert Nylen, ed. *Letters from the Nevada Frontier: Correspondence of Tasker L. Oddie, 1899-1902*. Reno, NV: University of Nevada Press, 2004.
• Earp, Josephine Sarah Marcus. *I Married Wyatt Earp*. Tucson, AZ: University of Arizona Press, 1979.
• Edwards, Jerome E. *Pat McCarran: Political Boss of Nevada*. Reno, NV: University of Nevada Press, 1982.
• Forstall, Richard L., *Population of Counties by Decennial Census: 1900 to 1990*, US Bureau of the Census, Washington, DC, 1995.
• Grover, David H. *Diamondfield Jack: A Study in Frontier Justice*. Reno, NV: University of Nevada Press, 1968.
• Hafner, Arabell Lee. *100 Years on The Muddy,* Springfield, UT: Art City Publishing, 1967.
• Hall, Shawn. *Shawn Hall's Nevada Ghost Towns*. www.nvghosttoems.com, 2013.
• *Harper's New Monthly Magazine*. New York, NY: Harper & Brothers, 1866.
• Lewis, Oscar *The Town That Died Laughing*. Boston, MA: Little Brown, 1955.
• Lillard, Richard G., *Desert Challenge: An Interpretation of Nevada*, New York, NY: Alfred A. Knopf, 1949.
• Lincoln County Nevada, *The Town of Pioche*, www. lincolncountynevada.com.
• McCracken, Robert. *History of Tonopah, Nevada*. Tonopah, NV: Nye County Press, 1990.
• McCracken, Robert. *Manhattan: The Land of Heart's Desire*. Tonopah, NV: Nye County Press, 2008.
• Moe, Al W. *Roots of Reno*. Charleston, SC: BookSurge Publishing, 2008.

- Nevada State Parks, Dept. of Conservation & Natural Resources, www.park.nv.gov/parks/belmont-courthouse, 2012.
- Raymond, Elizabeth. *George Wingfield: Owner and Operator of Nevada*. Reno, NV: University of Nevada Press, 1992.
- Rocha, Guy, *Nevada's Most Peculiar History: Brothel Prostitution, its Land Use Implications and its Relationship to the Community*, personal papers.
- *San Diego City Directories*, San Diego, CA, 1925-1931.
- Scott, Edward B. *Saga of Lake Tahoe*. Crystal Bay, Lake Tahoe, NV: Sierra-Tahoe Publishing Co. 1957 and 1973.
- Seagraves, Anne. *Soiled Doves: Prostitution in the Early West*. Hayden, ID: Wesanne Publications, 1994.
- Sweeney, James G., G.F. Talbot, F.H Norcross. *Revised Laws of Nevada*, Carson City, NV, 1912.
- Tefertiller, Casey, *Wyatt Earp: The Life Behind the Legend*, Hoboken, NJ: John Wiley & Sons, Inc., 1997
- *Tonopah Directory*, Southern Nevada – Consolidated Telephones and Telegraph Company, 1906.
- Travers, James W. *Tonopah, Past, Present, Future: History of the World's Greatest Mining Camp*, unknown publisher, 1902.
- Vanderwood, Paul J. *Satan's Playground: Mobsters and Movie Stars at America's Greatest Gaming Resort*. (Durham, NC and London, England: Duke University Press, 2010.
- Zanjani, Sally and Guy Louis Rocha. *The Ignoble Conspiracy: Radicalism on Trial in Nevada*. Reno, NV: University of Nevada Press, 1986.
- Zanjani, Sally, *Jack Longstreet: The Last of the Desert Frontiersmen*, (Athens, OH: Swallow Press/Ohio University Press, 1988.

INDEX

Welcome to Nevada History

Nevada's oldest cultural institution.

3000 manuscript collections
500,000 photographs
18,000 artifacts

Nevada Historical Society
Museum and Library
1650 North Virginia Street
Reno, NV 89503
775-688-1190

www.museums.nevadaculture.org

Central Nevada Museum

STEP INTO OUR PAST...

...and explore the rich and colorful
history of Central Nevada and the
early boomtowns of the west.

1900 Logan Field Rd., Tonopah, NV 89049
Phone: 775-482-9676
Hours: Tues.-Sat., 9-5 Free Admission

www.tonopahnevada.com/CentralNevadaMuseum

2011 Military Writer's Society of America Silver Medal for Creative Nonfiction

There's plenty of nerve-racking detail about the hazards of flying combat and of transporting the chief executive. I'm not sure which is worse.
– *Phil Scott,* **Smithsonian Air & Space Magazine, January 2012**

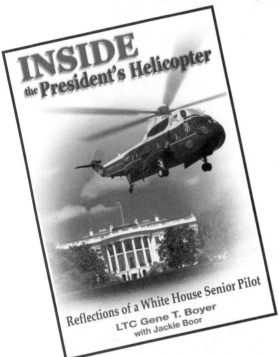

INSIDE the President's Helicopter

Reflections of a White House Senior Pilot
LTC Gene T. Boyer
with Jackie Boor

Sit down, buckle up, and get ready for an exciting ride with a White House helicopter pilot for Presidents Johnson, Nixon and Ford at the controls. Filled with candid observations about presidential personalities and private lives, LTC Boyer reveals scores of historic happenings that were never mentioned by the media. It's a fascinating inside look at the most important job in the world.

– *Flint Whitlock, co-author*
Capt. Jepp and the Little Black Book: How Barnstormer & Aviation Pioneer Elry B. Jeppersen Made the Skies Safer for Everyone

A story of high adventure, courage and history-making moments...a very human, up-close look at the Presidency.
– *Julie Nixon Eisenhower, NY Times best-selling co-author with David Eisenhower*
  Going Home to Glory: A memoir of Dwight D. Eisenhower

Inside the President's Helicopter takes the reader on an incredible journey through America's most controversial wars and presidential administrations— a real "back stage"view of the men and events that shaped world history.

– *Ken Sewell, NY Times best-selling author*
  Red Star Rogue

Hardcover $24.95
Paperback $17.95
E-book $9.95

ISBN-13: 978-1-934980-91-0
ISBN-10: 1-934980-91-9

Available at:
Amazon.com & cablepublishing.com

ABOUT THE AUTHOR

Jackie Boor began her freelance writing career in 1968 as a teen correspondent for two northern California newspapers and has worked as a reporter, ghostwriter, and forensic speech and debate coach. Her first major work, *Inside the President's Helicopter: Reflections of a White House Senior Pilot*, is the award-winning memoir of LTC Gene Boyer and was published in 2010. A resident of Sacramento, California, Jackie has long been fascinated by the dynamics of human communication and has built a multi-level career as a dispute resolution expert specializing in large group facilitation, problem solving, and civic engagement. Besides history and gardening, she enjoys golf and spending time with her family—both those in the present and from her past.